This Is Not the Way

by the same author

The Jewish People: Their History and Their Religion (with John D. Rayner)
To the Promised Land: A History of Zionist Thought
The Divided Self: Israel and the Jewish Psyche Today

This Is Not the Way

Jews, Judaism and Israel

DAVID J. GOLDBERG

faber and faber

First published in this edition in 2012
by Faber and Faber Limited
Bloomsbury House,
74–77 Great Russell Street,
London WC1B 3DA

Typeset by Faber and Faber Ltd

Printed and bound by CPI Group (UK), Croydon, CR0 4YY

A CIP record for this book
is available from the British Library

ISBN 978–0571–27161–0

10 9 8 7 6 5 4 3 2 1

In memory of Tony Judt
One relative whom I wish I had known better

'Thou wilt be missed, because thy seat will be empty'
First Samuel, 29:18

Contents

Introduction

This Is Not the Way was the title of Achad Ha-Am's first essay, written in 1889. Achad Ha-Am ('One of the People', the pen name of Asher Ginsberg, 1856–1927) was a Zionist before Theodor Herzl, his contemporary, ideological sparring partner and rival for public approval, had even heard of the word. The two men cordially detested each other. They were a complete antithesis, Herzl urbane, assimilated, an easy charmer of princes and commoners who could be economical with the truth when it got in the way of his inspiring orations and grandiose promises; Achad Ha-Am prim, schoolmasterly, worshipped by a small circle of acolytes, a stickler for accuracy who instinctively recoiled from flowery words and crowd-pleasing gestures. They hid their antipathy and mutual suspicion beneath exaggerated deference on Herzl's part and stiff formality from Achad Ha-Am. But the latter's barbed tribute after Herzl's sudden passing in 1904, that he had died at the ideal time, recalls Metternich's alleged response on being told of his adversary Talleyrand's death: 'Now what did he *mean* by that?'

A habitual carper and damner with faint praise, Achad Ha-Am wrote *This Is Not the Way* to pour cold water over the efforts and methods of the early pioneers in Palestine. The essay made his name and its Hebrew title – *Lo zeh ha-derech* – became a common figure of speech in Mandate Palestine and the early years of the State of Israel to describe going about things in the wrong way.

That is why I borrowed the phrase as the title for this book. I believe that the Jewish people worldwide, our religion of Judaism and the state that claims to represent the collective Jewish will are going about things in the wrong way.

This is not intended as yet another entry in the field of pro- or anti-Israel polemic. There are many others better qualified than I am to engage in that task. My larger concern, after spending virtually my entire career in teaching, expounding and defending Judaism, is to consider whether there is sufficient resilience and innate worth in our 3,500-year-old traditions and history to ensure the Jewish people's survival as a distinct culture into the future. Jews today are overwhelmingly secular. The majority might still mumble something vague about 'believing in God'; but belief comes way down the list when they are asked to say what makes them Jewish. Answers about 'tradition', 'history', 'family', 'community', 'Jewish values' are far more likely to occur.

In the Western world, where virtually all Jews now live, the level of 'marrying out', in the disapproving phrase of previous generations, is around 50 per cent. Previously, Jewish status depended on proof of maternal descent or a demanding conversion to Judaism. Jewish identity nowadays has become increasingly fluid and pick 'n' mix; yet the Orthodox guardians of the faith are more insistent than ever on observing the strict letter of conversion law. As a consequence, the gap in Israel and elsewhere between the 'black hats' bustling about with their seven or eight children in the garb of eighteenth-century

Polish noblemen and the ordinarily dressed majority with their 2.1 offspring has steadily widened, until they could almost be two different species of Jew.

With the erosion of belief, God has been replaced by Israel as the credo of the Jewish people, to the benefit of neither. Those 'Jewish values' that are always cited as evidence of the special Jewish contribution to civilisation – justice, a passion for freedom, love of one's neighbour, sympathy for the underprivileged, improving the world – ring hollow when set against the bleak reality of the Israel–Palestine conflict and the constant apologias that Diaspora supporters are required to make on Israel's behalf; and the harsh military occupation of another people's land, while fundamentalist settlers annex what they can of it, has coarsened and corroded the moral standards on which the Jewish state was founded.

Excessive reference to the Holocaust and dark allegations about resurgent anti-Semitism are two of the diversionary tactics used in the Diaspora by the Israel Lobby (which denies that any such entity exists, and to say that it does is tantamount to anti-Semitism) to deflect growing criticism of Israel. Is our preoccupation with anti-Semitism in danger of becoming a complex? And has the unique enormity of the Holocaust and its six million victims been trivialised by its exploitation for political purposes? What does it mean – following the decline of faith, the abatement of persecution and the fragmentation of community – still to identify as a Jew?

These are some of the broader issues that I try to explore in this book. I write as a Liberal Jew and perhaps it is appropriate at this juncture to explain a little about the various movements within Judaism, although where they differ on theological principles is made clear in the body of the text. By now, and due to controversies that regularly hit the headlines, non-Jewish readers are probably aware that Judaism is *not*, any more than Islam, the seamless, unified religion that for so long its advocates tried to present to the outside world.

Jewish life was regulated for over seventeen hundred years, from the destruction of the Second Temple by the Romans in 70 CE until the first glimmerings of the Jewish Enlightenment, by what is known as Rabbinic Judaism. In Europe it successfully kept at bay any attempts at a Jewish equivalent of the Reformation until the French Revolution. Afterwards, the march towards Jewish emancipation and citizenship was irresistible, and with it the desire to modernise Judaism. Reform Judaism, as it came to be called, began in Germany in the early nineteenth century. It spread slowly in Germany, Central Europe and Great Britain, and most spectacularly in the USA. Those who resisted its innovations were known as Orthodox; that is, conforming to traditional practice.

In the past two hundred years Judaism has further splintered as Jews responded to modernity. There are several variants of Orthodoxy, some not speaking to each other. In the USA, Conservative Judaism developed as a halfway house between Orthodox and Reform, while the Reconstructionist movement took up a position on the left. The Liberal movement in the UK (doctrinally close to American Reform) developed at the turn of the twentieth century, out of dissatisfaction with the slow pace of change initiated by the British Reform synagogues (doctrinally close to the American Conservative movement). In recent years a UK Masorti movement has pitched its tent halfway between United Synagogue Orthodoxy and the Reform movement. To try to simplify the confusion – or maybe compound it – non-Orthodox Judaism in its (American and British) Reform, Liberal and Reconstructionist manifestations – but not Conservative or Masorti – is generically referred to as Progressive Judaism.

Because my theological views have always been radical and my stance about Israel's treatment of the Palestinians one of moral indignation since the early 1970s, inevitably my many critics in Israel, Anglo-Jewry and beyond are going to read this book and react: 'There goes that self-hating Jew again.'

As 'self-hating' is the standard epithet for any Jew who does not toe the party line on any subject from Israel to building more faith schools in the Diaspora, it might interest readers to learn about the book's genesis and why I did *not* stick with its original working title of *Reflections of a Self-hating Jew*.

A few years ago I picked up on the furore following an October 2003 article in the *New York Review of Books* that called on Israel, 'a belligerently intolerant faith-driven ethno state' to transmute from 'a Jewish state to a binational one'. It was explosive stuff, written by Tony Judt, an English-born historian teaching in the USA; predictably, it caused a storm in Jewish circles, with the usual imprecations against its author for being self-hating and anti-Semitic. Discussing the repercussions *en famille* one day, a cousin wondered whether the author might be a relative, since on our maternal side the surname was spelt interchangeably as Yudt or Judt. A Google search confirmed that he was indeed kin; our *zeide* (grandfather) and his had been brothers. Several years before and without knowing of their connection, with an aunt I used occasionally to visit Tony's grandfather in his Jewish Old

Age Home in South London. He was known in the family as 'Heinech the Communist', a vigorous, intellectually sprightly man in his late eighties who would always greet me warmly and say, 'David, it's so good to have someone to be able to talk to properly. Not like these *alters*', gesturing dismissively to the row of *bubes* in armchairs placidly knitting for their grandchildren and evidently reluctant to engage in seminars with Heinech on Marx's critique of Capitalism.

I made contact with Tony and we got on well from the start, two outnumbered liberals in a mainly bourgeois extended family that did not take kindly to our opinions about Israel. In fact, he was braver than me. In Anglo-Jewry, critics may say rude things about you and write you abusive letters underlined in green ink and copied to the president of the Board of Deputies and the prime minister, but that's about it; in the USA, where violence is as American as cherry pie in H. Rap Brown's notorious dictum, some Jews are ready to resort to it when reasoned argument fails them. And Tony was more radical politically than me. I told him in one of our early email exchanges that not only did I not think much of his binational idea because, after all they had suffered, the Palestinians *deserved* to enjoy their own state, but also it was not very astute strategic thinking to tell the Israelis, a majority of whom had finally become reconciled to the idea of a Palestinian state on their doorstep, that no, we're going to scrap that idea after all, and ask them instead to share all that they had built up over sixty years with their Palestinian neighbours.

In 2008 Tony was diagnosed with amyotrophic lateral sclerosis (ALS) and became totally paralysed. Alas, he had not inherited his grandfather's longevity gene. Unable to move or write, but with a mind as sharp as ever, during the interminable night hours he would compose essays in his head by means of a mnemonic memory technique and dictate them to his assistant the next day.

We continued with our email exchanges. In the course of one, in which we had been discussing Grigor Rezzori's superb *Memoirs of an Anti-Semite* and the contemporary Jewish obsession with finding anti-Semites under every bush, I wrote, 'That gives me an idea for a great book title: *Reflections of a Self-hating Jew*. All I have to do now is write the book!'

So I produced a synopsis, gave it to my agent, and told Tony, who by now was in the final phases of his disease, that if ever it was published I would dedicate it to him. Because Faber Finds was reprinting a previous book of mine (*To the Promised Land: A History of Zionist Thought*) around then, I had a lucky entrée to the Editorial Director at Faber and Faber. He liked the synopsis and commissioned it; hence this book and its dedication to Tony Judt.

But I did change the title. When I am writing and people ask me what about, I usually reply evasively, because I am superstitious about jinxing the work in progress. This time, my stock answer to parry further questioning was to say that I had a great title and give it. Reactions varied. They ranged from 'Trust you!' through 'You wouldn't dare!' to grave reservations. In the end, it was the trio of my wife, a well-known writer and the chair of a religious organisation who persuaded me that it was not a good idea and would be misunderstood, even if I did make clear in the Introduction that the title was meant ironically and self-mockingly. As the writer said, 'David, the public doesn't do irony.' So the sobriety of Achad Ha-Am prevailed over my weakness for the bon mot in the eventual choice of title. After all, these are serious matters we are discussing.

As had the more famous and acclaimed dedicatee of this book, I have something of a reputation for non-conformity, being provocative, not suffering fools gladly, and needlessly criticising when silent discretion would be in the best interests of the Jewish people; to which my stock answer is that I merely point out when the emperor has no clothes on. 'Not in the public interest' is the excuse trotted out by rulers everywhere, from heads of democratic governments to the leader of the local parish council to the chair of a suburban synagogue, in order to suppress uncomfortable information.

One of the writers whose books I, as an adolescent with intellectual pretensions, would carry around to impress girls was François Mauriac, then modish, now largely forgotten. He was, I suppose, the French Graham Greene, exploring themes of sin, passion and Catholic guilt. In one of his novels – I don't remember which – he wrote a sentence that has stuck in my mind for well over fifty years. It was: 'Only the person without strong principles can be swayed by an unexpected argument.'

That is a very religious thought; some fundamental rules are non-negotiable. Of course we all understand about moral relativism, extenuating circumstances, tempering justice with mercy, and so forth. That is what makes Moral Philosophy such a rich, subtle and perennially fascinating discipline. But certain principles need to be insisted on, again and again. One I believe in unwaveringly, no matter how its context might change according to political circumstances, is that due to our history the most cherished Jewish value is Freedom and therefore it goes totally against the grain of Jewish ethics to subjugate or oppress another people. Heaven knows, I am the last person to presume to put myself forward as a moral paragon of any kind, but that principle of Freedom has consistently informed my approach to the Israel–Palestine conflict. The compliment I treasured most after a long rabbinic career was the message at my retirement service from the former PLO Head of Mission in London, Washington and Moscow, who wrote, 'With enemies like David I don't need friends.'

If that makes me a 'self-hating Jew', then so be it.

The Jews, Judaism and the State of Israel have frequently stirred me to pride, admiration and gratitude; they have also driven me to fury at their stubborn insensitivity, parochialism and self-absorption. But after years of disputing and disagreeing with them in usually unavailing attempts to get them to modify their ways, I still have to say alongside the prophet Hosea: 'How shall I give thee up, Ephraim? How shall I surrender thee, Israel?' For better or worse, it is my people, my religion, and my brethren's country, and it is to them that these reflections about our Jewish present and future are offered.

But before doing so, there is the pleasant task of acknowledging those who helped bring this book to fruition. Firstly, Neil Belton at Faber and Faber, who saw merit in the proposed subject and has been a sympathetic and discerning editor throughout; Vivienne Schuster of Curtis Brown, my long-time literary agent *extraordinaire* and dear friend; Max Hastings and Lucian Hudson, who steered me away from an error of judgement, although all the book's other failings are mine alone; Revd Dr Anthony Harvey, former Canon Theologian at Westminster, who provided me with an ideal Cotswold retreat in which to begin writing; and finally my wife Carole, who once again, supportively and good-humouredly, put up with the abstractedness, self-centredness and absent-mindedness that are characteristic of this author at work.

David J. Goldberg
London, June 2011

Zionism triumphant, the Diaspora subservient

It might be considered something of a turn-off to begin a book that hopes to analyse the condition of Jews, Judaism and Israel today with a raft of statistics. But there is no other way of setting Jewry in a global context. The extraordinary fact that 81.3 per cent of Jews live in just two countries – the USA and Israel – has a profound bearing on how we see ourselves and how we behave. After the Second World War, Leo Baeck, the respected leader of pre-war German Jewry who had managed to survive Theresienstadt concentration camp, used the image of Israel and the Diaspora as two foci of an ellipse to describe their relationship; nowadays, a truer analogy might be autocratic ruler and obsequious courtier. The relationship is skewed in favour of Israel. Before the advent of Zionism and the creation of a Jewish state, the regular concern of Diaspora communities throughout the centuries was expressed by paraphrasing a verse from Psalm 115: *Mah yomru ha-goyim* – 'What will the nations say? How will they judge us? How can we win the favour of hostile legislatures? What must Jews do to be granted social acceptance and civic equality?'

Nowadays, the regular concern of a deferential Diaspora is not 'What will the nations say?' but 'What will Israel say? How will the decisions we take or the judgements we make in our own communities go down in

Israel? And how do Israel's actions affect us as Jewish citizens of another country? Does the Diaspora have a future, or will it become merely an outpost of the sovereign Jewish homeland?'

Since Baeck proposed his two foci, the State of Israel has grown, prospered and assumed – by *force majeure* – the role of representative for all of Jewry. In 2004, Arik Sharon, then the Israeli prime minister, was asked by a French interviewer whether it was possible to distinguish between an anti-Semitism that should be condemned and legitimate criticism of Israel's policies. Sharon replied, 'Today there is no separation. We are talking about collective anti-Semitism. The State of Israel is the Jewish state and the attitude towards Israel runs accordingly . . . you cannot separate here.'

Not all Jews would accept that. I and many others feel bound to decline the blithe assumption that Sharon then, or his successors now, automatically speak for us in the name of Israel. But it is fair to say that most Jews in the world are probably happy with the formulation of Mortimer Zuckerman, a veteran American champion of Israel, that the Jewish state is 'the collective expression of the Jewish people'. Until the Six Day War of 1967, Diaspora Jewry paid lip service to the aims of Zionism without actually immigrating to Israel, wished the new state well and gave it financial support; since 1967, Israel has become the chief cause and *raison d'être* of Diaspora Jewry.

How did this transformation come about? To answer that question, some demographic data about the number of Jews in Israel and the Diaspora is required; hence the apologetic tone of my opening sentence for beginning with statistics, especially when we have to admit straight away that it is notoriously difficult to calculate accurately how many Jews there are in the world. According to the most recent estimate,[1] our number stands at around 13.4 million people. One of the reasons why it is so difficult to arrive at an accurate total is because in several countries – Arab and/or Muslim states, for example – the Jews who are still there prudently prefer not to advertise themselves as such.

But another, more important reason is that in open Western societies where there is rarely physical danger in identifying oneself as Jewish, an unknown number have either voluntarily opted out of any engagement with the Jewish community or else *do* regard themselves as Jews but are not recognised as Jewish by official communal organisations such as synagogues, representative bodies, or those who administer the admissions criteria of Jewish schools. As an illustration, the Jewish population of the United Kingdom is currently estimated at around 300,000 men, women and children, a steep decline from its supposed heyday in the 1970s, when it was said to number about 450,000.

I am sceptical about both figures. In the past there was a tendency to 'big up' our numbers, in order to maximise the Jewish community's importance. In the 1970s a former president of the Board of Deputies of British Jews, the community's oldest and once most influential representative organisation, would regularly proclaim: 'Speaking on behalf of Britain's half-a-million Jews . . .' He was both a Queen's Counsel and a Member of Parliament, therefore no stranger to hyperbole, and conscious that boasting of 500,000 followers had a more satisfactorily rounded ring to it than claiming to speak on behalf of merely 424,312 Jews, or whatever the true count then was.

The current relatively low figure is similarly suspect. It is extrapolated from annual numbers for Jewish births, marriages and deaths, plus synagogue membership according to Jewish households, registration in Jewish clubs, societies and other communal organisations, and then an intelligent guess as to how many unaffiliated Jews should be added on.

Doubtless this cavalier appraisal of their methods will infuriate those who toil away in the statistical and demographic units at the Board of Deputies and the Institute for Jewish Policy Research. It is a plain fact, though, that nowadays out-marriage – that is, marriage to a non-Jewish partner – accounts for well over 40 per cent of marriages involving a Jewish person. This means that the union is registered civilly, not under religious auspices, and as a consequence does not count as a 'Jewish' marriage and the future Jewish status of the children of such marriages is speculative. For instance, if the mother is recognised as Jewish by the religious authorities, then any children of hers are automatically granted Jewish status according to the *halachah* (religious law); but supposing they take on the religion of their father? And joining a synagogue (which is costly, since there is no state funding in the UK, as there is in much of mainland Europe, for the Jewish religion) – whether it is done to ensure an eventual Jewish burial or for less prosaic reasons such as providing a religious school education for one's children and encouraging a sense of 'belonging' – still attracts only around 70 per cent of those 300,000 UK Jews. Synagogue affiliation numbers have been artificially boosted in recent years by the surge in ultra-Orthodox places of worship.

My own gut instinct – and it is no more than that, based on nearly forty years' experience as a Liberal Jewish rabbi – is that there are around 100,000 more people in the UK who consider themselves to be at least Jew*ish* without 'going the whole way', in Jonathan Miller's celebrated disclaimer, than the official figure allows for. The rise in inter-marriage, the adoption of alternative, less formalised lifestyles and increasingly sceptical attitudes to the role of organised religion in society have made the traditional definitions of who is a Jew almost obsolete. As the authors of a recent report observe: 'Such shifts have led to Jewishness increasingly becoming a matter of choice rather than of birth, and making Jewish identity far more fluid . . .'

I shall return to the vexed question of Jewish identity in a later chapter. For the present, it is sufficient to reiterate from the example of the UK alone just how difficult it is accurately to gauge the number of Jews in the world.

Nevertheless, it is generally accepted by Jewish demographers that the State of Israel is about to overtake the United States – or has already done so, according to some triumphalist Israeli statisticians – as the largest single population centre of world Jewry. Tel-Aviv and its environs now have more Jews than Greater New York, once lauded as 'the greatest Jewish city in the world'.

According to Sergio Della Pergola, the doyen of contemporary Jewish demographers, a little more than four-fifths of world Jewry lives in just two countries: the United States and Israel.[2] Over half of all Jews (52.2 per cent) live in just five metropolitan areas: Tel-Aviv, New York, Jerusalem, Los Angeles and Haifa. Remarkably, 98.3 per cent of all Jews are congregated in just 15 countries: Israel, the USA, France, Canada, the UK, Russia, Argentina, Germany, Australia, Brazil, the Ukraine, South Africa, Hungary, Mexico and Belgium. Only 35 countries can claim Jewish communities of 5,000 or more. Most of the 200 or so countries in the world, including several where Jews had lived for millennia, such as Iraq, Syria and Ethiopia, are now completely bereft of Jews, or have tiny, unsustainable communities of fewer than a thousand people. If Jews rule the world, as our enemies claim, it is an extraordinary achievement for less than 0.2 per cent of the global population. As Jonathan D. Sarna, Professor of American Jewish History at Brandeis University, pointed out: 'For all that we Jews like to talk about "improving the world", the truth is that the vast majority of Jews no longer live in those sections of the world – Africa, Asia, and Latin America – that most need improving.'[3]

I thought of Della Pergola's statistics when officiating not so long ago at the *bat mitzvah* ceremony of the daughter of a friend. The ceremony took place where the family now live, on the Isle of Skye, estimated Jewish population perhaps a dozen, including a postmistress called . . . Rhoda Goldberg; not, so far as I could ascertain, a relation. What Della Pergola's figures would seem to suggest, I said in my sermon to the temporarily enlarged congregation of family and friends who had travelled to Skye for the occasion, is the ultimate vindication and triumph of Zionism. For the first time since the days of the Bible, the ancient Jewish homeland will be the largest single reservoir of Jewish population. In contrast, the Diaspora – the accustomed habitat of most Jews since being carried into exile after the destruction of the First

Temple by the Babylonians in 586 BCE – seems destined to shrink still further.

Population shifts of this size and significance have happened only rarely in Jewish history. The closest parallel occurred after the assassination of Tsar Alexander II in 1881 and the pogroms that followed. Around two million Jews left Eastern Europe between 1881 and 1914, overwhelmingly for America – the '*goldeneh medina*' (the golden country) in Yiddish parlance – but also for Great Britain, South Africa, Germany and anywhere else in Europe other than Russian territories. By way of comparison, the exile from Spain in 1492, poignantly remembered in Jewish legend as a tragedy on a par with the Babylonian exile of 586 BCE, dispersed, at the most generous estimate, 150,000 refugees. Between 1500 and 1648, attracted by economic opportunity and charters of protection, Polish Jewry expanded from 10,000–15,000 residents to more than 150,000. It was mainly Ashkenazi Jews from the Rhineland who settled there. The Spanish and Polish examples had long-term consequences for Diaspora history, but were nowhere near as momentous as the population explosion of American Jewry a century ago or the implications of Israel becoming the largest single concentration of Jews today.

Prophecy, Mark Twain supposedly remarked, is very difficult – especially about the future. And as Professor Sarna pointed out in his lecture, there have been previous, much exaggerated forecasts of the demise of Jewry. Around 800 BCE in the so-called Mesha Stone, the King of Moab boasts, 'I have triumphed . . . while Israel hath perished for ever.' In the event, Israel survived, and but for the Hebrew Bible (II Kings, chapter iii) who would ever have heard of Mesha, King of Moab?

In America, in 1818, one of the nation's wisest leaders, Attorney General William Wirt, predicted that within a hundred and fifty years Jews would be indistinguishable from the rest of mankind. He meant it positively. In the land of the free, Jews would no longer suffer from Old World discrimination. And almost on cue, in May 1964, *Look* magazine ran a cover story that received world-wide exposure, entitled 'The Vanishing American Jew'. It is hard to resist a smile when pointing out that nowadays William Wirt is long forgotten, and *Look* magazine has vanished not once but twice since 1964, whereas the American Jewish community is more vibrant and varied than ever before.

In 1952, the UK's foremost Jewish historian, Cecil Roth, delivered a lecture in New York on 'The Next One Hundred Years: An Historian's Forecast'. He announced sadly (Roth was an exponent of what Salo Baron, the leading Jewish historian of the twentieth century, decried as the 'lachrymose' interpretation of Jewish history, all persecution, pogrom and suffering[4]) that under Communism Russian Jewry would be completely lost to the Jewish people. Even if the Soviet Union collapsed, only 'a few thousand Jews would return to full Judaism . . . Russian Jewry has to be written off.' Instead, as we know, some 850,000 Russian Jews (in their cases the definition of 'Jew' has been elastic, for pragmatic *raison d'état*) have provided a vital boost to Israel's population since the 1990s, at least 100,000 more have emigrated to Germany, and in Russia itself and the Ukraine there has been a remarkable upsurge of Jewish visibility and activity, from Lubavitcher Chasidism and ultra-Orthodoxy, through Progressive Judaism, to humanist circles studying Jewish culture. New synagogue buildings, community centres and monuments to the Jewish victims of Nazism are unveiled regularly in the major cities of the Former Soviet Union, where long before Cecil Roth, Count von Plehve, the Tsarist Minister of the Interior, said, when asked in 1898 what would become of the Jews under a system of constant persecution, that one-third would die out, one-third would leave and one-third would assimilate without trace.

But even with these additional caveats, all the demographic indices do seem to point inexorably towards Israel becoming the indisputable population centre of world Jewry. Particularly at a time of global recession, with unemployment among young people in the United States and the United Kingdom at its highest level for decades, *aliyah* (literally 'ascent', i.e. immigration to the Land of Israel) becomes an attractive option. Unlike most other economies, the Israeli one is buoyant. According to the *Jewish Chronicle*, the newspaper of record for British Jewry, 'The recession has seen the largest influx of British Jews making *aliyah* for a quarter of a century.' Immigration is also on the rise from South Africa, North America (up by 15 per cent) and France.[5] The Palestinian impasse may be more intractable than ever, but from an economic and demographic point of view Israel is booming.

In the classic formulation: Is this good or bad for the Jews? Two further notes of caution need to be inserted before trying to answer that question. Firstly, immigration to Israel may be up, but so is emigration from Israel. There are sizeable Israeli diasporas in New York, Los Angeles, London, Paris, Rome and many other big cities. At any given time around one million of Israel's five-and-a-half million Jewish citizens are living or working abroad. For a large number of Israelis, especially the young, who have the opportunity to set up home elsewhere, the relentless political situation with its ever present threat of terrorist attacks, the frequent call-ups of reservists to serve on the West Bank and the border with Gaza, the menace of Iran's nuclear potential and the quotidian tension that affects every aspect of existence is a price no longer worth paying. Better a quiet life somewhere else. In that respect, the exodus of young, talented and disillusioned Israelis is reminiscent of the situation with White South Africans during the bleak late apartheid years.

Secondly, the immigration figures need to be broken down into their component parts. It is predominantly the religious Orthodox who are making *aliyah*; in other words, those sections of world Jewry most likely to choose to live in settlements on the West Bank, to be hard-line about retaining every place mentioned in the Bible rather than willing to give it up for a peace treaty, to be exempted from military service, and to receive generous welfare benefits from the state for their large families while themselves engaged in the spiritually rewarding but materially unproductive work of studying Rabbinic codes all day.

So is it good or bad for Jews to put most of our eggs in the Israel basket? Briefly summarised, my argument (which I have made in an earlier book[6]) was that even in the unlikely event of world Jewry immigrating en masse to Israel, there will within a generation still be more Arabs than Jews living between the Mediterranean and the Jordan, due to their respective birth rates (even allowing for the disproportionately large families of the Orthodox); that historically the Jews have been a diaspora people much longer than they have been a nation state; that Israeli and Diaspora Jews are becoming two different types, due to the success of early Zionism in creating a new Jewish identity as far removed as possible from the subservient Diaspora stereotype; that over centuries of dispersion Diaspora Jewry learned strategies of adaptability, discretion and judicious alliance-making in order to survive, whereas Israeli Jews seem to take a perverse delight in eschewing diplomatic niceties; that physically a Jew today is safer in New York, London or Paris than in Tel-Aviv or Jerusalem and has as much opportunity to lead a full Jewish life and study Jewish religion, history and culture in all its ramifications; that it is in the Diaspora and through intercourse with other peoples that the Jewish genius has flowered most productively and made its most distinctive contributions for the benefit of humanity; and finally, that in the terminology of Isaiah Berlin's essay on the hedgehog and the fox,[7] Diaspora Jews are the fox, knowing many diverse things, whereas Israelis are the hedgehog, knowing just one big thing.

As may be imagined, the book was not to the taste of Israel's most ardent supporters in the UK and the USA. In London, I was invited to participate at the popular annual Jewish Book Week, and then hastily disinvited after excerpts from the book appeared in the *Jewish Chronicle* and another Jewish magazine. Of course I have no evidence of any pressure being brought to bear on the organisers of Jewish Book Week ('Israel Lobby? What Israel Lobby?') but as Henry Kissinger once famously noted, even a paranoid has enemies.

So yes, I do have more regard for the Diaspora's achievements than they are usually accorded in the Zionist version of Jewish history. *My* reading of Jewish history is to see the value of discrete, widely scattered communities, whether of five million, five thousand, even five hundred Jews, or indeed the estimated dozen on the Isle of Skye, each tenaciously preserving its own traditions and culture, each intermingling with its non-Jewish neighbours as local circumstances dictate.

The history of the *Nidchey Yisrael* ('The Scattered of Israel') synagogue in Bridgetown, Barbados, is illustrative. Built originally in 1654, it is one of the two oldest synagogues in the Western hemisphere, the other being in Curacao. Destroyed by a hurricane in 1831, it was rebuilt by the community. It was rededicated on 29 March 1833. The *Barbados Globe* of 1 April 1833 carried a front-page report: 'About 3 of the clock on a bright and sunny afternoon . . . the people of the Hebrew Nation in Bridgetown, Barbados, commenced to assemble in the courts and avenues of their synagogue . . . They were joined by a number of the most respectable inhabitants, the ladies of grace, fashion and beauty . . . to witness the interesting and impressive ceremony before them.' The paper's editor predicted that 'It was a day that would ever stand eminently distinguished in the annals of the Hebrew Community of the town.'

But the steady fall in sugar prices meant that by 1900 only seventeen Jews remained in Barbados. In 1929, the synagogue in disrepair and its adjacent cemetery a rubbish tip, the last practising Jew in Bridgetown had the building deconsecrated and negotiated its sale to a local lawyer. The Bevis Marks synagogue in London acted as trustee and custodian of the Torah scroll, its breastplate, and other ceremonial artefacts. Valuable furnishings and possessions were sold off privately.

Ironically, it was shortly thereafter that a steady influx

of Jewish immigrants began to arrive in Barbados, refugees from the worsening political situation in Europe. Seemingly, though, it was too late to reacquire the community's former property or halt its structural decline, and in 1983 the Barbadian government sequestered the land in order to build a new courthouse on it. But a few wealthy individuals, aided by the American Jewish Congress, the Commonwealth Jewish Trust, the Canadian Jewish Trust and private benefactors, bought back the building. The synagogue was restored to its original specifications, and the cemetery cleaned up. Nowadays, there is an excellent museum on site detailing the history of Caribbean Jewry, and the lovely synagogue holds weekly Eve of Sabbath services for the sixty or so local Jews and visiting tourists. That is what Jews do. We enjoy visiting places of historic Jewish interest, sighing over former glories, marvelling at the resilience and tenacity of our forebears, and making a donation towards the upkeep of communal institutions.

It is because of examples such as this, multiplied a hundredfold throughout the lands of our dispersion, that I cannot be happy at the prospect of the Diaspora slowly dissolving into a remnant and the great majority of Jews packing up to go and settle in Israel. For that to happen, admittedly, would require an apocalypse beyond imagining to overwhelm world Jewry, one that dwarfed the Holocaust in magnitude.

But the voluntary liquidation of the Diaspora and the ingathering of the exiles in their ancestral homeland would be the consummation of the Zionist vision; not merely achieving *Lebensraum* but bolstering *numbers*. Since the state was established in 1948, the constant plaint of its leaders has been 'If only we had more Jews.'

More Jews to populate the Galilee; more Jews to make the Negev bloom; more Jews to counter-balance the increasing numbers of Arab citizens of Israel; more Jews to provide a bulwark against the three-times-higher Palestinian birth rate in Gaza and the West Bank. All this because the greatest threat to Israel's long-term viability in a hostile Arab environment is not the military but the demographic one.

Despite its remarkable success in at least reaching numerical parity with the powerful, enviably wealthy, self-confidently assimilated American Jewish community in little more than sixty years, Israel will not consider that the central tenet of Zionism has been fulfilled until all the Jews in the world who reasonably can have made *aliyah*. Realistically, barring the apocalypse I mentioned, it is an impractical goal and Zionist ideologues and emissaries to the Diaspora must surely know it, even while spouting the line that there is a worldwide resurgence of anti-Semitism disguised as anti-Zionism, which is putting all Diaspora communities at risk.

Why on earth would a secure, well-established bourgeois Jew from London, Paris, Sydney or Miami – who supports Israel financially through the Joint Israel Appeal and other charities, has family and friends who live in Israel, takes two holidays a year there, sends his kids in their gap year to work on a kibbutz or do a course at the Hebrew University – possibly need to *live* there? Our typical London suburban Jew lobbies his local MP and is quick to write a letter of complaint to the BBC or the *Guardian* whenever he detects anti-Israel bias in their reporting. He is an honorary Israeli by association, regards it as his second home. But when push comes to shove and despite his growing unease about anti-Semitic incidents reported here and in other countries, usually occasioned as a result of controversial Israeli actions, he will find a dozen pressing reasons to stay put rather than make *aliyah*. His business . . . his aged mother . . . the children's education . . . what would he *do* in Israel? . . . perhaps when he retires. As with British expats in southern Spain, there are colonies of elderly Diaspora Jews in Israel speaking only enough Hebrew to order a cup of tea or give instructions to the Filipino cleaner, quaintly retaining their accustomed Diaspora way of life, having little contact apart from hellos and goodbyes with the native population because of the language barrier, but instant experts on the mood of the country and what Israel will do next, thanks to the English-language *Jerusalem Post* or the online English edition of *Ha'aretz* newspaper that they read daily.

(Incidentally, the same scenario applies, *mutatis mutandis*, to the Palestinian diaspora of at least two million people who have built their lives elsewhere. Hamas and the PLO leadership might routinely demand an unequivocal Right of Return for all those Palestinians who had been displaced in the 1948 war, which Israeli politicians in turn adamantly reject for its potentially catastrophic effect on the population ratio and therefore the Jewish character of the state. Privately, both sides know they are playing at gesture politics. As I used to say of Edward Said, a scholar whom I knew slightly and admired greatly, and one of the persistent advocates of the Palestinian right to return, could anyone seriously imagine *him* giving up his professorship at Columbia University, his proximity to power and his New York apartment, in order to go back and live permanently in

Ramallah? Buying a symbolic vacation apartment there, maybe . . .)

Analysis by the Jewish Agency of immigration figures to Israel includes categorisation according to age, but not according to whether the applicant is religious or secular. If it did, my conviction is that, whatever their age, those making *aliyah* nowadays are more likely to be political hawks than doves.

Why do I assume that? Because if they are young and religious, they will have no qualms about retaining territory captured in the 1967 war. They have been taught that the Five Books of Moses are divine and true for all time. A staple of TV reporting from Israel is to interview some young couple from Brooklyn or Golders Green on their austere Judean hillside settlement, surrounded by like-minded and equally fecund families, he with beard, side curls and skullcap, she in headscarf and long grey skirt befitting the modesty of a married woman, while they passionately assert that this has been our land since time immemorial; it was promised to the patriarchs and their descendants by God. (Only they won't take His name in vain, so use a Rabbinic synonym like *Ha-Shem*, meaning *The* Name, to refer to the Deity.) Who dares gainsay a divine command and give up what the Almighty has decreed?

If they are young and secular, they will have belonged to a Zionist youth movement, perhaps gone on that grotesque 'March of the Living', where Jewish teenagers are taken on a trip to Auschwitz and then Israel, to hammer home the hardly subliminal message of 'Never Again' and that from the ashes of the death camps arose the phoenix of the reborn Jewish state. At the very least, with their youth group from synagogue they will have

enjoyed a summer in Israel and been thrilled by the
bustle, variety and exuberance of the country, the swag-
gering machismo of young army recruits with their rifles
slung carelessly over their shoulders, and the devil-may-
care rudeness of daily life that is a surly adolescent's
dream come true. As David Hare mused in his mono-
logue *Via Dolorosa*, one experiences more emotions in
a morning in Tel-Aviv than an average Swede manages
in a year. It is a heady, liberating indoctrination for a
young Diaspora Jew. So they arrive keen to join the army,
to do their bit to protect the state and become part of
a society where due to service on the front line their
youthful generation has earned experience, responsibility
and respect beyond its years. They dismiss the bleeding-
heart anxieties about Palestinian rights voiced by their
university contemporaries in the Diaspora and affect to
see the Middle East realistically for what it is ('a tough
neighbourhood to live in', in the popular formulation
used to explain away the second *intifada* of 2001 and repeated by Ehud Barak after the Israeli raid that left nine
dead in June 2010 on a Turkish ship bound for Gaza as
part of a sanction-breaking flotilla), and they are predictably robust about how to deal with the Arabs.

If they are elderly religious immigrants they have come
to fulfil a lifelong dream: to spend their last years and
be buried in the holy soil of the Holy Land. One cannot
over-emphasise the importance of this millennial yearning in the psyche of a devout Jew. 'My heart is in the
East and I am at the edge of the West', as the medieval
Spanish poet Judah Halevi (*c*.1075–*c*.1141) wrote in one
of his best-known poems. He himself, according to legend, finally made it at the end of his days to Jerusalem,
where he was gazing in rapt wonder at the city walls

when a galloping Arab horseman rode him down. So the elderly religious immigrant will walk the narrow alley-ways of East Jerusalem in order to pray at the Western Wall, absorbed in holy thoughts, oblivious to danger and hostile glances from the Palestinian residents, un-aware of and indifferent to the political situation because frivolities such as newspapers and TV have no place in the home, but utterly convinced of one inexorable fact; that *Ha-Shem* intended Jerusalem and all the sites around it, such as the Tomb of the Patriarchs in Hebron, to be forever Jewish. Which leaves little room for territorial compromise.

And if they are elderly secular immigrants, they will have squared their consciences about Israeli military gov-ernment of the Occupied Territories ('Disputed' Territ-ories is the currently preferred euphemistic designation, although religious settlers have no such inhibitions and baldly call them by their biblical names of Judea and Samaria). They regard the ugly Security Wall brutally bi-secting the landscape as an unfortunate necessity to deter suicide bombers. They parrot the standard PR line that Israel is desperate to negotiate about the West Bank's future status and a Palestinian state, but can find no serious Palestinian partner to negotiate with. Anyway, these elderly secular immigrants live in Tel-Aviv or a coastal resort, not a settlement, don't like visiting Jerus-alem's Old City ('too many *meshugganer frummers* [mad ultra-Orthodox] there'), have never risked travelling to Hebron or Jericho so what goes on in the Territories is none of their business, but regard it as a *chutzpah* of America or any EU country, most of which didn't have such a proud record of helping Jews escape the Nazis, to tell Israel where she can or can't build. Nobody pushes us around now, although, granted, the Likud government could be a bit more sensitive in its relations with its allies.

I am parodying such responses, but not by much. These sentiments are expressed regularly in the correspondence columns of the Jewish press and on the internet, where American Jewish loyalists usually add as a rider to their diatribes against European critics of Israel that 'we' saved your ass during World War II but shouldn't have bothered and left you to Hitler. The pervading message from all these internet sites that invite readers' comments is that Israel is used to standing alone against international hostility and anti-Semitic calumnies, with only Diaspora Jewry for support.

But Diaspora support is not what it once was. The tacit consensus that Diaspora communities do not criticise Israel publicly but convey concerns to the appropriate government minister privately has long since been fractured. A representative communal body such as the Board of Deputies still tries to maintain the line that its role is to stand behind the government of Israel, come what may. The majority of Board delegates (whatever their religious denomination) subscribes to that view, but a vocal minority has provoked increasingly rancorous debates over controversial military actions such as Israel's Operation Cast Lead into Gaza in January 2009.

Dissenting organisations such as Peace Now, Independent Jewish Voices and Jews for Justice for Palestinians may wax and wane and attract largely the same left-of-centre constituency but their entry onto the communal stage always provokes exaggerated alarm from a Jewish establishment anxious to maintain a façade of unity over Israel before the non-Jewish public.

For a few months, until I grew disillusioned with a

group of articulate Jewish intellectuals who preferred splitting ideological hairs to action, I was on the organising committee of Independent Jewish Voices (IJV for short). Indeed, I was responsible for devising the slogan 'A Time to Speak Out' that introduced its first full-page advert in *The Times*, signed by over eight hundred Jews, many of them well known in academic, legal and theatrical circles.

The effect was electric. Every news agency picked up on the story, as did radio and TV. On the day of the advert's appearance I was invited to speak about the reasons for forming IJV on the BBC's *Newsnight*, along with a pleasant Orthodox rabbi to oppose me. Mysteriously, he discovered two hours before the programme was due to be transmitted that suddenly he had to take evening prayers. Apparently Melanie Phillips, the *Daily Mail* columnist and formidable attack dog of neo-conservatism, had been suggested by a communal organisation to replace him. She savaged me and IJV, barely allowed me to get a word in edgeways, and ended up in a row with Jeremy Paxman. It was hardly my finest hour and little comfort to my bruised ego when sympathetic viewers tried to console me afterwards by saying that at least I had reacted to her tirades with dignity.

I recall this humiliation at Melanie's hands to illustrate the panicky reaction of the powers-that-be to the possibility of criticism against Israel being voiced on TV by a Jew speaking on behalf of eight hundred other Jews, who were dismissed by Melanie as well-known self-hating Jews never previously involved in the community, unrepresentative of anyone but themselves, who had courted cheap publicity by adding their names to an anti-Israel advertisement. In the storm of protest that followed the

IJV initiative, one letter writer to the *Jewish Chronicle* demanded to know where the sum of £30,000 to pay for the advert had come from. Actually, it cost £12,000 and every signatory gave around £20 each to cover its cost (some more, some less); but why spoil a juicy conspiracy theory with facts? As to Ms Phillips, on her blog the next day she branded IJV as 'Jews for Genocide', which even her keenest admirers thought was somewhat excessive.

Despite such occasional alarums, generally it is easy enough in the UK for Jewish critics of Israel to ignore and evade communal censorship. The liberal ethos of the BBC and several broadsheet newspapers ensures them a ready hearing. The community's watchdogs may bark but in most cases are too British and gentlemanly to know how to bite. Nor do they muster sufficient power or respect. Four years ago a highly regarded and well-known Israeli journalist was disinvited from giving the keynote address at the Zionist Federation's annual conference in London after daring to use the word 'apartheid' to describe the legal inequalities in place on the West Bank. It was the Zionist Federation that made itself look cowardly and silly by justifying its decision to cancel his invitation on the ground that he had 'encouraged the demonisation of Israel and the Jewish people'.

In the USA, it is a different story. There, organisations such as the Anti-Defamation League (ADL), the Zionist Organisation of America (ZOA) and AIPAC (American-Israel Public Affairs Committee) wield great patronage and influence and are quite open about using it on Capitol Hill to have meetings cancelled, invitations withdrawn and the pro-Israel credentials of candidates for office scrutinised, declaring all the while that to suggest there is such a thing as an Israel Lobby is an anti-Semitic slur.

Such bristling outrage at the very suggestion of American Jews using their muscle in the perceived best interests of fellow Jews in Israel is strange at first glance. Despite their veneer of success, wealth and self-confident acculturation in American society, it betokens a deep-rooted unease among Jews there about accusations of dual loyalty. There are historical reasons for this. The execution of Ethel and Julius Rosenberg as Soviet spies in 1953 sent shock waves through the Jewish community for years, and the more recent case of Jonathan Pollard, convicted of spying for Israel in 1987 and given a life sentence, assuredly was not 'good for the Jews'. In May 2010, Alan Dershowitz, a Harvard law professor and Israel's most strident advocate, declined the flattering invitation from Prime Minister Binyamin Netanyahu to use his flamboyant oratory and forensic skills as Israel's UN ambassador with the explanation that he would not give up his American citizenship or lay himself open to the accusation of dual loyalty.

Irish Americans lobby, Hispanic Americans do it, Armenian Americans do it, everyone is doing it. Lobbying is as American as apple pie. There is a gun lobby, an automobile lobby, pro- and anti-abortion lobbies, an oil lobby, a green lobby, and a lobby for every letter of the alphabet, each with its offices and PR firms and channels of influence in Washington.

But few are as brash, up-front and effective as the Israel Lobby – or quicker to deny its own existence. At times, the keenness of Israel's American warriors to leap into action and snuff out any whiff of anti-Semitism masquerading as anti-Zionism results in behaviour that has an effect directly counter to the one intended. In 2007, the Catholic University of St Thomas, Minnesota, rescinded an invitation to Nobel Laureate Desmond Tutu after pressure from the ZOA, which had accused him of anti-Semitism. Explained the university's vice-president, 'We had heard some things he said that some people judged to be anti-Semitic *and against Israel policy* [my italics] . . . he's compared the State of Israel to Hitler and . . . making moral equivalences like that are hurtful . . . to the Jewish community.'

Tutu's allegedly offensive comparison came from a speech delivered in Boston five years previously, on 13 April 2002. The date and context is important. It was during the brutal siege by the Israeli army of Jenin refugee camp as part of Operation Defensive Shield, the invasion of the West Bank in response to an appalling terrorist atrocity two weeks before that had killed 29 and wounded 150 civilians as they celebrated a communal Passover meal in the resort of Netanya. Luridly exaggerated rumours of massacre and wanton destruction in Jenin were fuelled by Israel's decision to bar reporters and TV crews from covering the fighting.

In his speech, Archbishop Tutu paid fulsome tribute to Jewish support in the apartheid struggle, reiterated Israel's right to secure borders, voiced his distress at Palestinian suffering, called on the Israeli and Palestinian peoples to live together in peace based on justice 'because it is God's dream', added that to criticise Israel in the US was immediately to be dubbed anti-Semitic since 'the Jewish Lobby is powerful – very powerful' and continued, 'Well, so what? This is God's world . . . We live in a moral universe. The apartheid government was very powerful, but today it no longer exists. Hitler, Mussolini, Stalin, Pinochet, Milosevic, and Idi Amin were all powerful, but in the end they bit the dust.'

That is the extent of the 'moral equivalences' for which the Zionist Organisation of America branded a noble Christian and champion of freedom for all peoples as an anti-Semite. Not even Nelson Mandela has escaped the slur, for having said that aspects of Israeli policy towards the Palestinians reminded him of apartheid.

This habit of labelling critics of Israel as anti-Semitic backfired spectacularly in the furore surrounding Stephen Walt and John Mearsheimer, two previously obscure American academics propelled to prominence by the smear campaign mounted against them by the (non-existent) Israel Lobby. In 2002 they had been commissioned by the *Atlantic Monthly* to write a paper on the influence of the Israel Lobby on US foreign policy. The paper was rejected, for reasons that neither side has explained. A condensed version of it appeared in the coyly Marxist and rather-too-pleased-with-itself *London Review of Books* in March 2006 under the title 'The Israel Lobby'. I read it at the time and thought that for a supposedly scholarly piece it was long on generalised speculations and short on hard facts.

America's Israel supporters thought otherwise. A sustained assault was launched on the two authors by columnists in leading newspapers from – geographically – the *Boston Globe* through the *New York Times* and *Wall Street Journal* via the *Washington Post* and *Chicago Sun-Times* down to the *Los Angeles Times*. The ubiquitous Alan Dershowitz debunked what he called the newest version of the Jewish conspiracy theory. Charges of academic malpractice, shoddy scholarship, drawing from neo-Nazi websites and – of course – anti-Semitism were levelled against Walt and Meersheimer.

Having been turned into notorious anti-Semitic

celebrities, the two professors did the obvious thing and enlarged their paper into a book, published in August 2007 under the title *The Israel Lobby and US Foreign Policy*. Once again, it garnered shoals of adverse publicity to boost sales and delight their publishers. Strenuously denying that they were anti-Semitic (although after what they had been subjected to from Jewish opponents *I* would have been!), the authors reiterated their thesis that there is a 'loose coalition of individuals and organisations who actively work to steer US foreign policy in a pro-Israel direction'.

Even this watered-down accusation failed to dampen Jewish wrath. Once again, the big guns, including former Secretary of State George Shultz writing in *US News and World Report*, were unlimbered to demolish the two academics. In the UK, Anthony Julius, the solicitor who represented Princess Diana in her divorce from Prince Charles and in his alter ego as a literary critic has written an acclaimed study of T. S. Eliot's anti-Semitism and an inordinately long, overwrought and mind-numbingly turgid account of English anti-Semitism from medieval times to the present[8] – was wheeled out in the *Jewish Chronicle* to give it as his considered judgement that if not outright anti-Semites, Walt and Mearsheimer were a new strain of the virus, 'proto-anti-Semites', who gave aid and comfort to the real ones by perpetuating 'the Jewish conspiracy myth'.

The phrase about sledgehammers and nuts suggests itself. Surely it would have been more mature and productive to engage with Walt's and Mearsheimer's argument, rebut its factual inaccuracies and point out that since Israel is America's staunchest ally in the Middle East it is hardly surprising that lobbyists should be furthering their joint interests. But like its less important UK counterpart, that is not how the American Jewish establishment sees its role. And like its UK counterpart, it is belatedly discovering that its Israel-right-or-wrong philosophy is not to everyone's taste, particularly those among the Jewish young who have reservations about how the Palestinians are treated.

In the 10 June 2010 edition of the *New York Review of Books* the lead article was by Peter Beinart, an Associate Professor of Political Science at the City University of New York. His piece appeared under the succinct headline, 'The Failure of the American Jewish Establishment'. The article began by relating that in 2003 several prominent Jewish philanthropists had hired Republican pollster Frank Luntz to discover why Jewish college students were not doing more to rebut campus criticism of Israel. His findings were salutary. 'Six times we have brought Jewish youth together as a group to talk about their Jewishness and connection to Israel. Six times the topic of Israel did not come up until it was prompted. Six times these Jewish youth used the word *they* rather than *us* to describe the situation.'

When Luntz probed the students' views on Israel, he encountered some firm convictions. Firstly, 'They reserve the right to question the Israeli position' and 'resist anything they see as "group think".' They wanted 'an open and frank discussion' about Israel and its flaws. Secondly, 'Young Jews desperately want peace.' They empathised with the plight of the Palestinians, and when shown ads depicting Palestinians as violent and hating Israel criticised them for being unfairly stereotypical.

Peter Beinart summed up Luntz's findings as follows: 'Most of the students, in other words, were liberals, broadly defined. They had imbibed some of the defining values of American Jewish political culture: a belief in open debate, a scepticism about military force, a commitment to human rights. And in their innocence, they did not realise that they were supposed to shed those values when it came to Israel . . .'

That corroborates my own experience over the years with idealistic UK Jewish students. Hardest of all for them to swallow is the unacceptable paradox of observing a robustly democratic Israel within its pre-1967 borders, but in the Occupied Territories a military administration under which one group of subjects, the Israeli citizens, enjoys full rights, while a much larger, disenfranchised group, the Palestinians, enjoys none of any significance.

Yet because in the UK, the USA and other centres of strong Zionist support, such as South Africa, France and Australia, the communal leadership persists in its myopia over the moral anxieties caused by continued rule over territory conquered in 1967 and refuses to budge in its public stance of obligatory, unwavering support for Israel, it is steadily alienating those young Jews who might otherwise hold Israel dear and defend her sovereign right to exist within secure and internationally recognised borders. They live overwhelmingly in liberal democracies where equality under the law, multiculturalism and co-existence are the norm. In Beinart's words, 'There are a great many Zionists, especially in the Orthodox world, people deeply devoted to the State of Israel. And there are a great many liberals, especially in the secular Jewish world, people deeply devoted to human rights for all people, Palestinians included. But the two groups are increasingly distinct. Particularly in the younger gener-

ations, fewer and fewer American Jewish liberals are
Zionists; fewer and fewer American Jewish Zionists are
liberal . . . If the leaders of groups like AIPAC and the
Conference of Presidents of Major American Jewish Organisations do not change course, they will wake up
one day to find a younger, Orthodox-dominated, Zionist
leadership whose naked hostility to Arabs and Palestinians scares even them, and a mass of secular American
Jews who range from apathetic to appalled.' This sub-
stantiates my observation that people who make *aliyah*
nowadays are more likely to be religiously Orthodox and
to form a constituency that favours a greater religious
say in civil legislation and tougher measures to deal with
Palestinian unrest.

But instead of taking stock and altering course, the
Diaspora establishments just shout louder about anti-
Semitism. In the dock alongside Nelson Mandela and
Archbishop Tutu have been placed Mary Robinson, the
former UN High Commissioner for Human Rights; Amnesty International ('bigoted, biased and borderline anti-
Semitic' in the snappy sound bite of Abraham Foxman,
the indefatigably loquacious director of the ADL); Human Rights Watch; Christian Aid; Save the Children –
and a Jew, Judge Richard Goldstone, who presided over
the UN commission that investigated accusations of war
crimes by both Israel and Hamas during the 2009 invasion of Gaza. Israel declined to give evidence to the
commission, preferring to launch its own investigation,
and along with its Diaspora loyalists excoriated Goldstone – a distinguished and experienced jurist – for his
naivety in being gulled by testimony with a clear anti-Israel bias. Israeli human rights organisations were accused
of feeding him false information and Naomi Chazan, a

veteran Knesset member and civil rights campaigner, was charged with treason by a Likud member.

The abuse against Goldstone took a more sinister turn when he was prevented from attending his grandson's *bar mitzvah* in Johannesburg in spring 2010 due to threats of violence. A similar threat deterred Rahm Emanuel, then President Obama's chief of staff, from celebrating his son's *bar mitzvah* in Israel. Incidentally, President Obama was described in the official newspaper of Shas, the ultra-Orthodox party representing Jews of North African and Middle Eastern descent, and a vital component of any Israeli coalition government, as being 'an Islamic extremist'.

As one dispiriting example follows another, well-meaning Diaspora Jews express shock and concern, to show their attachment to the once decent, humane, liberal, 'beautiful' Israel of their memories. If such an Israel ever actually existed rather than in whitewashed dreams, it breathed its last with the accession to power of Menachem Begin and the Likud coalition in 1977. Since then, apart from a brief interlude under Yitzchak Rabin, Israel has moved steadily rightwards domestically and with regard to the Occupied Territories, in both cases due to the proliferation of the ultra-Orthodox and the influx of hard-line Russian immigrants.

For those Jews no longer willing to delude themselves, there is something morally repugnant in the behaviour and attitudes of Israel's foreign minister, Avigdor Lieberman, who has publicly stated that he wants to revoke the citizenship of Israeli Arabs unwilling to swear a loyalty oath to the Jewish state; who tried to prevent two Arab parties that opposed the 2009 Gaza invasion from running candidates for the Knesset; who declared that

Arab Knesset members who met with Hamas representatives should be executed; who wants to jail Arabs
who publicly mourn on Israel Independence Day, and
wishes permanently to deny citizenship to Arabs from
other countries who marry Israeli Arab citizens – and yet
he is defended and excused by Diaspora apologists dutifully playing monkey to his organ grinder's tunes. 'He's
not saying expel them. He's not saying punish them,'
explained – inevitably – Abe Foxman to the Jewish Tele-
graphic Agency. Malcolm Hoenlein, the executive vice-
chairman of the Presidents' Conference, assured listeners
after the election that brought Lieberman to power that
his agenda was 'far more moderate than the media has
presented it'.

Perennial Diaspora optimists detect signs of hope in
anti-Establishment groups such as Independent Jewish
Voices, its American equivalent For the Sake of Zion,
and the American networking site J Street as forces for
change and a means of bolstering the bruised and
battered Israel peace camp. I wish I could share their optimism. I have been connected with several Israeli initiatives looking for a solution to the Israel–Palestine conflict
and the restoration of civility to political discourse in the
public arena. Without exception they have all flickered
then expired, blown away by the gusts of extremism.

Nowadays, sadder and wiser after more than thirty
years of offering my modest support from the pulpit,
in articles, on the radio and TV, in public appearances
and frequent visits to Israel, to the beleaguered voices of
moderation and liberalism that still remain in the country, I watch sadly from the sidelines, helping instead
small, quixotic causes such as Daniel Barenboim's West-
East Divan Orchestra, the Neve Shalom–Wahat al Salam

Arab–Israeli communal village, and a similar centre in Akko; they are oases in the wilderness, with no political clout or power to affect the bitterly entrenched attitudes of the majority, but heartening examples that with good-will, willingness to listen to the other's story and a genuine desire to overcome inbred hatreds, it *is* possible for Israelis and Palestinians to live, work and make music together in harmony.

Opinion polls are highly volatile, but they do reflect public attitudes at any given time. In 2009, a poll by the Israel Democracy Institute found that 53 per cent of Jewish Israelis – and 77 per cent of recent immigrants from the former USSR – supported the idea of encouraging Arabs to leave the country. In March 2010, another poll reported that 56 per cent of Israeli high-school students – and over 80 per cent of religious high-school students – would deny Israeli Arabs the right to be elected to the Knesset.

As Peter Beinart noted in his *NYRB* article, 'Israeli governments come and go, but the Netanyahu coalition is the product of frightening, long-term trends in Israeli society; an ultra-Orthodox population that is increasing dramatically, a settler movement that is growing more radical and more entrenched in the Israeli bureaucracy and army, and a Russian immigrant community that is particularly prone to anti-Arab racism.' He quoted Shulamit Aloni, one of the brave, moderate and idealistic politicians I used to support, saying, after a posse of settlers had forced a large bookstore to stop selling a book critical of the occupation, 'Israel has not been democratic for some time now.'

Aloni made her comment before an incident in the Knesset when Anastassia Michaeli, a member of Avigdor

Lieberman's party, rushed to attack physically Hanin Zo-abi, the first-ever female member of an Arab party in the Knesset, as she tried to explain from the rostrum why she had joined the Gaza aid flotilla boarded by the Is-raeli navy. Other members rose from their seats to help Michaeli. Only with great difficulty were the ushers able to protect Zoabi from bodily harm. She comes from a large Palestinian family that has lived in Nazareth for centuries. Michaeli was born in what was then Lenin-grad, elected Miss St Petersburg, became a model, met and married an Israeli, converted to Judaism and immig-rated to Israel. She was not censured for her assault on a fellow Knesset member, but Zoabi was stripped of her parliamentary privileges.[9]

Yet the Diaspora Israel Lobby automatically continues to defend the indefensible. In May 2010, a petition from American Jews said that the building of more settlements in the West Bank and Arab districts of Jerusalem was 'morally and politically wrong and feed the de-legitim-isation process that Israel currently faces abroad'. The chairman of the Jewish National Fund UK responded with the asinine comment, 'The Israelis are not stupid natives waiting for their brothers and sisters across the ocean to tell them how to compromise their security.'

Stupid certainly not, but currently in thrall to a Great-er Israel vision that is impervious to demography and international opinion. Allied to parochial religious fun-damentalism at home, it threatens the future survival of the state as either Jewish or pluralist or democratic. Then Israel will have become part of the Middle East with a vengeance, if not in the way envisaged by its founders. And the rest of the world's Jews would be well advised to remain where they are in the Diaspora rather than answering the call of *aliyah*.

Nahman of Bratzlav (1772–1811) was a revered leader of early Chasidism. He used to tell a parable about some courtiers who brought their king distressing news. The harvest had been gathered in, but whoever ate of the crop became mad. No other food was available. What should be done – eat of the harvest and go mad or die of starvation? The king decreed: 'We all must eat of this crop, but a few of us must remember what the effect will be, to remind us that we are mad!'

My fellow Diaspora Jews need reminding that in our knee-jerk defence of Israel and enthusiasm to accuse anyone who dares criticise the state of being an anti-Semite, we are all in danger of going mad. It is worth investigating how this courtier-like deference to the sovereign demands of the State of Israel came about.

2

Creating Israel's foundation myth

With the benefit of hindsight, two events can be identified as forever altering the balance of the relationship between Israel and the Diaspora. The first was the trial of Adolf Eichmann in Jerusalem in 1961. The second was the Six Day War of 1967.

By the end of Second World War, most of the institutions, synagogues, schools, communal services and infrastructures of Jewish life in mainland Europe had been destroyed or seriously impaired and two-thirds of Europe's Jews had perished in the Holocaust. The Jews in Poland and the USSR had suffered terribly under Nazi occupation. How many had survived there and in Hungary, Czechoslovakia, Romania and the Baltic countries could be only guessed at as the Soviet Iron Curtain divided Europe. What was known was that approximately 250,000 Jewish refugees, or DPs (Displaced Persons) in bureaucratic parlance, were in desperate need of succour and resettlement.

The *Yishuv* (the Hebrew name for the Jewish 'settlement' in Palestine) was still nominally limited to the immigration quota set in the British government's 1939 White Paper – a total of 75,000 newcomers over a five-year period, and thereafter subject to Arab consent. Boats attempting to land illegal immigrants were intercepted by the Royal Navy and their passengers either interned on Cyprus or sent back to Europe. After victory parades on VE Day, over 100,000 people took to the streets of Tel-Aviv shouting, 'Open the gates of Palestine!'

There was, effectively, only one Diaspora community that could offer large-scale assistance: the Jews of America. Only the American Jewish community had the size and 'clout' to influence its national government to alleviate the crisis. President Truman needled his British ally with repeated requests that 100,000 immigration certificates should be granted immediately.

The number of Jews in Great Britain – as it was known then – had been boosted by the pre-war arrival of escapees from Hitler's Germany and Austria and some 50,000 youngsters on *Kindertransports*. But the country was exhausted by the war, financially impoverished, overwhelmed by the burden of containing Indian nationalism, vainly trying to hold the ring in Mandate Palestine between militant Zionists and vengeful Arabs, and desperately wanting to turn the question of Palestine's future over to the United Nations. It was no time for communal bodies such as the Board of Deputies – mindful then, as always, of its role as Court Jew in presenting the community in the best possible, least troublesome, light – to importune HM's government.

The French community, of roughly similar size before World War II, had been traumatised by the mass roundups and deportations of Jews under the Vichy administration. Its representative body, the *Comité representatif des Israélites de France* – CRIF for short – had been set up only after the liberation of France in 1944. The South African, Canadian and Australian Jewish communities were of negligible influence.

As befitted its size and wealth, and a nagging sense

that perhaps it could have done more to save Europe's Jews from Hitler given the prominence of Jewish advisers in Roosevelt's administrations, American Jewry led the way. The American Jewish Joint Distribution Committee (the 'Joint') was at the forefront of aid agencies helping survivors rebuild their lives. And the USA narrowly lost out to the USSR as the first to recognise the new State of Israel when it was voted into being by the United Nations in late 1947. With an election imminent, Harry Truman was conscious of the potential impact of over five million Jewish votes.

Since the 1930s, American Jews, encouraged by two leading Reform rabbis, Stephen S. Wise and Abba Hillel Silver, who held senior positions in the World Zionist Organisation, had been more sympathetic to Zionism's aims than any other Diaspora community. Now they had come through triumphantly. There was cheering and dancing in Times Square as the result of the UN vote was broadcast.

And, for twenty years, that was about it. Having done their (generous) bit by helping Holocaust survivors, promoting the UN resolution that called for partition of Palestine into a Jewish state and an Arab state, and buying Israel Bonds, American Jews went back to consolidating their own position in their own country, which was about to enter the boom decades of the 1950s and 1960s. Despite increasing prosperity, American Jewry's donations to Israel steadily declined in the years leading up to the Six Day War. In a study conducted in a Midwestern Jewish suburb in the late 1950s listing in order of importance the indices for being considered a good Jew, 21 per cent of respondents ticked 'Support Israel', while 58 per cent opted for 'Help the underprivileged'.[1]

It was a time of unprecedented opportunity for American Jewry to consolidate its status in the mainstream of national life. Hundreds of thousands of Jewish servicemen had fought in World War II. Most of them were second- or third-generation Americans. They came home to take advantage of the GI Bill of Rights and the new opportunities in an expanding economy. They shared in the feel-good factor from having fought a just war against evil in Europe and the Pacific and had earned their place in the sun as America began to explore its limitless potential. Their homeland was the America of social mobility, affluent suburbia, Reform temples and Jewish country clubs, not the plucky little Israel of economic hardship, collective farming and socialised health care, all of it too uncomfortably reminiscent of the Communist society of the USSR, America's new deadly enemy.

In those days, unless they were 1930s-vintage 'lefties', American visitors did not feel that much at ease in Israel, not least because they had to make do with margarine instead of butter, due to the Eisenhower administration's punishment of Israel for having colluded with Great Britain and France in their attack on Egypt in 1956 after Nasser had nationalised the Suez Canal. American Jewry's muted indifference to the butter embargo imposed by a furious John Foster Dulles, the Secretary of State, was reflected in the presidential election a month later, when Eisenhower actually increased his share of the Jewish vote.[2]

In the United Kingdom and France, because one's *pays d'origine* and Israel were in alliance, the Jewish communities responded more or less unanimously in support of the Anglo-French invasion and its stated aim to protect the Canal and create a buffer zone between Egyptian and Israeli forces. Jews, especially in France, which was faced with rebellions in its Moroccan and Algerian colonies, took a staunchly pro-government, pro-Israel line. In the UK, there was more vocal but strictly limited Jewish dissent.

As a modishly radical sixth-former in 1956, I parroted the Labour Party protests endorsed by most of its Jewish MPs, that Anthony Eden and the Tories were guilty of old-fashioned gunboat imperialism. I was threatened with being thrown out by my parents, who took the simpler line that Israel deserved all the help she could get against enemies like Nasser. Too young to have absorbed the momentous implications of the 1947 vote for statehood and the 1948 War of Independence, it was not until 1957 that I made my first visit to Israel, while travelling for two years between school and university. Like all adolescents before and since, I was bowled over by the exuberant vitality of the young state. It was such a release from Diaspora circumspection to realise that everyone else around was also a Jew (unless obviously an Arab), that it wasn't necessary to lower your voice when talking about Jewish topics or to assess the listener's reaction when you told someone your foreign-sounding name and, worse still, were asked to spell it.

But I do remember a deeply unhappy Egyptian Jewish family billeted on the kibbutz where I was working who did not share my naive sense of wonder. They had been expelled from Alexandria, along with all its Jews, in retaliation for the 1956 Sinai Campaign. The father, a physically soft, emotional man who hated working in the fields, wept constantly for the bank, the servants and the good life that he had been forced to leave behind – for this! – gesturing in despair around the communal dining hall of the kibbutz. That was when I first understood that the Zionist phrase about 'ingathering the exiles' had a fine ring to it but concealed a multitude of different realities for the ingathered.

It took the kidnapping from Argentina of Adolf Eichmann, and his trial in Jerusalem, to stir American Jewry from its self-absorption and towards a reappraisal of Israel's role in Jewish life. Where American Jewry leads, the rest of the Diaspora is rarely far behind. By capturing and bringing to trial a leading Holocaust perpetrator, the Israeli government had asserted to the watching world its custodianship of the memory of the Six Million. No matter that its original intention in putting Eichmann on trial had been different; to educate uncomprehending younger Israelis, the native *sabras*, in the history of their Diaspora ancestors. In his lengthy presentation of the prosecution case against Eichmann, Attorney-General Gideon Hauser hammered home the theme of a persistent anti-Semitism that went as far back as Pharaoh in the Bible persecuting the Children of Israel and had continued unabated throughout history, until the worst and most recent example of Nazism. His pedagogical message to the Israeli young was hardly subtle; that only in their own country could Jews feel safe and free and avoid the fate of their grandparents' generation.

The response of the Israeli young to Eichmann's trial was not at all what David Ben-Gurion and his educators had wished for. Instead of discovering an empathy with the 350,000 survivors from Europe who had been absorbed since 1947, the *sabras* expressed bafflement and contempt at the way so many Diaspora Jews had gone so passively to their deaths. Why had they not fought back, as Israelis would have done? At least those who took up arms in the Warsaw Ghetto or joined partisan bands had shown the right spirit. If it emerged that these fighters had also belonged to Zionist youth groups, that simply vindicated the innate sense of superiority felt by *sabras* over the Diaspora.

In the United States, too, the reaction was not at all as anticipated. There, the usual representative bodies such as the American Jewish Congress and the Anti-Defamation League had warned that coverage of the trial could exacerbate anti-Semitism. An unflattering portrait would emerge either of the Jew as perpetual, hapless victim, or of a Shylock obsession with vengeance at the expense of the nobler Christian virtue of forgiveness. Eminent Jewish jurists expressed their doubts about the legality of having kidnapped Eichmann.

In the event, American public reaction was almost universally favourable. The perception of a brave little Israel taking the fight to former Nazi tormentors outweighed legal quibbles about the trial's validity or the nuanced, uncomfortable reports that Hannah Arendt sent back from Jerusalem to *The New Yorker*. 'Self-Hating Jewess Writes Pro-Eichmann Series for New Yorker Magazine' was how one Jewish newspaper headlined a piece about her.

Furthermore, the trial had a liberating effect on Jews themselves. For the first time since the war, they could talk publicly about the Holocaust as a specifically Jewish tragedy, instead of it being a topic referred to by rabbis in their sermons behind the closed doors of the synagogue. Survivors were encouraged to relate their experiences. It is hard to credit at this distance of time that for many years afterwards it simply wasn't done for former inmates of Auschwitz and other concentration camps to talk about what they had been through. Silence and a stiff upper lip was how one coped. For a survivor to lift an arm and inadvertently reveal a tattooed number prompted an embarrassed hiatus in conversation. It was a revelation of something shameful.

We have been inundated in recent years with the memoirs of survivors and of the children and even grandchildren of survivors. A raft of histories, plays, films and TV documentaries have charted every aspect of European Jewry's suffering under Nazism between 1933 and 1945. Survivors or their children hold conferences, oral-history seminars and reunions, and have become adept at addressing school groups. Latterly, a complex social hierarchy has evolved, in which having survived a death camp ranks higher than merely having been forced to flee, and being the descendant of a Polish or East European survivor is more 'authentic' than being the descendant of a German refugee who managed to escape before 1939.

In London about twenty years ago, there was an exhibition of photos taken by a Wehrmacht soldier – strictly against orders – during the liquidation of the Warsaw Ghetto. A noted historian introduced the exhibition and other communal bigwigs added their two bits' worth. Finally, a handsome woman in her seventies spoke. She had lived through the ghetto siege. Her simple words were electrifying, the testimony of someone who had really been there. Afterwards I thanked her for such a moving account and wondered if she had thought about writing down her story. She laughed and said that at a recent reunion of Warsaw Ghetto survivors in New York she had been introduced as 'Magda, the only one of us who is *not* writing her memoirs!' Neither her amused response, nor mounting the exhibition of photos, would have been conceivable before the Eichmann trial in 1961. The trial and conviction of Eichmann catapulted the Holocaust into international consciousness, just as, thirty-two years later, Steven Spielberg's film *Schindler's List* would do afresh for a new generation.

Six years after the Eichmann trial, the Six Day War established Israel's position at the centre of the Jewish world. Until then, the Jewish press in various countries would tend to highlight on its front page stories of local interest, especially when, as during the mid-1960s, Israel was going through a bleak phase of higher emigration than immigration, emerging tensions between the relatively prosperous Ashkenazi and the disadvantaged Sephardic communities, and a stagnant economy. News from the Middle East was dominated by the doings of President Nasser of Egypt.

But ever since the stunning victory of June 1967, Israel has been the automatic lead story in the Jewish media worldwide. Within weeks, the *Jewish Chronicle*, reflecting Anglo-Jewry's sense of priorities, took the editorial decision to reserve its first five pages for news from Israel, saving some momentous event of Jewish concern in the UK or elsewhere. Nowadays, with so much critical international attention focused on Israel, its spokesmen are wont to ask plaintively why it is that such a tiny country has so many reporters permanently assigned there, and why it attracts so much more column space than somewhere of similar size and population, such as Wales or Austria.

The reason is, of course, that Wales and Austria tend to keep out of serial wars with their closest neighbours and are not geographically situated at the likely flashpoint of the next global conflagration. But, until 1967, Israel more or less had its wish of avoiding excessive media coverage. After the 1956 Sinai Campaign, apart from occasional incursions by *fedayeen* from Egypt and Jordan, promptly paid back with harsh retaliation to send a deterrent message, and needling provocations with Syria around the Sea of Galilee, Israel's borders stayed relatively tranquil.

We now know much more from previously embargoed material and the reminiscences of Egyptian military and diplomatic figures who were closely involved about the calculations that prompted Nasser into his disastrous decision to present Israel with an explicit *casus belli* by closing the Straits of Tiran to her shipping. We also know more about the Soviet Union's devious and misleading role in the build-up to war, and the confident assessments of both Israeli and American military intelligence that it would take Israel only seven to ten days to defeat the Egyptian and Syrian forces.[3]

None of this was apparent at the time. A beaming Nasser appeared on TV screens surrounded by smiling pilots and soldiers. In contrast, Levi Eshkol, the Israeli prime minister, looked old and sounded hesitant. He was one of the veteran guard of Labour politicians who had made *aliyah* as idealistic pioneers, changed their family names with their demeaning Diaspora resonances to something defiantly new Hebrew and worked their way up through the murky world of pre-state *Yishuv* politics that in its plotting, double-dealing and shifting alliances resembled nothing so much as the *shtetl* (small-town) environment from which as young Zionists they had fought to escape. Until Ben-Gurion's retirement, Eshkol had been a canny finance minister always receptive to a mutually advantageous deal, with a pithy Yiddish sense of humour and turn of phrase. Reputedly he greeted one big businessman looking for a favour by brushing aside all courtesies: 'You're a busy man, I'm a busy man. Let's begin at the end.'

Adequate in peacetime, he was badly out of his depth at a time of war. The Israeli public pressed for Moshe Dayan, hero of the Sinai Campaign, to be made minister of defence in a government of national unity. Diaspora Jewry mobilised as never before, holding large public rallies of support and fund-raising on an unprecedented scale. Even so, a sense of alarm and foreboding spread from Israel to the Diaspora. The Jewish Agency called for volunteers from overseas to work on kibbutzim and help out with essential services in place of all the reservists who had been called up. Diplomatic efforts at the UN were getting nowhere. War was inevitable.

More than forty years on, I can still vividly recall my feelings as I took a lonely stroll round the playing fields of Trinity College, Dublin, where I was reading Semitics in preparation for training for the rabbinate, and made the decision to volunteer. After that exciting year in Israel in 1957, working with the sheep and horses on the kibbutz to which Ben-Gurion had retired in order to inspire Israeli youth to settle in the Negev rather than opting for the soft life in Tel-Aviv – remember, Israel was just nine years old then – I had returned home to take up a scholarship at Oxford. I promised myself (and a pretty Israeli girlfriend) that I would come back after university. With a qualification one would be of more use to Israel. That's what all of us said who had been bitten by the Israel bug. Few of us did return permanently.

But now in 1967, barely twenty-five years after the

Nazi Holocaust, we Jews were being threatened with a second extermination. Arab propaganda was crowing about the imminent destruction of Israel and promising to drive the Jews into the sea. It seemed more honourable to choose to die fighting in Israel than to survive through the good fortune of living in the Diaspora. When I announced my decision even my parents accepted it without dissent, and middle-aged men mumbled that if only they were twenty years younger and without a family they would have been on the plane with me.

In the event, my ultimate quixotic sacrifice, and that of many thousand other volunteers, was not required. By the time I arrived on the fourth day of the war and was assigned to a kibbutz, it was clear that Israel had won without my help. What heady, jubilant days! The harvest festival of *Shavuot* fell a couple of days after victory. In a rare display of imagination the government announced that pilgrims would be allowed to visit the site of the Western Wall in Jerusalem, the one surviving remnant of Herod's Temple, under Jordanian control and barred to Jews since 1948. I joined the vast throng, estimated at 200,000, as it snaked round the city walls to the Temple Mount. Palestinians under curfew watched sullenly from their windows in the Old City. In the background, as a reminder of recent fighting, the regular detonation of un-exploded mines could be heard.

At one point I looked back at the flowing stream of people on foot and thought that a pilgrim festival in Temple times would have been like this. It was a powerful religious connection between past and present. Personally, I am left unmoved, even hostile, by shrines, relics, tombs, mementos, vials of Jordan water and splinters of the true cross, and do not think that retention of the Western Wall or any holy site is worth a single Jewish or Arab life. But on that *Shavuot* afternoon in newly united Jerusalem I did feel the potency of religious symbols and why zealots will happily die for them.

In those exhilarating days it was easy to fall into quasi-religious terminology to describe wondrous events. The most popular song was *Yerushalayim shel Zahav*, 'Jerusalem the Golden', a lyrical evocation of the sense of awe at being able to return to the Old City with its golden dome on the Mosque of Omar and visit the Dead Sea again by way of Jericho. Almost the worst abusers of religious metaphor were Reform rabbis of the largest synagogue movement in the USA with nearly three million members. One expected Orthodox Jews to detect God's guiding hand in the deliverance. But Reform rabbis? Supposedly devotees of Reason, successors to the *Wissenschaft des Judentums* (Scientific Study of Judaism) school of mid-nineteenth-century German scholarship influenced by Hegel, they slipped easily into describing Israel's victory as 'miraculous', 'a divine intervention', 'the day that the Lord has made', 'the Almighty remembering His people Israel'.

Starting in America, Jewish theologians began to develop a schema that posited a causal connection between two landmark events: from destruction in Europe to redemption in the Land of Israel. Israel's miraculous escape from the valley of the shadow was partial recompense for the enormity of the Holocaust. There had been no equivalent in Jewish thought to the 'Death of God' debate among Protestant theologians in the late 1950s and 1960s. Philosophically speaking, asking why God had been absent in Auschwitz was no different in kind from the agonising problem that the biblical prophets had confronted about God's inscrutable purposes in allowing the destruction of the First Temple or rabbis had been faced with during the exile from Spain, the Crusades, medieval pogroms, and the Chmielnitski massacres that decimated Ukrainian communities in the mid-seventeenth century. But the very magnitude and industrial scale of the Nazi attempt to wipe out Jewry dwarfed all previous disasters. In the modern, scientific age it was bound to pose more urgently than ever before the question of whether God – certainly in the attributes of omnipotence and omniscience ascribed to Him in traditional Jewish theology – really existed.

Rather than pursue the implications of such a blasphemous suggestion, Jewish thinkers nervously skirted around it, tweaking God's attributes here, quoting Eli Wiesel's overwrought Chasidic parables about the death camps there, invoking the Free Will defence as a last resort. Don't ask: Where was God in Auschwitz? Ask: Where was Man? In the USA, Richard Rubenstein, a Conservative-trained rabbi and academic, published a book influenced by fashionable existentialism, *After Auschwitz*,[4] which argued that it was no longer possible to sustain belief in a supernatural deity, that we live in a cold, dark, unfeeling cosmos from which God has permanently retreated and in which He plays no active part. It was a best-seller and won Rubenstein notoriety and opprobrium for his pains. Generally speaking, Jews gathered in their synagogues and recited an unchanged liturgy that praised God's awesome power, majesty, goodness, mercy, and compassion for the oppressed. Few might believe it, but there was a comfort of sorts in repeating familiar words.

Into this absence of faith, victorious Israel stepped to

fill the void. Israel and Judaism became synonymous. Now, suddenly, there was a new Redeemer to turn to. Zionism became the substitute for Jewish belief. The re-unification of Jerusalem and the capture of the West Bank, so redolent with place names from the Bible, dis-proved the dangerous notion that the Holocaust had precipitated a permanent rupture with the Jewish past. God moves in mysterious ways . . . There was a danger-ous whiff of messianism in the air.

Just as Israel had declared herself the guardian of the memory of the Holocaust with the seizure and trial of Eichmann, so now with victory in the Six Day War a rejoicing Diaspora granted her the protectorate over *all* Jewry. The new buzz phrase for Diaspora fund-raisers, rabbis, educators, youth workers and communal leaders became 'the centrality of Israel in Jewish life'. A tri-umphant Israel was not only the beacon for world Jewry but also the guarantor of Diaspora survival. Major Jew-ish organisations rushed to relocate their headquarters in unified Jerusalem.

Such euphoria was not confined to Jews. When I re-turned to Ireland three months later, people would clasp my hand and say, 'I just want to congratulate you on your remarkable victory.' Modestly accepting the plaudits seemed more gracious than pointing out that Di-aspora Jews were not the same as Israelis.

My own response to a second lengthy sojourn in Israel had been characteristically ambivalent. On the one hand, I promised myself – and the very attractive divorcee who pruned roses with me in the kibbutz orchard (I have to acknowledge in retrospect that my success with Israeli women probably had less to do with my good looks and inherent qualities than that I represented a meal ticket to greener pastures for them) – that I would finish rabbinic studies then think about helping to establish Progressive Judaism in Israel, which in those days was either aggressively secular or atavistically Orthodox.

On the other hand, I was wary about buying into the then prevalent notion that the Diaspora was doomed and the Jewish future lay only in Israel. I married in 1969, and when I mentioned to my new wife that I still harboured residual guilt feelings about not having settled in Israel, she briskly announced that in that case I would be going there alone, which could be said to have settled the issue for me. But it was a deeper intellectual and emotional dilemma than that.

Throughout Jewish history there has always been a tension between particularism and universalism; whether to be, in the biblical description of the soothsayer Balaam, 'a people that shall dwell apart' (Numbers 23:9) or, in Isaiah's phrase, to be 'a light unto the nations' (Isaiah 42:6). This tension has played itself out in many different times, countries and circumstances. As one relatively recent example, when Hermann Cohen (1842–1918), an eminent neo-Kantian philosopher of the Marburg School, was told that Zionism aimed to produce a happy new breed of Jews, he riposted sardonically, 'Aha, so they want us to be happy now, do they?' A persistent critic of Jewish nationalism, Cohen held the opinion that the Jewish destiny was 'to go on living among the nations as the God-sent dew, to remain with them and be fruitful for them'.

For better or worse, I have always counted myself among the Jewish Universalists, preferring to take my chances in wider society, learning from other cultures, mixing with other peoples. I have been known to remark flippantly, but mean it seriously, that the revered rabbis of the Talmud were great scholars, teachers and wise men, but would have benefited even more had they read some Plato and Aristotle instead of scornfully dismissing 'Greek wisdom' as a distraction from studying God's laws recorded in the Bible.

The symbiosis that emerged after 1967 between the Holocaust and Israel, memorialising the one by sacralising the other, has had baneful ramifications. The most serious is that every Jewish or non-Jewish critic of Israeli policy – and there has been much to be critical about – must tediously preface any comments with a lengthy acknowledgement of the unique horror of the Holocaust and therefore a full understanding of why Israel, established as a refuge for the survivors, should be so concerned about her security and reluctant to jeopardise it without cast-iron guarantees of peace from all her Arab neighbours. Any words of judgement have been vitiated in advance by the obligatory preface that 'I feel your pain', in tribute to Jewry's past suffering. Thus Israel's creation myth is accepted at face value and manipulated by unscrupulous politicians, of whom Binyamin Netanyahu is the most recent example, to justify their obduracy over withdrawing from Palestinian territory.

It is indeed true that some 350,000 Holocaust survivors eventually made their way to the newly created State of Israel. But it is just that – a myth – to perpetuate the idea that Israel was brought into being by a guilty world wanting to make restitution for its indifference to Jewish suffering under Nazism. Recent archival research has plausibly shown that any linkage between the two events is more fanciful than real.[5] There is no evidence that any of the countries that voted at the United Nations by 33 votes to 13 to partition Palestine into a Jewish and an Arab state were prompted by 'guilt' rather than the usual considerations of realpolitik.

America and the Soviet bloc together sponsored the crucial resolution. Harry Truman (not a known Jewish sympathiser) and Joseph Stalin (a paranoid anti-Semite) had specific domestic and geopolitical reasons for acting in concert. For one, it was securing the Jewish vote in the forthcoming presidential election. For the other, it was loosening Great Britain's ties in the Middle East and establishing a Soviet presence there. And those South American countries that supplied the lion's share of favourable votes had no cause to feel guilty about the Jewish catastrophe in distant Europe, but every cause to be aware of their military and economic reliance on their American neighbour. The eminent Zionist historian David Vital, after examining British and American foreign policy immediately post-war, dismissed as 'absurd' the theory that Israel was born, so to speak, of the Holocaust – a bone thrown to survivors by benevolent powers in belated contrition for their indifference to Jewish suffering.[6]

But because it has become a given of Israel's foundation narrative to stress the transition from the Holocaust in Europe to the creation of a Jewish state where such horrors would never happen again, as though the second was a natural progression from the first, we regularly witness the unedifying spectacle of Israel reminding the rest of the world of Jewry's victim status, in order to justify its own bullying behaviour. As Avraham Burg, the former Knesset Speaker and one of the diminishing band of Israeli doves, astutely observed, 'Victimhood sets you free.'[7] You can excuse almost any error of judgement on your part and condone however much pain you inflict on others – usually without even offering a formulaic expression of regret – if you can put it down to a tragic birth and traumatic upbringing among implacable enemies forever bent on your destruction.

The most avid exponent of this victim-therefore-aggressor line was Menachem Begin, Israel's first Likud prime minister. In his case it has to be said that his brooding obsession with the destruction of European Jewry was genuine, not the calculated ploy it has become since in the hands of Israeli politicians and lobbyists. He kept on his office wall a map marking all the destroyed Jewish communities of Europe. (I have seen something similar in Ramallah on the office wall of Hanan Ashrawi, the Fatah politician; a map of pre-Israel Palestine showing all the Arab villages obliterated in the 1948 War.) Begin would stand visitors in front of the map and harangue them on why, therefore, Israel could not give up territory captured in 1967 or contemplate a Palestinian state alongside. As his behaviour grew increasingly erratic during the 1982 invasion of Lebanon, Begin took to comparing Arafat to Hitler and the PLO to Nazis. In 1993, Likud's current leader and prime minister, Benyamin Netanyahu, who, unlike Begin, has managed successfully to conceal any guiding principle in his career apart from that of acquiring power, wrote a self-serving autobiography[8] in which he repeatedly equated the Palestinian goal of statehood with Nazism, described an Israel that withdrew from the West Bank as a 'ghetto-state' with 'Auschwitz borders' and compared international pressure 'to gouge Judea and Samaria out of Israel' to Hitler's effort to wrench the Sudetenland from Czechoslovakia in 1938.

Another consequence of regarding the transition from

Holocaust to Israel as a natural progression, with the indescribable bestiality inflicted on Jews by Nazism furnishing the explanation for why Israel is understandably inflexible in dealing with Palestinians, is that the Holocaust itself has been trivialised in the process. On frequent occasions, in Israel and the Diaspora, individually or collectively, Holocaust survivors have protested that invoking their name in defence of some morally dubious or militarily excessive action by Israel dishonours the memory of those who perished. As we have noted, Prime Minister Begin was particularly culpable in that respect, but its effect can be detected in other, more insidious ways.

There is now, for example, a confusing plethora of commemorative days from which to choose to mark the Holocaust. Tony Blair's government instituted a national Holocaust Day, its purpose to universalise the 'lessons of the Holocaust' (whatever that means) and its annual approach the occasion for ritual protests from Muslim organisations that either won't take part or want their own day of remembrance. Then in the Jewish calendar there is *Yom ha-Shoah* (Holocaust Day) on the anniversary of the Warsaw Ghetto uprising, an addition to, but not to be confused with, Israel's Memorial Day, which falls a week after Independence Day celebrations. The day observed in the religious calendar for recalling the victims of the Holocaust is *Tishah b'Av* (the Ninth of Av), the date on which, according to tradition, both the First and Second Temples were destroyed, and pious Jews fast and recite the Book of Lamentations. Finally, a date increasingly favoured by those of German descent is the anniversary of *Kristallnacht* (Night of Broken Glass), 9 November 1938, when Nazi thugs went on a rampage of killing, burning and looting that effectively heralded the end of Jewish life in Germany.

Almost every Western country has its own Holocaust museum. The USA has a superb museum in Washington, finally unveiled after intense controversy between competing Jewish organisations claiming ownership of the project. In Berlin there is the comprehensive Museum of German Jewish History, housed in a magnificent building designed by the architect Daniel Libeskind, and a haunting Holocaust Memorial by Peter Eisenman, covering nearly five acres a few hundred yards from the Brandenburg Gate on one side and the site of Hitler's bunker on the other; a graphic illustration, in the very heart of its capital, of Germany's shame and remorse.

In the UK there are two major venues that commemorate the Holocaust: the original *Beth Shalom* (House of Peace), a small, deeply moving centre privately set up by a Quaker family that had been overwhelmed by its visit to *Yad Vashem* (The Hand and the Name), the Israeli Holocaust Museum outside Jerusalem; there is also the larger, more impersonal exhibition at the Imperial War Museum, although what connection the Holocaust has with British military history is not readily discernible. A Holocaust museum opened recently in Warsaw, a belated gesture from a country never historically noteworthy for warmth towards its large Jewish population. Now that the USSR has disintegrated, former Soviet satellites are rapidly catching up with sculptures, monuments and permanent exhibitions to memorialise their Jews butchered during the German advance on the Eastern Front. An Israeli sculptor friend is currently working on a huge memorial for Babi Yar, the notorious ravine outside Kiev where approximately 100,000 Jews were massacred by

German troops in 1941. Until now, the inscription on the plinth of the sculpture there in bombastic neo-heroic style mentions only the 'Soviet citizens' who were slaughtered at Babi Yar.

An obligatory port of call for every visiting statesman to Israel, *Yad Vashem* once was a profound experience for all who toured the site. Nowadays, with its sponsored buildings, noisy groups of schoolchildren and large plaques dedicated to generous benefactors, it has a brash Florida feel to it.

Holocaust archives, research centres and university chairs also abound, often in rivalry with each other. The Simon Wiesenthal Centre in Los Angeles, named after the famous Nazi hunter but with which he disavowed any connection, seems to depend for its funding on shrilly proclaiming evidence of resurgent anti-Semitism in Europe or unearthing yet another wretched Latvian geriatric hiding under an assumed identity who might have been implicated in a mass killing of Jews seventy years ago. At the Hebrew University in Jerusalem there is a professorship in Holocaust Studies endowed by the exotically named Vidal Sassoon Centre for the Study of Anti-Semitism. The Steven Spielberg Institute does altogether more valuably enduring work recording and collating for posterity oral testimonies from the dwindling number of Holocaust survivors.

When one considers what a thriving growth industry the Holocaust has become, providing gainful employment for an army of teachers, researchers, historians, archivists, university assistants, tenured professors, fundraisers, museum employees and ancillary staff, the tasteless but pertinent flippancy of an American Jewish comedian comes to mind: 'There's no business like Shoah business.'

When all is said and done, this automatically assumed synonymous relationship between the Holocaust and Israel is to the benefit of neither historical truth nor the future of the state. Not to the memory of the Holocaust, because too much repetition diminishes its salutary impact and reduces its unique evil to banality. And not to the well-being of Israel, because using the Holocaust as *raison d'être* and incontestable justification frees her from ultimate responsibility for her actions and having them judged by the usual criteria applied to all other nations at the bar of international opinion. And that in turn can fuel an anti-Zionism that may or may not shade over into anti-Semitism.

3

Anti-Semitism and anti-Zionism

Mordecai Kaplan (1881–1983) was born in Lithuania and taken to the USA as a child. He was the founder of the Reconstructionist movement. Kaplan was one of the foremost figures of twentieth-century American Judaism, a traditionally trained scholar thoroughly versed in Rabbinic literature and codes, yet receptive to secular knowledge and alert to the nuances of contemporary Jewish life. In his best-known, frequently reprinted book he famously remarked, 'If Judaism is reduced merely to an awareness of anti-Semitism, it ceases to be a civilisation and becomes a complex.'[1]

In that case, we modern Jews are suffering from a severe pathological condition. The three pillars around which classical Jewish thought revolved used to be: God, Torah and the People Israel. Nowadays they are: anti-Semitism, the Holocaust and the State of Israel.

That anti-Semitism, the Holocaust and Israel are intimately bound up with each other is self-evident. Just as there was a causal link between anti-Semitism and the Holocaust, so there was between anti-Semitism and the Zionist struggle to create a Jewish homeland that was intended to solve 'the Jewish problem' and to ensure that the Holocaust could never happen again.

But History rarely unfolds predictably, in such clear-cut patterns. In the short term – meaning the six decades of its existence – the State of Israel, far from solving the problem of anti-Semitism, has exacerbated it, and failed to increase the collective security of its Jewish citizens or alleviate the existential anxiety of Jews around the world. And when Jewish representatives insist, as the Israel PR Lobby does, on an axiomatic linkage between anti-Semitism and anti-Zionism, as though they are two aspects of the same seamless, linear continuity, not only are we guilty of sloppy, ahistorical oversimplification but we are also failing to treat a subject vital to our well-being with the intellectual rigour it deserves.

The first corrective point that needs to be made is that European Christian anti-Semitism and Arab Muslim anti-Semitism differ greatly in origin, theological animus, duration and magnitude.

European anti-Semitism grew out of religious hatred for the accursed Jews who had rejected the true Saviour and killed him. From the time that Christianity became the official religion of the Holy Roman Empire under Constantine (325 CE), the treatment of Jewish communities was determined by ecclesiastical law and depended on the whim of individual Christian rulers and their bishops, usually based not on dogma but on a prudential calculation of how valuable Jews were to the local economy: whether it was more beneficial to plunder them financially and drive them out or to allow them to remain under royal and Church protection and bleed them through taxation instead. All of this was done with theological validation, the Jews' lowly estate as witnesses to the triumph of Christianity being their punishment for having demanded the crucifixion of the Son of God. Such a justification in Church teachings for reviling, mistreating, torturing, killing, forcibly converting or expelling another group of people simply because they were Jews – a *religious* motive – is more accurately called Judaeophobia than anti-Semitism. When Shylock speaks of the 'lodged hate and certain loathing' he feels for Antonio, Shakespeare equally well might have been describing the normative Christian attitude of his time towards Jews. The villainous potency and enduring fascination of Shylock as the archetypal Jew is such that most people automatically assume that *he* is the merchant of Venice, when in fact it is Antonio.

The term 'anti-Semitism' itself was first coined in 1879 by Wilhelm Marr, a German gutter journalist and – sadly inevitable, somehow – the baptised son of a Jewish actor. He used it to justify *Judenhass* (Jew-hate) on the ground that the Jews were an alien 'race' of mixed Asiatic stock polluting the pure Aryan peoples among whom they had settled. This new phenomenon of anti-Semitism was primarily economic and racist, grounded in fear of the spectacular success and visibility of newly emancipated Jews in the professions, banking, commerce, academia and the stock market. Instead of using Christian holy writings as its warrant, anti-Semitism quoted evidence from the current pseudo-science of anthropology to 'prove' the inherent superiority of Aryanism over Semitism.

But of course new anti-Semitism rehashed the old, familiar tropes from medieval Judaeophobia. The malign stereotypes from sermons, popular ballads and folk mythology were given a fresh minting: the Jew as member of a sinister race, set apart from all others not merely by his rituals but by his collective character; arrogant even in his debasement, secretive, cunning, grasping, obsessive about money; scattered throughout the world and

forming an international brotherhood even more powerful than that of the Freemasons; his hidden hand and
shady contacts controlling the banks and media in
whichever country that his tribe infiltrated; never to be
fully trusted on account of dual loyalties.

This paranoid admixture of fear, envy, hostility and
grudging admiration was the typical anti-Jewish discourse of Christian Europe from medieval times until
Nazism. Bigoted, phobic, discriminatory, and an incite-
ment to violence against Jews, it is not unreasonable to
insist that such an unremitting diet of negative charac-
terisation, from a poetic masterpiece such as Geoffrey
Chaucer's *The Prioress's Tale* to the vapourings of
Richard Wagner about Jewish decadence in music, created the climate in which blaming the Jews for all of
society's ills and offering a nostrum for 'the Jewish problem' was the stock in trade of every demagogue; and
the respected Prussian historian Heinrich von Treitschke
(1834–1896) could declare with reference to the immigrants pouring over the Polish border – albeit with no
inkling in his wildest imaginings of how the slogan would
be acted on by Hitler and his henchmen – that 'the Jews
are our misfortune'.

In his controversial novella *The Portage to San Cristobal of A.H.*,[2] a philosophical disquisition on the imagined capture and trial of a ninety-year-old Adolf Hitler
in the Amazon jungle, George Steiner gives the last,
powerful speech in his own defence to Hitler himself.
Hitler blames it on the Jews for having learnt his master-
race theory from their 'covenant of election, the setting
apart of the race, *das heilige Volk*, like unto no other . . .
My racism was a parody of yours, a hungry imitation.
What is a thousand-year *Reich* compared to the eternity

of Zion?' He continues that there had to be a solution, a *final* solution, because of the three impossible burdens that the Jews had bequeathed to humanity. Firstly, their creation of an invisible, omnipotent, all-seeing, all-knowing God: 'We are as blown dust to His immensity. But because we are His creatures, we must be better than ourselves, love our neighbour, be continent, give of what we have to the beggar . . . The Jew invented conscience and left man a guilty serf.' Secondly, theirs was the responsibility for Jesus and his demands of man that 'he renounce the world, that he leave mother and father behind, that he offer the other cheek when slapped, that he render good for evil, that he love his neighbour as himself . . .' And thirdly, theirs was self-incrimination for the fact that Marx and his minions, with their cry of equality for all and justice on earth, 'the congregations of Bolshevism – Trotsky, Rosa Luxemburg, Kamenev, the whole fanatic, murderous pack – were of Israel'; it had been only small, incremental steps 'from Sinai to Nazareth, from Nazareth to the covenant of Marxism'.

Three times the Jew had pressed on mankind 'the blackmail of transcendence' and 'the bacillus of perfection'. It was the Jew's voice that cried out to remind us we are made in the divine image and must do His will, that in losing life we gain life eternal, and from each according to his abilities, to each according to his needs. Mankind was sick to death of being infected by the Jewish 'virus of utopia' and had barely raised a hand when Hitler set about his extermination cure. The Jew liked to think of himself as chosen to be mankind's conscience; in reality, as the reaction to Hitler's policies had demonstrated, the Jew was only mankind's *bad* conscience, and getting rid of him would let the world breathe in peace.

It is a dazzlingly sustained devil's advocate defence (only a Jew could have dared to present it). But interestingly, the final and most provocative argument that Steiner puts in Hitler's mouth, the one that caused the greatest controversy when the book first appeared – that he should be honoured by Jews, recognised as their true Messiah maybe, because by means of the Holocaust he had done more to create Israel than Herzl ever did, and had given Jews 'the courage of injustice' to drive out the Arabs – that argument would raise few flickers of disagreement today. The connecting link discerned by Jewish theologians and an army of fund-raisers after the 1967 victory, between destruction in Europe and rebirth in Israel – 'The Holocaust was the necessary mystery before Israel could come into its strength', in the words given to Hitler – had not yet become common currency when Steiner wrote his book. It would be satisfying mythology to maintain that Israel was created solely out of the bravery, skill and military resourcefulness of its pioneers; but the generally acknowledged and galling fact is that in the ten years between 1935 and 1945 Hitler and his National Socialist German Workers' Party did more to accelerate the reality of a Jewish state than all of Zionism's efforts had managed in the previous fifty.

If we turn to consider Muslim anathema of the Jews, it has been of shorter duration, more sporadic and less malignant than its European counterpart, at least until recent times. In the words of Professor Bernard Lewis, the leading authority on Jewish–Muslim history, who over the years has moved from a position of liberal sympathy for Islam to advising George Bush about the invasion of Iraq, so can be quoted in support by doves and hawks alike: '[The situation of Jews under Islamic rule] was never as bad as in Christendom at its worst, nor ever as good as in Christendom at its best.' He elaborated that 'there is nothing in Islamic history to parallel the Spanish expulsion and Inquisition, the Russian pogroms or the Nazi Holocaust', but added the caveat that there was nothing in the experience of Jews under Islam 'to compare with the progressive emancipation and acceptance accorded to Jews in the democratic West during the last three centuries'.[3]

In another, earlier work,[4] Lewis makes the point that 'There is little sign of any deep-rooted emotional hostility directed against Jews – or for that matter any other group – such as the anti-Semitism of the Christian world . . . On the whole, in contrast to Christian anti-Semitism, the Muslim attitude towards non-Muslims is one not of hate or fear or envy but simply of contempt.' That contempt for those benighted enough not to acknowledge the ultimate Koranic revelation and the supremacy of Muhammad was formalised in the so-called Pact of Omar in the early eighth century, which in return for guaranteeing security of life and property and freedom of worship to non-believers required Jews and Christians to accept inferior *dhimmi* status and payment of the *jizya* (poll) tax to the local Muslim ruler.

As in Christian Europe's treatment of the Jews, the stringency or leniency with which these rules were applied – and ancillary ones about not building new synagogues, wearing distinctive clothing, not riding horses and not employing Muslims – varied from ruler to ruler and depending on Jewish utility to the state. But Lewis points out a crucial contrast between Muslim and Christian treatment of the Jews in medieval times: 'In Islamic society hostility to the Jew is non-theological.'[5] It was not related to any specific statement of belief or motivated by a particular historical incident. Unlike with Christianity, Islam's anti-Jewish bias was not genetically encoded in the very birth pangs of the new religion. It was, rather, as Lewis acutely puts it, 'the usual attitude of the dominant to the subordinate, of the majority to the minority, without that additional theological and therefore psychological dimension that gives Christian anti-Semitism its unique and special character'. For centuries throughout the territories of the Ottoman Empire, conditions for Jews were generally benign.

How was it, then, that all the classic themes of European anti-Semitism metastasised to find their lurid modern equivalent in an avalanche of pamphlets, school textbooks, university theses and Internet postings throughout the Arab world? The one word answer is: Zionism. From 1897 onwards, the influx of pioneers into Palestine had a baneful impact on Muslim–Jewish relations, and the 1948 establishment of Israel confirmed the rupture. An infidel government in the midst of *Dar al-Islam*, the House of Islam, where Muslim rule and Islamic law should prevail, is an intolerable affront that abrogates the *dhimma* pact and can be rectified only by a canonically obligatory perpetual state of struggle known as *jihad*, usually translated as 'holy war'.

Since the beginning of the twentieth century, there had been growing Arab resentment that the proper relationship between Muslims and *dhimmi* unbelievers was being subverted by the expanding influence of Western powers in the region. This aggrieved sense of the old order being overturned by inferior *dhimmi* found one channel of expression through the translation from the original French of anti-Semitic literature produced during the Dreyfus Affair. As it happens, the translations were done mainly by Arab Catholics, Maronites and Uniate Christians, working with European consuls and traders to oust local Jews from positions of influence in the crumbling Ottoman Empire in favour of their own Christian nationals. The most notorious of all anti-Semitic forgeries, *Protocols of the Elders of Zion*, a Russian fabrication based on a French lampoon of Napoleon III, which purports to unveil a Jewish plot for worldwide domination, was published in Cairo in 1927.

During the Second World War, the Grand Mufti of Jerusalem, Haj Amin al-Husseini (1895–1974), took refuge in Berlin, from where he broadcast Nazi propaganda to the Arab world. In the summer of 1940 and again in 1941, he presented proposals to the German government on behalf – so he said – of an inter-Arab representative committee, for German–Arab co-operation to achieve common ends. His draft proposal included a clause to the effect that Germany and Italy would recognise the right of Arab countries to solve the question of the Jewish elements in Palestine and other Arab countries 'as required by the national and ethnic [*volkisch*] interests of the Arabs, and as the Jewish Question was solved in Germany and Italy'.[6] The regular anti-Semitic charge that Jews manipulated the organs of state was modified to suit an Arab audience. In 1942, as American troops were about to land in North Africa, the Mufti broadcast that 'The Americans are the willing slaves of the Jews, and as such the enemies of Islam and the Arabs.' Two years later he declared, 'No one ever thought that 140 million Americans would become tools in Jewish hands . . .'[7]

Other staples of Christian anti-Semitism, including accusations of Jewish well-poisoning and the Blood Libel, proliferated both preceding and after the establishment of Israel in 1948.[8] Pogroms in Baghdad, Tripoli, Cairo and Tangier that followed the Arab defeat were almost as bad as anything against Jews in medieval Europe. Nowadays, a comprehensive literature of anti-Semitic works, either translated or adapted from European originals, is available in Arabic; indeed, there are more translations and editions of the *Protocols* in Arabic than in any other language, and it is required reading in departments of Comparative Religion at several reputable Arab universities. Apparently it was the custom of King Faisal of Saudi Arabia (1901–1975) to present copies of the *Protocols* and other anti-Semitic tracts to his visitors. He solemnly informed an interviewer from a popular Egyptian magazine that while he was in Paris on a recent visit the police had discovered the bodies of five murdered children whose blood had been drained by some Jews, subsequently arrested, in order to mix it in the bread [*sic*] that they eat on their annual day of vengeance.[9]

The king is dead; long live the same old obsession with Jews' eating habits. A teacher at the university named in the King's honour told readers of a Saudi daily that the Jewish ritual of 'spilling human blood to prepare pastries for their holidays is a well-established fact'. For Purim goodies, she elucidated, 'the victim must be a mature adolescent who is . . . either Christian or Muslim', unlike the Passover cannibalism that had so upset King Faisal thirty years previously, when 'children under ten must be used'.[10]

My own experience of the pernicious ubiquity of the *Protocols* concerned the London Central Mosque in Regent's Park. When the mosque opened in 1978, my synagogue council sent a welcoming gift. Along with the vicar of St John's Wood Church and the mosque's director, Dr (later Sir) Zaki Badawi – the shrewdest and most effective spokesman yet to emerge from the UK Muslim community – we arranged a series of regular Trialogue meetings between the three faiths, the first of their kind ever held in this country, attracting audiences of several hundred people. The clergy of mosque, church and synagogue met monthly for lunch together, and groups of doctors, teachers and social workers held sessions to discuss common issues.

The contacts continued throughout the Israeli invasion of Lebanon in 1982 and its aftermath, although there were growing tensions. Eventually Dr Badawi, the Revd John Slater and I decided to drop the public meetings, because the atmosphere had become too confrontational and combative, stirred by unfolding events in the Middle East. Those who refuse to acknowledge that the Israel–Palestine conflict has been the major factor in the rise of Arab anti-Semitism and the consequent embitterment of Muslim–Jewish relations worldwide are deluding themselves as wilfully as those Labour ministers who refused to accept that the London suicide bombings of July 2005 by British-born Muslims had anything to do with the 2002 USA–UK decision to invade Iraq.

A couple of years after we stopped the meetings, Dr Badawi quit the mosque in the aftermath of the Salman Rushdie controversy over *The Satanic Verses*. His successor was a charming Saudi Arabian, who, true to that country's favoured method of conducting diplomacy, preferred behind-the-scenes negotiation to public visibility. After a cordial introductory get-together, the mosque's ten-year relationship with its local church and synagogue gently tapered away.

Not long afterwards, a congregant told me how shocked he had been to see a copy of *Protocols of the Elders of Zion* on sale in the mosque bookshop. I wrote to the director in a carefully modulated tone of 'more in sorrow than in anger' to say how disappointed I was, given the warm relationship between our two places of worship and my own close friendship with his predecessor, to hear that such a scurrilous anti-Semitic forgery should be on sale to mosque visitors. He wrote back with effusive apologies, assuring me that it had been an unfortunate 'oversight' committed by an underling, and the book would be withdrawn.

And so it was, but from school textbooks to supposedly 'scholarly' works for the advanced student, whether in Middle-Eastern countries or in the wider world, modern-day Muslim readers have at their disposal the whole gamut of European anti-Semitic mythology and iconography. Anti-Jewish cartoons in the Arabic press use caricatures and stereotypes descended directly from the Nazi propaganda rag *Der Stürmer*. Holocaust denial is a commonplace.

Although they started from different theological premises and in different social and economic milieux, old Christian and new Muslim anti-Semitism have merged in a common typology.

So we Jews do have justifiable cause to be concerned. Anti-Semitism has always been a light sleeper and requires constant monitoring. Jewish students regularly report examples of harassment and intimidation from Islamic societies on university campuses.[11] In recent years there has been an increase in vandalism against synagogues and cemeteries, and attacks against Jewish persons and property have also risen, most markedly in France, where relations between the state and its large Muslim community are sensitive and fractious.

I was visited recently by the moderator of a European-based and European Union-accredited Council of Religious Leaders. His brief was to ask my opinion about the current level of anti-Semitism in the UK. I said light-heartedly that I was hardly in the best position to answer, since it would be a very odd person indeed who on my being introduced to him as a rabbi replied, 'How do you do. By the way, I hate Jews.' But my impression was that although criticism of Israel had become sharper and more widespread, on the whole British Jewry did not feel any more vulnerable on account of the upsurge in anti-Semitism that according to alarmist reports in the American and Israeli press was supposedly sweeping Europe. My visitor then told me that in his area of London, where few if any Jews live, members of the local Hindu, Jain, Sikh and Zoroastrian communities – which historically have had minimal contact with Judaism – had confessed to him how angry they have become with Jews generally, on account of Israel's treatment of the Palestinians.

That sobered me, because a generalised prejudice against all due to the actions of some is how bigotry spreads its poison and prepares the ground for certitudes beginning, 'The trouble with Jews/Blacks/Muslims/Pakistanis is . . .' So vigilance is certainly called for, but lugubrious hand-wringing that 'they're all out to get us' and a masochistic pleasure in uncovering evidence of yet another allegedly anti-Semitic thought, word or deed, impairs rational judgement and a calibrated response. This applies particularly to Israel's American vigilantes, as a couple of examples will illustrate.

In 2005, the indefatigable Abe Foxman of the ADL cited international criticism of the security wall that Israel was building to deter incursions by suicide bombers from the West Bank as 'proof' that anti-Semitism was rampant. Even more lurid and overwrought, Phyllis Chesler's best-selling book (among American Jews, at least), *The New Anti-Semitism*, detected evidence of 'a global war against the Jews' and asserted 'in our contemporary world anti-Zionism is nearly inseparable from anti-Semitism'.[12]

So there you have it. But just as hoping to stifle criticism by invoking the Holocaust at every opportunity eventually demeans it, so too crying 'Anti-Semite' at every critic of Israeli policy choices eventually reduces the potency of that charge to the level of a playground taunt.

Surely it should still be possible for us Jews to recognise a difference in kind, degree and gravity between, say, the case of Bishop Richard Williamson, a steadfast Holocaust denier, being welcomed back into the Catholic fold and Silvio Berlusconi, Italy's buffoonish former prime minister, cracking a crass Holocaust joke that played on the stereotype of the money-grasping Jew;[13] or that when a foolish Crown Court judge, summing up in the trial of seven anti-Israel activists accused of damaging an arms factory, directs the jury a propos Operation Cast Lead that it must look 'coldly and dispassionately' at evidence that points to Israeli war crimes, adding, 'It may be as you went through what I can only describe as horrific scenes, scenes of devastation to civilian population, scenes which one would rather have hoped to have disappeared with the Nazi regimes of the last war, you may have felt anger and been absolutely appalled by them, but you must put that emotion aside',[14] he is flouting every canon of judicial impartiality and giving vent to his own subjective emotions but, even so, his anti-Israel bias hardly puts him in the same category as, say, the notorious revisionist historian and Nazi apologist David Irving.

Admittedly more difficult to pick one's way through were the drink- and drugs-fuelled tirades of Mel Gibson, the Hollywood star, and John Galliano, the sacked Dior designer. My instinct is that Gibson *could* be an anti-Semite. He is a fundamentalist Christian with a literal belief in the Gospel narratives, and his 2004 film *The Passion of the Christ* reinforced malign Jewish stereotypes. The crafty Caiaphas is surrounded by ugly, beady-eyed priests, whereas Mary Magdalene is played by the gorgeous Italian actress Monica Belluci and the 'Christian' characters are noticeably better looking and dentally enhanced than their 'Jewish' opponents. Well-meaning Pontius Pilate is hoodwinked by Caiaphas and his vengeful crew. That is the line taken by the last of the Gospels, John's, which sought to ingratiate the new religion of Christianity with its Roman rulers. Crucially, the explosive alleged line of Caiaphas that 'His blood is on us and our children' – which gave rise to the charge of deicide and justification for the punishment of Jews in perpetuity – is omitted in the film's subtitles but retained on the soundtrack, as those few of us who have some knowledge of Aramaic can attest. And Gibson's infamous outburst in July 2006 when arrested for driving under the influence that 'the Jews are responsible for all the wars in the world' sounded like the *in vino veritas* of someone who has drunk deep of, and believes, anti-Semitic conspiracy theories.

On the other hand, Galliano's offensive diatribe of October 2010, the one that prompted his dismissal, sounded like the slurred ramblings of someone coming apart at the seams. Only a complete loss of mental and emotional self-control could explain why anyone would use a bar in the Marais district, historically the Jewish quarter of Paris, to announce that he 'loved' Hitler and not enough Jews had gone to the gas chambers. That repellent remark was echoed regularly by opposing fans on the terraces of football clubs with substantial Jewish support, such as Ajax in Amsterdam or Tottenham Hotspur in London, until the law stepped in. It shared ancestry with chants about the Munich air disaster or the Hillsborough tragedy with which Manchester United and Liverpool teams are still taunted. As Sam Goldwyn might have said: never underestimate the bad taste of the general public. But bad taste about the Holocaust, however gross, is not the same as anti-Semitism.

One of the great safety valves for Jews during centuries of European persecution was a wryly deprecating sense of humour, even to the Jewish definition of an anti-Semite being someone who dislikes Jews more than is necessary. The similar level of indignation and identically parroted rent-a-quotes in response to Bishop Williamson, Berlusconi, Judge Bathurst-Norman, David Irving, Mel Gibson, John Galliano et al., despite the very different level of their offences, would suggest that we are in danger of losing that ability to discriminate between real and imagined anti-Semitism that sometimes is provided by employing a soupçon of humour to give ourselves a more reasoned perspective on alleged anti-Jewish prejudice.

It was precisely the unremitting humourlessness with

which Anthony Julius tracked down in *Trials of the Diaspora* every anti-Jewish reference, whether banal or baneful, in English literature and journalism from medieval times to the present that made it such an indigestible read. It was in support of his thesis, expanded over 588 pages of text plus nearly two hundred more of exhaustive notes, that there is something sinister in current attacks on Jews and the State of Israel that he puts down to 'the persistence in this country of an obdurate, harsh anti-Semitism resistant both to reason and considerations of decency'.

A strong indictment; but in a disparaging review[15] that has probably made me an enemy for life, I poked fun at what first alerted Julius, aged eleven, to the ubiquitous nuances of anti-Semitism. He was, he tells us, travelling in a train with his father and a non-Jewish business associate, tactfully given the alias of 'Arthur'. The two grown-ups were chatting amiably until 'Arthur' said something along the lines that his daughter had a special friend, a Jewish child, and, 'I must say, the child has got the most beautiful manners.'

What a traumatic exposure to anti-Semitism for the young Julius! My earlier generation, as I wrote in the review, was made of sterner stuff. Our gym teacher at primary school would simplify choosing football sides by dividing us up into Jews versus Christians, or 'Yids against Yoks' as we Jewish boys called it; and it was a dare among us who would respond loudest to our teacher Miss Fisher's 'Good morning, children' by substituting a P for the F in our 'Good morning, Miss Fisher' back.

Autres temps autres mœurs. In those post-war days schoolchildren learned the limerick 'Taffy was a Welshman, Taffy was a thief'; 'to Jew' someone was a common idiom; every little girl had a gollywog among her dolls. As evidence of their respectability, boarding houses put notices in the window saying, 'No Irish or Blacks'; outside American country clubs in the South it was: 'No dogs, niggers or Jews'. My mother would not hang out washing on a Sunday, out of deference to our Christian neighbours. Playground fights between Jews and Christians were a regular occurrence (for some reason, Catholic girls were the most uppity) and as we Jewish kids tended to be weedier and more bespectacled – another stereotype – than our assailants, we would shout our gibes from behind the back of our Jewish champion, a youngster so big and muscled that in the derogatory Yiddish epithet he could have been a *shaygets* (gentile lout), who rode into the lists on our behalf like a medieval knight. When it came to weekly Scripture class, Jewish pupils were sent to sit at the back of the class and told to get on with their reading, but we listened, of course, ears burning, while the Gospels recounted terrible things about how the Jews had mistreated gentle Jesus; which did not prevent us from taking any part from the Virgin Mary to Herod to Father Christmas (I played him once) in the annual Nativity play.

There is no way of knowing whether or not such mixed messages and frank expressions of religious antagonism made me and my contemporaries more or less sensitive to anti-Semitism than succeeding generations are. Nowadays, it is certainly to the good that religious and ethnic minorities have legal protection from insult and injury. But it does strike me as somewhat excessive to get into a lather about a well-meant albeit condescending compliment to a Jewish girl with beautiful manners, and to deduce therefrom that it is part of an insidious English variant of the anti-Semitic virus.

Generally speaking, Julius's book had a lukewarm reception from UK reviewers. Either that confirms his thesis, or – more likely – demonstrates their critical bemusement on being asked to accept that the low-grade, ignorantly boorish, *ad hominem* kind of anti-Jewish prejudice typically expressed by the English upper classes and their literary chroniclers, such as G. K. Chesterton, Hilaire Belloc and Evelyn Waugh, or by thriller writers such as John Buchan, Agatha Christie and Eric Ambler, for whom the villain's Jewishness is usually code for 'wily foreigner', fulfils Julius's tortuous definition of anti-Semitism as 'beliefs about Jews or Jewish projects that are both false and hostile and, secondly, the injurious things said to or about Jews or their projects, or done to them, in consequence of those beliefs'. But not since 1947–48, when Britain was vainly trying to keep control in Mandate Palestine and Irgun terrorists were attacking and killing British soldiers, has there been any noticeable level of anti-Jewish feeling in the UK to justify Julius's lucubrations.

In America, however, *Trials of the Diaspora* was given an enthusiastic welcome by the Jewish community (few of whom would have the patience to wade through its acres of legalistic prose and pseudo-anthropological jargon), doubtless because it confirms the conviction tirelessly peddled by the Israel Lobby and Jewish defence organisations that Europe is going through the worst bout of anti-Semitism since Hitler. 'How are things?' Jewish visitors from the USA will enquire in lowered voices, as though the community here spends most of its time cowering in cellars.

Harold Bloom praised Julius's book extravagantly in a *New York Times* review, applauding the immensity of his achievement in unmasking the 'English literary and academic establishment, which essentially opposes the right of the State of Israel to exist, while indulging the humbuggery that its anti-Zionism is not anti-Semitism' – which must be the most preposterous generalisation ever penned by that distinguished literary critic.

True, there *is*, and always has been, a form of braying, Hooray Henry antipathy to Jews among the stately-home-owning, hunt-following fraternity of the English shires – possibly because they were perennially in hock to Jewish bankers. In one of his many books about Winston Churchill, the historian Martin Gilbert records an exchange between Winston's father and an aristocratic country-house guest. 'What, Lord Randolph,' enquires the guest, 'you've not brought your Jewish friends?' 'No,' Randolph Churchill is reputed to have replied, 'I did not think they would be amused by your company.'[16] My scepticism about the story's veracity is only because Randolph Churchill is not known for having said anything else witty in his life. But I can vouch for the veracity of a pretty, blonde and blue-eyed Jewish friend of my wife who regularly accompanies her non-Jewish husband, a well-known public figure, on country-house weekends. She enjoys discomforting any dinner partner who gives vent to anti-Jewish remarks by enquiring sweetly, 'Oh, didn't you know that I'm Jewish from Golders Green?' On one occasion her husband was so outraged by anti-Jewish comments at the dinner table that he insisted they leave immediately, even though it meant forgoing the next day's shooting – in his case a severe deprivation.

Using the indispensable gift of humour to keeps things

in perspective, shortly before he died Tony Judt and I had an email exchange in which we reminisced about amatory conquests in our youth; two elderly Jewish men fondly recalling what a hit we had been in our undergraduate days with 'gels' from the shires. Both of us slight, nimble of mind and body, good with the schmooze, so unlike the big, stolid, huntin'-shootin'-and-fishin' types they were destined eventually to marry, we cut a swathe through these posh, languid, cut-glass-accented English beauties who were captivated, no doubt, by our dark, Semitic energy, as though Benjamin Disraeli had been reincarnated for their entertainment. One brawny, rugby-playing swain threatened to break my neck at a college ball, for having too evidently found favour in the eyes of his date, concluding his minatory outburst with the words: 'What is it about you f***ing Jewish men?' I had not realised until then that we are also the objects of penis envy among jealous Gentiles . . .

Undoubtedly it is the element of insouciant cockiness (no pun intended) allied to a quick intelligence that so riles our detractors. What *right* have Jews got to act so superior, given their subservient history? But it is true of all nations and peoples that they seek to find something unique about themselves. For Cicero it was to be able to say *Civis Romanus sum*. Joseph Chamberlain thought that the greatest card to be dealt in the hand of life was the good fortune to be born an Englishman. A few years ago I was invited to a glittering banquet in Vienna, at which the presidents and prime ministers of various recently created Balkan states were making a pitch for admission to the expanding European Union. They expatiated on the glorious history and culture of their country and the rapid economic development that made it so well

fitted to take its place in the EU. The prime minister
of Albania was last of the five speakers. He confessed
that his country could not claim the glorious cultural
patrimony of its neighbours, or their level of industrial-
isation, but he reminded his audience that Ferrando and
Guglielmo, the two affianced officers in *Così fan tutte*,
had disguised themselves as Albanians!

It may be imprudent to confess it, but we Jews *do* have
a sense of innate specialness and cleverness, perhaps as a
consequence of the 'Chosen People' doctrine that Steiner had Hitler learn from the Jews, or because centuries
of being victimised and physically circumscribed meant
that only the mind was free to roam and value the ac-
quisition of learning for its own sake. In the days when
it was still deemed necessary to reassure sceptical native citizens about Jewish civic loyalty and that our brave
boys weren't fighting Hitler in a 'Jewish war', books with
faintly embarrassing titles like *The Jewish Contribution
to Civilisation* or *Jewish Nobel Prize Winners* would be
published. But it is a fact that in every Western democracy the Jewish presence in arts, sciences, academia's
higher slopes, the media and philanthropy is out of all
proportion to the size of the community.

And it was even more marked under repressive Communist regimes. In a mere twenty years from being emancipated after the 1917 Revolution until the outbreak of
the Second World War, Russian Jewry – less than 2 per
cent of the general population – made up nearly 15 per
cent of all Soviet citizens with higher education. Thirty-
three per cent of young Jewish men and women between
the ages of nineteen and twenty-four were college students, compared with 5 per cent of that age group in
the general population. In Moscow and Leningrad, Jews

made up roughly 40 per cent of doctors, 70 per cent of dentists, 30 per cent of writers, journalists and the publishing profession and almost 20 per cent of scientists and university professors – a pre-eminence as striking as that of German Jewry before the rise of Nazism.

So yes, we *are* adaptable and quick-witted, two causes of offence to the anti-Semite. But, as Julius perceptively points out in what is by far the best part of his book – his analysis of English literary anti-Semitism from Chaucer through Shakespeare, Marlowe and Dickens to his own bête noire, that fine poet but primly constipated anti-Semite T. S. Eliot – whereas English writers seem to take the Jew's greater intelligence for granted, their heroes compensate and come out on top by virtue of possessing the inestimable quality of *character*. It is a common refrain of the English empirical tradition to be suspicious of effete intellectuals, high-flown theory, and those who are 'too clever by half', plumping instead for the more manly values of no-nonsense straight talking, baffled decency and fair play. The dialectic is not merely Jew–Christian. It is also a contrast between Johnny Foreigner and the Upright Englishman. Agatha Christie's Belgian detective Poirot fills the 'Jew' role to a T, down to sneers about his eccentric, alien ways, with the added little joke about his murky origins, since people constantly mistake him for a Frenchman. Steady, dependable Captain Hastings, the quintessential English antithesis to the flashy Belgian/Jewish outsider, is in awe of Poirot's deductive brilliance, but there can be no doubt in the reader's mind which one of them you would rather have by your side on a tiger shoot.

A compendium of anti-Jewish, anti-foreign prejudice, yes, but is this an example of the 'obdurate, harsh anti-

Semitism resistant both to reason and considerations of decency' that prompted Julius to write his book? Surely not. Perhaps naively, I prefer to take refuge in an anecdote once told me by the late Rabbi Dr Louis Jacobs, my revered Talmud teacher and probably Anglo-Jewry's greatest scholar yet. For a few years in the 1950s the philistine Manchester Jewish community was undeservedly blessed – I grew up in Manchester and know whereof I speak – in having both Louis Jacobs and Alexander Altman, the historian of the Jewish Enlightenment who later left for Brandeis University, as its communal rabbis.

An exhibition was staged at the Central Library in Manchester of rescued treasures and artefacts of German Jewry. The Lord Mayor made a crass opening speech, stumbling over names and evidently with no idea of the rich history of destroyed German Jewry. When Jacobs mentioned this as they left together, Altman replied, 'Yes, in the smallest Black Forest town before the war the Lord Mayor would have made a polished speech quoting Goethe, Heine and Moses Mendelssohn. But when the Nazis marched in he would have been the first to welcome them. That Manchester mayor, on the other hand, just would have known instinctively that what the Nazis were doing to the Jews was wrong.'

I am less sure now than I was forty years ago about the essential decency and tolerance of the British character. Apart from experience teaching me to be more realistic and less idealistic about human nature and to recognise how thin the veneer of civilisation is, I live in a capital city where one-third of the population is made up of ethnic minorities. The culture and civic values I grew up with in a homogeneous, overwhelmingly white society are no longer universally shared. Nevertheless, it would shock and surprise me beyond telling if the UK ever succumbed collectively to the 'obdurate, harsh anti-Semitism', the bigoted racism, or the hysterical Islamophobia of which vocal minority elements in our society are guilty. I would expect a free citizenry, a democratically elected Parliament and an independent judiciary to detect the dangers early and nip extremism in the bud.

Ultimately, the accusation of anti-Semitism often depends on the subjective eye of the accuser. For example, Julius thinks that Labour Party posters in the 2005 election campaign depicting Michael Howard, the Jewish leader of the Conservative party, as Shylock, or those associating him and another Jewish MP, Oliver Letwin, with pigs, 'evidenced a culpable ignorance of anti-Semitism's long pre-Holocaust history'. For my part, I regarded them as borderline and pandering to protean anti-Jewish associations, but possibly I was ultra-sensitive to inferences because Michael Howard is a member of my synagogue and although we disagreed politically he has always been very helpful personally (whereas Julius is a prominent Labour supporter). On the other hand, Julius was justifiably upset by snide and pejorative references to him in the *Daily Telegraph* at the time he represented Princess Diana in her divorce from Prince Charles; he was a 'Jewish intellectual', an 'outsider' not 'Establishment', and would 'win lots of money' for his client according to an anonymous Cambridge don who had taught him. For my part, these were merely the sort of veiled, shorthand clichés routinely used by the press for its readers to identify exotic Jews/Arabs/Asians – preferably ennobled, filthy rich and embroiled in a scandal. But then I hadn't been stigmatised personally.

However vehemently Jews may disagree about the

prevalence and growth of anti-Semitism – and I am clearly on the sceptical end of the spectrum – I have maintained for years that I would far rather be Jewish than black or Muslim in any one of today's polyglot European states with their badly fraying multicultural-ism. Thirty years ago in the UK, official statistics and the anecdotal evidence of white youngsters with black friends confirmed beyond argument that black teenagers were four times more likely than their white counter-parts to be randomly stopped and interrogated by the police on 'sus' (suspicion).

Nowadays, Muslims have replaced blacks as the bogy-men and Islamophobia is more virulent and widespread throughout Europe, especially in traditionally liberal countries such as the Netherlands, Sweden and the UK, than anything we Jews can claim to have experienced since 1945. In addition to fear of Muslim suicide bombers, mass immigration is at the heart of the prob-lem, as cheap labour with its distinctive garb and cus-toms and incomprehensible languages has flooded into prosperous Central and Northern Europe. What initially was hailed as a celebration of multicultural diversity is now perceived as a threat to the cultural integrity of the host country. As a consequence, right-wing, nationalist parties have steadily increased their support, particularly among the urban proletariat fearful of losing jobs to foreigners. One of the more endearing delusions of Com-munism was to imagine that the workers of the world would ever unite, rather than protect their own sectarian interests.

All of this should have a familiar and salutary ring to it for Jews. By the turn of the twentieth century, a pop-ular and media backlash had begun in the UK against the tide of Russian Jews – swollen to around 150,000 in all – that since 1881 had been fleeing to Britain to avoid Tsarist persecution. They settled mainly in London's East End. The British Brothers' League was formed to stop the country becoming 'the dumping ground for the scum of Europe'. Supported by MPs, borough and county councillors, ministers of religion and, of course, trade unions, the Brothers' League held large rallies calling for restrictions on the further immigration of 'destitute foreigners'. It was in response to public agitation, the flavour of which was caught by an editorial in the *Manchester Evening Chronicle* demanding 'that the dirty, destitute, diseased, verminous and criminal foreigner who dumps himself on our soil and rates simultaneously shall be forbidden to land', that the Aliens Act of 1905 was passed by Parliament. Immigration controls and deportation mechanisms were introduced for the first time in Great Britain, but the Act made exemption provision for asylum seekers from religious or political persecution, so that those elements wanting to halt Jewish immigration were comprehensively outmanoeuvred. And so our forebears, and we their descendants, have lived here more or less happily ever after.

That is why I have little patience for the 'circle the wagons' mentality that affects much of the Jewish communal establishment in the UK and the USA. Whatever the level of alleged anti-Semitism masquerading as anti-Zionism that we are supposed to be the victims of nowadays, it is small beer compared with the very real anti-Jewish prejudice borne by our Ashkenazi ancestors a century ago, less than a pinprick when set against the Judaeophobia suffered by European Jewry in the Middle Ages, and positively benign in contrast with the suspicious antipathy shown towards Muslim, black and Hispanic minorities in present-day Europe and America.

In my opinion, the best riposte to adopt towards any anti-Jewish gibes, sneers and innuendo is the lordly disdain affected by Disraeli, who never failed to emphasise his Jewish roots and answered a taunt in the House of Commons with the words, 'Yes, I am a Jew, and when the ancestors of the right honourable gentleman were brutal savages in an unknown island, mine were priests in the Temple of Solomon.'

I used Disraeli as my model a few years ago, when a newspaper asked me to write an article about the storm of protest that had engulfed the French ambassador to the UK. He had gone to dinner at the home of Conrad Black, the media proprietor, and his wife Barbara Amiel, the newspaper columnist and ardent Israel defender, where he delivered himself of the opinion that Israel was 'a sh**ty little country' that caused too much trouble. Unsurprisingly, the ambassador's remarks soon became public. Outraged Jewish groups demanded his resignation and recall to Paris.

In my piece I wrote that I certainly agreed with the demands of the protestors for the ambassador's recall. The only possible explanation for his extraordinary comments at the dinner table of two well-known Israeli supporters was that he had been drunk or remarkably ill briefed about his hosts; either way, he had demonstrated his incompetence to represent a great country such as France . . .

That is why I think that in seeking so sedulously to detect and analyse every errant strain of anti-Semitism and anti-Zionism as Julius did in his magnum opus, and as the Anti-Defamation League and their Diaspora counterparts do more shrilly and less fastidiously, they are all barking up the wrong tree. The social and geo-political climate has changed, but they are not willing to recognise it. Hair-splitting about who is or is not anti-Semitic and whether or not anti-Zionist rhetoric is a new variant on the oldest hatred is twenty years out of date.

One of the most astute and balanced observers of contemporary Jewish life in Europe is the Italian-born, Paris-domiciled intellectual historian Diana Pinto. In a recent lecture,[17] she outlined the three stages that European countries have travelled from anti-Semitism through Philosemitism to what she defined as *Asemitism*. Anti-Semitism has not been a respectable option for any European political party to dare hint at since the Holocaust; even Jobbik, the growing Movement for a Better Hungary, accused by its opponents of being neo-Fascist, homophobic and anti-Semitic, strenuously denies the charge and points to its support for Israel.

Stage 2, Philosemitism, was the over-compensation of a shamed post-war Europe to the revelation of Nazi atrocities: solemn, head-covered national leaders dutifully attending remembrance services and the unveiling of public memorials; the Pope visiting synagogues as an act of contrition; all those books, plays and films about the Jewish experience in Europe; the middle-class vogue for claiming a Jewish ancestor somewhere down the line, a Claudia Roden Jewish cookbook on the kitchen shelves, Woody Allen everyone's favourite comic philosopher; the compulsory use of Yiddish words such as *chutzpah* or *schmooze* in modish articles by au fait journalists.

By contrast, Pinto argues, contemporary *Asemitism* is neither pro nor anti, but treats the Jews in a calmer, more detached manner, as a group that definitely 'belongs' in each individual country, its rights and security protected by law, but that is treated in identical fashion to every other civic minority. The special status once conferred on Jews, historically by Christian rulers before the Enlightenment, and in the recent past by secular governments in the aftermath of the Holocaust, is being replaced by a new indifference – 'indifference' to be understood in its original etymological meaning of not according special importance to 'difference'. Instead, Jewishness is no longer regarded as being unique, but simply one of several minority settings in the modern, multicultural world. In an age of globalisation we are no longer the only diaspora people. We are no longer the only discrete immigrants. As an illustration, European politicians today are more exercised over 'the Muslim problem' than they are by 'the Jewish problem'. We have to learn to 'time share' with other cultural identities and ethnic groupings, each with its own demands for recognition and favourable treatment. Jewish communities in Europe and elsewhere are losing their special status, to the perplexed bafflement of the communal leadership, for centuries accustomed to exerting discreet pressure behind the scenes through the good offices and influence of 'court Jews'.

It is a challenging analysis, and offers a fresh slant on the anti-Zionism-is-anti-Semitism-in-disguise debate. Everyone would agree that anti-Semitism – meaning blanket hostility to all Jews *qua* Jews – is a despicable creed and should be beyond the pale of any civilised society, along with homophobia, Islamophobia and racism. Anti-Zionism too belongs in that dustbin if, rather than judging each conflagration involving Israel on its merits, it asks instead why Israel, alone among the nearly two hundred member states of the United Nations, has the right to exist, when the legitimacy of several arguably more controversial countries or 'failed states' is never called into question. Perhaps it is a back-handed compliment to demand that the Jewish state must behave 'better' than others – Steiner's 'virus of utopia'.

But Zionism as a national movement and ideology should no more be protected from critical analysis than capitalism, socialism, theism, secularism, colonialism or Islamism. Not every ant-Zionist is automatically the loony president of Iran or a Hamas suicide bomber. There are perfectly respectable intellectual arguments that often have been voiced by Jews themselves to query the goals of Zionism and the actions of Israel. In its early, Herzlian days, Jewish socialists and Bundists (members of the Jewish workers' movement) were distinctly lukewarm about the dream of creating a Jewish state. They rejected Zionism as economically retrograde and harmful to the cause of international socialism. Isaac Deutscher, the Marxist historian and 'non-Jewish Jew', accepted the 'historical necessity' of a Jewish state after the Holocaust, but always favoured internationalism over Jewish nationalism.

For a brief time during the Palestine Mandate, a small group of prominent *Yishuv* Zionists, including luminaries such as Arthur Rupin, whose soubriquet was the 'father of Zionist settlement', Judah Magnes, the first chancellor of the Hebrew University, and faculty members Hugo Bergmann, Martin Buber, Ernst Simon and Gershom Scholem banded together in an organisation called *Brit Shalom* (Covenant of Peace). They advocated bi-nationalism as the only equitable solution for a land claimed by two peoples. Their good intentions were blown away in the rising tide of Jewish and Arab nationalism. But in recent years a number of Jewish academics on the political left – for example, Tony Judt in the USA, Eric Hobsbawm in the UK and Shlomo Sand in Israel – have resuscitated the idea of a bi-national state as the answer to the intractable Israel–Palestine conflict. However much or little other Jews may think of their proposition, it is a perfectly valid one to put forward. If the reader is wondering, incidentally, how a Jewish anti-Zionist can possibly also be an anti-Semite in disguise, Judt, Hobsbawm, Sand et al. qualify in another category. They are 'self-hating' Jews.

With a sense of historical perspective allied to calm debate and reasoned analysis, it should be possible, and would be helpful, to distinguish between anti-Semitism and anti-Zionism, particularly when the latter is not questioning Israel's right to exist but asking critical questions of government policy vis-à-vis Israel being *the* Jewish state rather than a state for *all* its citizens, settlement building, and the viability of offering to trade land for peace. Conflating anti-Semitism and anti-Zionism as one and the same and insisting on an inseparable link between the two – a *collective* anti-Semitism, as it were – may deter criticism in the short term. As with overuse of the Holocaust, familiarity eventually breeds indifference, until the excuse no longer holds up.

Then both Israel, which likes to describe itself and be regarded as the collective expression of the Jewish people, and those Diaspora cheerleaders who have enthusiastically encouraged that identification will have to find a better defence than blaming all criticism of Israel on covert anti-Semitism.

Instead, they might try to agree on an answer to the

definitional problem that has perplexed the Jewish people at least since Rabbinic times: Who is a Jew?

4

Who is a Jew?

Solomon ibn Verga was a Jewish historian whose life spanned the fifteenth and sixteenth centuries. The dates of his birth and death are uncertain, but he witnessed the 1492 expulsion from Spain. In his best-known work, *Shevet Yehudah* (*The Rod of Judah*), he tells a story about a boatload of Jewish refugees. Ravaged by the plague, they were forced to land their boat on a desolate coast. Among the infected castaways were a husband, his wife, and their two young sons. As they struggled on through the wasteland, the wife died. The man carried his two sick children until he fainted from hunger and fatigue. When he awoke, he found the two boys dead by his side. He staggered to his feet and cried out, 'Sovereign of the Universe, much You have done to make me forsake my faith. But know for a certainty that nothing You have brought, or may still bring, upon me will make me change. In spite of all, a Jew I am and a Jew I shall remain.'[1]

It is an affecting little anecdote, and even if not necessarily true, it makes a good point. As Italians say: *Si non è vero è ben trovato*. And the point it was making is that a Jew's identity and his faith are inextricable. The one defines the other.

That, certainly, was the case in medieval Europe, and not only for Jews. It was religion that identified a person, not nationality. First of all you were a Catholic, Protestant, Jew or Muslim and only secondarily from a city state in Italy, Spain, the Rhineland or Morocco. What you prayed, and to whom, was your ID card. A traveller knew he was among fellow Jews in Granada, Córdoba or Toledo during the centuries of amicable conviviality between Muslims and Jews by listening to the distinctive chants emerging from behind a front door like any other in the street on a Saturday morning, just as a Catholic in Germany after the Counter-Reformation would know quickly which church he was in from the incense (or lack of it) and the ritual.

Until the Reformation, there was no differentiation for a European Christian between ethnic origin and religious faith. You were Catholic, *tout court*, and submitted to papal doctrine. Because the Middle Ages lasted much longer for Jews, it was not until the Age of Enlightenment granted them limited access to wider society that they could even consider modifying their religious observances or – more radical still – discarding them. This discarding process was accelerated by the egalitarian ideals of the French Revolution.

In fact, in their avidity to enter the mainstream, Jews abandoned Judaism in droves. Despairing preachers likened it to a plague epidemic. Moses Mendelssohn, 'the German Socrates' and founder of the Jewish *Haskalah* (Enlightenment) movement – by modern standards a strictly observant Jew – had six children, only one of whom remained within the faith. His son Abraham, father of the composer Felix Mendelssohn-Bartholdy, had his children baptised because 'Christianity is the religion of the majority of civilised men'. The poet Heinrich Heine converted in order to gain admission to the Bar (at which he never practised), masking his decision with the wry flippancy that 'The baptismal font is the entrance ticket to European culture.' His friend Edward Gans converted to obtain a chair in philosophy at the University of Berlin, where one of his students was Karl Marx, baptised at the age of seven.

In some ways, Jewish women were even more prone to the temptation of apostasy than the men. If wealthy and vivacious, they entertained Christian suitors in their salons, could quote Goethe's 'elective affinities' to justify their liaisons, and knew that conversion and marriage to a nobleman might lead to residence in Venice, Paris or London, where their shameful origins could more easily be glossed over.

Rahel Varnhagen (1771–1832) was a case in point. The daughter of a Berlin merchant, she presided over a select literary salon frequented by princes, diplomats and distinguished foreigners. With Goethe and Heine, Schleiermacher and Fichte among her acquaintances, she had a strong influence on the Romantic movement in Germany. Consciously living her life as a work of art, its central focus and the spur for several love affairs – invariably with men considerably younger than herself – was to escape the straitjacket of Jewishness and subsume it under some grander, more universal aesthetic. She was a complex woman, neither beautiful nor even conventionally attractive but of remarkable intelligence and allure and her biography was written, appropriately, by Hannah Arendt.[2]

Rahel converted in 1814 and married a Prussian diplomat and man of letters, Karl August Varnhagen von Ense, fourteen years her junior. According to her husband, on her deathbed, after a happy marriage, she said, 'I am here a refugee from Egypt and Palestine and find help, love and care with you . . . What was to me for so long the greatest reproach, the bitterest suffering and misfortune, to be a Jewess, not for anything would I now wish to give it up . . .'

At the time of the French Revolution, about four and a half thousand Jewish families lived in Berlin. Half of them had converted to Christianity by 1823, when a conservative reaction against the universal ideals of French Enlightenment thought took hold in Germany. The automatic connection between being counted as a Jew and practising Judaism had broken down. And, with it, the traditional markers for defining Jewish identity also crumbled. It took time – almost two hundred years – for the unmistakable results of that disintegration to become apparent even to the most purblind Jewish traditionalist, but old religions (see also the Catholic Church) are extremely conservative and dismissive of any evidence that threatens their hegemony.

Absolutism and theocracy are the Enlightenment's natural enemies. In his book *In Defence of the Enlightenment*,[3] the philosopher Tzvetan Todorov describes the features common to all entrenched religious structures – obscurantism, authoritarianism and dogmatism – as hydra heads that keep growing back because they are perpetual human characteristics. People prefer to defend the exclusivity of their group rather than embrace universal ideals. We mouth concepts of freedom and truth as being integral to our religion's value system and applying to all peoples, but in actuality want to remain safe and comfortable within familiar boundaries. In time, these features become as typical of reformed religions as they were of the founding institution from which they originally broke away. I have Progressive Jewish colleagues –

whose expression of Judaism is not recognised as 'authentic' by Orthodoxy or dismissed as 'another religion' – who are as pernickety in querying Jewish status and reluctant to grant it as any ultra-Orthodox rabbi. Having control over another person's identity is a seductive power.

The result of vainly trying to insist on the Rabbinic definition of *Who is a Jew*, despite the breakdown of Rabbinic Judaism over the last two hundred years, is that modern Jewish identity is fluid, fractured and self-defining, depending on your religious grouping (or lack of one), or indeed on whether you even bother to seek Rabbinic validation of your status. What it means to be Jewish is a personal response and differs from one individual to the next. A professing Protestant who denied the resurrection of Jesus (although Alan Bennett did once deliver the witticism that 'The Church of England is so constituted that its members can believe almost anything – but of course none of them do'), a practising Catholic who abjured Vatican authority, an observant Muslim who rejected Muhammad as the true Prophet – those are logically untenable categories. The person subscribing to them is, at best, a 'lapsed' Protestant, Catholic or Muslim. While studying in Ireland over forty years ago, I met so many Catholics who would explain vociferously and at length their reasons for no longer accepting the dogma of papal infallibility and going to Mass that it grew quite tiresome. I found myself wondering: why can't they just lapse *quietly*?

But a modern-day Jew who is a secular atheist, indifferent to the State of Israel, does not associate with the Jewish community in any meaningful way and has a Christian spouse who is bringing up their children as

Catholics, nevertheless will still most likely answer in the affirmative if asked whether they are Jewish. Nowadays, contrary to the case of the grief-stricken father in ibn Verga's story, it is no longer axiomatic to link Jewish identity to Jewish faith. Ethnicity is a greater pull than religious practice.

The standard definition of *Who is a Jew*, codified by Rabbinic authorities over centuries, is that a Jew is someone born of a Jewish mother, or who chooses to convert to Judaism. It was not always so. If we take the biblical Hebrews or Israelites to be the Jewish progenitors, then in their time descent went through the paternal, not maternal line. Every genealogy listed in the Bible is 'B the *son* of A', naming the father, as it is in the Gospel of Matthew when tracing the line of Jesus. King Solomon might have had one thousand foreign wives according to legend, but their offspring all would have followed the Solomonic family tree.

Nobody can be sure when or why, but at some time in history this reflex assumption changed. Scholars suggest it was during the Maccabean era (165 BCE onwards) that maternity, not paternity, came to be the determining factor in Jewish status, probably because it was a lengthy period of wars, invasion and upheaval and a mother is more readily identifiable as the parent of a young child. As Freud observed, paternity is always a matter of surmise. Whatever the reason, the ruling was codified in the Mishnah and the Talmud and henceforth became universally valid.

Conversion to Judaism is a trickier issue. Rabbinic sources on the topic are copious. Whether the reaction is welcoming or not to the would-be convert depended on the historical context. In benign times, when Jews were free to proselytise on an equal footing with other religions and cults of the ancient world, the rabbis were fulsome in their praise of converts. A typical Talmudic quote, from *Pesachim* 87b, is that God dispersed Israel among the nations for the sole purpose that proselytes should wax numerous among them. It is no accident that some of the most highly regarded Talmudic sages, including Meir and Akiba, were said to be the descendants of proselytes. And earlier still, the pastoral idyll of the Book of Ruth, the Moabite woman who marries Boaz and becomes the great-grandmother of the greatest of all Israel's heroes, King David, is understood by biblical scholars to be a literary riposte to the harsh decree of Ezra that the returning Babylonian exiles should divorce their foreign wives.

In hostile times, on the other hand, when Judaism was under threat and it was an offence to proselytise, the rabbis were prudently more cautious in their welcome. A notorious and oft-cited quote in the name of Rabbi Chelbo (*Yebamot* 109b), to the effect that proselytes are like an 'eruption' or 'scab' on Israel, loses some of its offensiveness when the comparable text in a different tractate (*Kiddushin* 70b) makes it clear that the rabbi is indulging in a jocular play on words rather than intending to be taken literally. That even in dark days sincere converts were welcomed is evidenced from the following famous passage: 'The Rabbis teach: If anyone comes nowadays and desires to be a proselyte, they say to him: "Why do you want to become a proselyte? Do you not know that nowadays the Israelites are harried, driven about, persecuted and harassed, and that sufferings befall them?" If he says, "I know it, and I am not worthy", they receive him at once . . .' (*Yebamot* 47a).

As in all instances where Scripture and ancient sources are cited in support, you pick and choose those examples that accord with your own viewpoint. Orthodox authorities, who are stern in their requirements of intending proselytes – excessively so in the UK, where they have the unenviable reputation of being the strictest in the world – will cite those quotations that appear to validate their approach. Progressive authorities, on the other hand, who take a distinctly more sympathetic attitude to would-be converts, quote those sources that bolster their approach. As Blake's couplet puts it:

> Both read the Bible day and night,
> But thou read'st black where I read white.

The result is that nowadays the *halachic* (legal) formula of who is a Jew might be shared by the several religious groupings in the modern Jewish world, but their interpretation of it varies widely. The anarchic situation has now been reached whereby some Orthodox Rabbinic authorities don't even recognise the conversions of other Orthodox Rabbinic authorities! The inhibitingly strict London *Beth Din* (literally 'House of Judgment' – Rabbinic Court) has several times refused to recognise converts accepted by a *Beth Din* in Jerusalem, creating a delicious conundrum for lawyers to solve; if one is Jewish when boarding the plane in Israel, at what precise point on the flight over to London does one cease to be Jewish and revert to Gentile status?

It almost goes without saying that the Orthodox will not recognise a Progressive conversion; but that is less an issue of principle than of politics. Progressive Judaism, as did the Protestant Reformation, threatens the primacy of its older sibling. Authority is at stake, and by withholding recognition from other branches of Judaism and their converts, Orthodox Judaism is desperately trying to maintain a monopoly on the religious fabric of Jewish life that has steadily been prised from its grasp since the Enlightenment. For many centuries Rabbinic Judaism (a more precise term than 'Orthodox Judaism'; Orthodox (i.e. conforming to traditional faith) is an early-nineteenth-century nomenclature, applied only in order to define Jewish traditionalists *after* the early Reformers had made their innovations) was remarkably successful in giving a uniform structure and coherence to scattered Diaspora communities East and West. There might be minor local modifications, but essentially the *halachah*, as interpreted by generations of rabbis since Talmudic times, provided the ground rules for Jewish living, from admitting a convert, sanctifying a marriage and burying the dead, to making a chicken ritually fit for consumption or specifying which actions were permitted on the Sabbath without infringing the prohibition against work. Rabbinic Judaism set the norms for all Jewry from the completion of the Mishnah (*c.* 200 CE) until the last decades of the eighteenth century.

But since the dawn of the nineteenth century it has not been the only game in the Jewish town. That is why Orthodoxy has ambivalent feelings about all the so-called 'benefits' that have accrued to Jews as a result of the Enlightenment, emancipation and modernity generally. There really was a conference held in Jerusalem on the bicentenary of the French Revolution that asked: Was the French Revolution a good or bad thing for the Jews?

All Jews except fundamentalists would unequivocally answer 'a good thing'. Loosening the rigid structure under which Rabbinic Judaism suborned all Jews unless they deliberately cut themselves off from the community was deemed a worthwhile price to pay for admission to the opportunities on offer in an open society. East European *shtetl* (small-town) life in reality, not as portrayed with the saccharine sentimentality of *Fiddler on the Roof*, was superstitiously pious, but poor, dirty, petty and restricting, with an overwhelming pressure on its inhabitants to conform. The majority of early-twentieth-century immigrants to America threw off its shackles with joyful alacrity. Modification of traditional practices took longer in Germany, France, the Low Countries and the UK, only because Poland or the Ukraine was a lot nearer geographically and the *heim* still exerted a strong pull.

My maternal grandparents came over from Poland to London in 1919. They were old-fashioned devout. Their eight children were to a greater or lesser degree Orthodox, apart from the black-sheep son who married a non-Jewess and left in disgrace for Australia. (Jewish black sheep and their blonde wives were a steady source of immigration for the Colonies.) It was the same on my father's side – originally from Russia, they left after the 1881 pogroms that followed the assassination of Tsar Alexander II – except that in his family it was a daughter who 'married out' and ended up in colonial Malaya.

Thus my generation of cousins is an eclectic mix of nominally Orthodox, Progressive, secular, free-thinking, university-educated, maternally or paternally Jewish, and intermarried – a fairly typical modern Jewish family. Our children's generation has added black and Oriental genes to the mix. It amuses me that theologically I sit far to the left of second cousin Lord Jonathan Sacks, the Orthodox Chief Rabbi, but politically somewhere to the right of late second cousin Tony Judt and with Sacks probably the best-known contemporary progeny of the destiny that joined two immigrant families together over seventy years ago. As an undergraduate onlooker at family gatherings that began convivially but frequently degenerated into bust-ups between one set of relatives and another over a new or long-simmering *broiges* (Yiddish, 'grudge'), I would reflect that from Polish or Russian *shtetl* to Oxbridge college in three generations was quite a large social and intellectual leap to make and was bound to leave some emotional dysfunctionality in its wake. But then, as the formidable journalist Ann Scott James told her son Max Hastings, *all* families are dysfunctional.[4]

To return to the question: Who, nowadays, *is* a Jew? As I suggested in Chapter 1, it is both a broader and a larger category than is recognised by officialdom. Despite all the efforts of Rabbinic custodians to safeguard *limpieza de sangre* (purity of blood) as zealously as the Spanish Inquisition, we Jews are a stubbornly mongrel people, one factor that has contributed to our adaptability and survival. It is only inbred clans that end up with Habsburg chins or haemophilia, whereas there is an astonishing variety about the Jewish physiognomy and physique.

It is simply not possible to know how many millions of people have entered and exited Judaism over the centuries. We know the famous ones who joined the Jewish people. Queen Helena and the ruling family of the tiny Mesopotamian kingdom of Adiabene, who had converted and come to live in Jerusalem shortly before the Romans razed it in 70 CE; the Black Sea kingdom of

the Khazars, who allegedly converted en masse in the
tenth century and are taken by some fanciful scholars
such as Arthur Koestler and more recently Shlomo Sand
to be the original Ashkenazi Jews;[5] the bizarre case of
nine families, some forty people, from the town of San
Nicandro in Apulia who decided in the 1930s to convert
to Judaism, thirty of them migrating to Israel in 1949;[6]
Marilyn Monroe, apparently, in order to marry Arthur
Miller (however skimpy her tuition under American Reform auspices, I doubt that too many Orthodox admission boards would have rejected her); likewise Elizabeth
Taylor. Those are some of the famous ones. We don't
know the anonymous, unrecorded legions that joined
Judaism over the millennia, either out of conviction or
for the purpose of marriage.

In 1975, when I joined the synagogue that would remain my pulpit until retirement nearly thirty years later,
two elderly men shared the duties of Honorary Librarian.
Max and Willie, as they told me to call them, chatted
away amiably together while they sorted books. It was
obvious from their heavily accented English that they had
been German refugees. I would greet them on my visits
to the Library with the affable condescension displayed
by busy young people towards the old – a barely concealed impatience that I ruefully recognise being directed
towards me nowadays – but apart from saluting them
and their wives at services I learned little more about
them.

Then Willie died and I was deputed to officiate at
his funeral. I went round to visit his widow, a straight-
backed, severely handsome woman, in their flat in a
converted Edwardian mansion in Swiss Cottage, where

so many German refugees had settled before and after the Second World War.

That was when I got an inkling of Willie's stature. While I was there, a condolence telegram arrived from Willy Brandt, the former chancellor of West Germany, followed by one from Helmut Schmidt, the current chancellor; then a telephone call came from the German ambassador, asking at what time the funeral would be.

His widow Tanya told me Willie's story. In the early 1930s he had been one of Germany's most brilliant young scientists with a glittering career ahead of him, tipped as a future Nobel laureate. He met and fell in love with Tanya, a Jewish opera singer. When Hitler came to power Willie was warned that marrying a Jewess would ruin his career, but true love prevailed. They eloped to Switzerland and before the war started in 1939 crossed over to England.

They were interned on the Isle of Wight as enemy aliens, until the authorities were alerted to Willie's detestation of Nazism and exceptional scientific abilities. With typical military perversity, the army assigned Willie to – the Pioneer Corps.

At war's end he was sent back to Germany to oversee the rebuilding of the Ruhr's devastated industries. He was one of the architects of Ludwig Erhard's 'economic miracle' and was appointed vice-chancellor of Karlsruhe University. When the Queen visited the Ruhr region on her first official visit to Germany after the war, her sharp eyes spotted the British army medal beneath his academic robes. Willie took great delight in explaining how he had earned it.

After retirement from university life, he and Tanya returned to England. They had not been able to resettle in post-war Germany. It held too many bad memories. Here in London, Willie finally took the decision to convert to Judaism, forty years after first meeting Tanya. They now lie side by side in our cemetery.

Similarly, we know the well-documented cases of those who, for their own good reasons, departed from Judaism. The early Christians, for example, who believed that Jesus of Nazareth was the risen messiah; the great Moses Maimonides for a while, forced to convert to Islam (a fact conveniently overlooked in most Jewish textbooks); the ancestors of Michel de Montaigne; Heinrich Heine; Benjamin Disraeli's father; Karl Marx's father; Gustav Mahler and every other musician, academic and public figure looking to ease their advancement in Austria and Germany; Hugh Montefiore, Bishop of Birmingham; Cardinal Lustiger, Archbishop of Paris; Saint Edith Stein, canonised by the Vatican in 1998. Those we know. We don't know the forgotten millions who left their ancestral religion to escape persecution, better their social standing, out of conviction that Christianity or Islam was the true faith, or for marriage purposes.

I remember reading *Ivanhoe* as a child, with beautiful Rebecca, the tragic Jewess, sired so surprisingly from the loins of her crafty, money-grubbing, stereotypical father Isaac, and wondering how many medieval Jewish fathers with a beautiful daughter would have wished to help her escape the hardships and discrimination of ghetto life by marrying her off to a Christian nobleman. One of the less felicitous sound bites of Orthodox spokesmen is to assert that intermarriage has done more damage to Jewry than Hitler. However concerned they are by falling Jewish numbers, the analogy is obscene.

It is statistically impossible to arrive at a quantitative

estimate of how many have joined Jewry over the centuries against how many have left. In my rabbinic career I have witnessed both sides of the coin and variants of it. Years ago, I was called on to conduct the funeral of the last man with a reserved space in his family's catafalque in our synagogue cemetery. The grandfather who had erected the catafalque for himself and his descendants had been a well-known Edwardian business magnate. His great-granddaughter and daughter of the deceased, Lady X, came to see me with her husband, a distinguished career diplomat, to discuss arrangements. 'Please could you explain to us', asked Lady X, 'the form of the funeral service? We are all Christians, you know.' It disconcerted me momentarily on entering the prayer hall at the commencement of the funeral service to see that most of the mourners were on their knees in prayer. Afterwards our elderly sexton, who had worked for the synagogue since the 1920s, said to me, 'I can remember when on the High Holydays that large family filled the front two rows of the sanctuary.' Three generations later, only a few scattered cousins acknowledge being Jewish.

Likewise, the son of a family with years of devoted service to the wider Anglo-Jewish community, a boy I had known and been fond of since his years in Religion School, decided to convert to Christianity under the influence of his deeply committed and practising fiancée. His family were devastated, and asked me to reason with him. I stopped trying to dissuade him when I recognised that, although – to my way of thinking – he was misguided, his motives were patently sincere. My wife and I were invited to his church wedding. We thought long and hard about it, and decided to go. Among other reasons, such as demonstrating support for his parents, I did not want him to feel that he was being cast off by Judaism because of his convictions. Claiming to be a religious liberal requires actions as well as words.

Another family took years to forgive me for failing to deter their daughter from marrying and embracing the religion of her Christian husband-to-be . . . a vicar. They were reconciled with her (and me) only after the first grandchild was born. When I first joined my synagogue as its student rabbi in 1968, I noticed an elderly, devoted couple sitting there – well, *religiously* – at every Sabbath service, he wearing a clerical dog collar. Curious, I enquired about them and was told she was Jewish, he a Unitarian minister and that they had been married for over forty years. The undertaking they had given each other was that every Saturday he would go with her to synagogue and every Sunday she would sit in his congregation.

It is only fair to add that I can also cite examples from my congregation of young people who have gone the other way – to ultra-Orthodoxy. Reason and Conscience tend to be the watchwords of reformed religions, but as Isaiah Berlin observed in one of his essays,[7] for all their humanity, civilisation and learning, and success in keeping within the fold myriads of Jews who otherwise would have strayed, the reformed branches of Judaism cannot instil in their followers the enthusiasm and zeal of a living spiritual force such as Chasidism. In Berlin's words, 'the Baal Shem [founder of the Chasidic movement] was destined, in the end, to triumph over Moses Mendelssohn'.

I recall one university-educated young woman from a family proud of being third-generation Liberal Jews, who was introduced to and married a rabbi from the largest

Chasidic sect, the Lubavitcher. The thing that upset her favourite uncle most about her wedding in Jerusalem was not the strict segregation of the sexes, nor the wig that henceforth she would have to wear because long hair is a female snare and a wife should be attractive only to her husband, but that his book-loving niece would not be allowed secular literature of any kind in the house.

A former long-distance walking companion of mine has two very pretty daughters. One of them joined us for a stretch of the Pennine Way some fifteen years ago. As she bounded youthfully ahead of us, this easily smitten rabbi could not help but notice how fetching she looked in her shorts and T-shirt. Then, at university, she was, as the saying goes among distraught North-West London Jewish parents, 'aished'. *Aish* ('Fire') is an organisation that seeks to rekindle in the young an ardour for traditional Judaism. Like the Moonies and other evangelical groups such as the Alpha Course, it is particularly effective on campus with vulnerable students or among the lonely in big cities. After being 'aished', the next step for this young woman was 'sem' (seminary) in Jerusalem, there to study Jewish codes and ritual observance.

I was going out to a conference in Jerusalem and her parents asked me to take some items for her. We arranged to meet for tea at a kosher hotel. I had known this girl since her childhood, and my first instinct was to give her a kiss and a hug. But something about her severe hairstyle, plain white blouse and grey skirt down to her ankles warned me that such an affectionate greeting would be inappropriate. We shook hands formally. A few days after my return to London, along with all the male relatives and friends on her contacts list, I received an email saying that she had been studying the Rabbinic concept of *Tzeniut* (Modesty) and would we please understand that from now on she would be avoiding any embrace or physical contact with us, such intimacies being reserved only for a future husband.

The parents of both these young women installed new ovens and meticulously separated meat and dairy utensils in two dishwashers so that their children and grandchildren could continue to eat in their houses. In submerging their own feelings and going to such lengths to maintain family unity, those Liberal Jewish parents strike me as having behaved more truly in consonance with the proper spirit of religion than their self-absorbed children who, in order to be ritually punctilious, disregarded the graver ethical trespass of causing pain to loved ones.

On the credit side, I can count the several hundred students whom I taught or supervised during their successful conversion to Judaism. More pleasing still were those cases in which I had conducted a Wedding Blessing for a mixed-faith couple where the non-Jewish partners, while being fully respectful of Judaism, had their own valid reasons for not wishing to convert, although they were happy for any children to be brought up as Jewish. In several instances the couple would come to see me after a few years of marriage and children, and the non-Jewish partner would explain that he or she now wanted to convert, to feel fully part of the family group when the Sabbath candles were lit and *Kiddush* (Sanctification) made over the wine, rather than remaining a sympathetic outsider. Their decision always pleased me, because apart from anything else it signified that theirs was a solid and mutually supportive partnership.

And I have known many cases of a child or grandchild making their way back to Judaism after their family had abandoned it. It was common among some Holocaust survivors to feel so angry or disenchanted with their religion on account of what had befallen them as Jews, that they did everything possible to protect their children from a similar fate. (Israel, Benjamin Disraeli's father, had a less plausible reason. He renounced Judaism after a row with the elders of the Bevis Marks synagogue over his annual subscription.)

The child of one such survivor family came to see me about thirty years ago. I recognised her from her frequent attendance at services and cultural events at the synagogue. She told me her story. She was an only child and her refugee parents had never acknowledged they were Jews. She had been baptised and brought up as Christian, been sent to a girls' boarding school, been married in church, had mothered two boys and played the *grande-dame* role in the village where she and her City-banker husband lived. But all the time she had an intense curiosity about her origins and was increasingly drawn to Jewish company and culture. It caused an irretrievable rupture with her husband. They divorced and she went in search of her roots. Now she wished to convert – or, as she preferred to think, 'return' – to Judaism. She studied and was accepted. Not long afterwards she was introduced to a Progressive rabbi and married him.

Their marriage could not be solemnised in an Orthodox synagogue because of course the Orthodox would not recognise her Progressive conversion. But I know another survivor's tale, that of a Polish Jewess smuggled out of the Warsaw Ghetto as a child. It was impressed on her by her Christian rescuers never to mention her Jewish origins. She survived the war in a convent and eventually was taken to Israel by an uncle but could never settle there, so returned to Poland, where she married a Catholic, denying her Jewishness until her dying day. But because she herself was of impeccable Jewish stock, her son, with a Catholic father and no Jewish knowledge or education whatsoever, nevertheless could have been married in the strictest Orthodox synagogue in the country, had he so wished, being the child of a halachically recognised Jewish mother. In the event, after a period of Judaic instruction, he chose me to officiate at his wedding.

Similarly anomalous is the case of a well-known Anglo-Jewish writer whose first, Irish wife converted and married him in a Progressive synagogue. The marriage ended in divorce, as did his second attempt at the triumph of hope over experience. Finally and third time lucky, he found happiness with a Jewish bride. By now a celebrated author who wittily lampoons the Jewish bourgeoisie in his novels – displaying in the process his own convoluted and unresolved problems about being Jewish – he has moved steadily rightwards in recent years, especially in defending Israel and ferreting out alleged anti-Semitism in the country's critics. His nuptials were conducted by no less an eminence than the Chief Rabbi. Because his first two marriages to non-Jews were not recognised by Orthodoxy as religiously valid, they were not deemed to count and he could stand unblemished under the marriage canopy, to be eulogised by the religious head of the Orthodox community. Personally, I find such institutionalised hypocrisy on the part of Orthodoxy unpalatable (it recalls the Catholic Church and its selectively flexible approach to annulment – especially if you are a Kennedy from Boston) and blanking out two previous wives for the sake of an Orthodox Rabbinic imprimatur somewhat slippery on the part of the writer.

If the law allows such logical inconsistencies, the law is an ass. But scratching away at the *Who is a Jew* issue is a constant feature of modern Jewish life, a displacement activity to evade graver anxieties. It resurfaces regularly in Israel. Significantly, whenever the country has suffered a trauma such as the surprise attack of the 1973 Yom Kippur war, or is beset with intractable problems vis-à-vis what is euphemistically called the 'peace process' and the government is in danger of imploding, that is when the controversy always seems to reopen.

In August 2010 the Likud-led coalition of Binyamin Netanyahu was desperately searching for a way out of the latest *Who is a Jew* impasse, precipitated by proposed amendments to the conversion law tabled by Knesset member David Rotem of the far-right *Yisrael Beiteinu* (Israel Our Home) party. His proposals would have given ultimate authority over conversions to the Orthodox Chief Rabbinate of Israel, thereby and predictably alarming all non-Orthodox religious movements and secular liberals. True to past form, threat, counter-threat and dark mutterings about irreparable danger to Jewish unity followed, until yet another unsatisfactory and temporary compromise was cobbled together to put the issue on the 'long finger' as the Irish say, while a committee takes its time to submit alternative proposals on how to redraft the bill to the satisfaction of all concerned (by when the Messiah will have come).

The back story to Rotem's failed attempt to facilitate the conversion process for those wishing to be recognised as *religiously* Jewish as well as having Israeli citizenship, is the so-called Law of Return, passed by the

Knesset in July 1950. It entitles anyone with one Jewish grandparent – a deliberate retort to Nazi race definition – to become an Israeli citizen, along with their spouses and family. Speedily enacted at the time to solve the homeless status of the refugee remnant of the Holocaust, with hindsight the Law of Return can be recognised as a temporary expedient that has served its purpose, is no longer relevant, and will not be remembered as the wisest piece of legislation since Solon the Lawgiver. It remains on the statute books, though, because it still has inestimable political utility. Its blatant inequity allows those messianic settlers from Brooklyn or New Jersey to settle on Judean hilltops and proclaim it their God-given entitlement, while expatriate Palestinians whose families have lived on the land for generations have no such legal recourse.

Also, it gives remarkable latitude to those looking for a better life – especially from the former Soviet Union – suddenly to discover that they had a Jewish grandparent, after all. The Law of Return grants them automatic Israeli citizenship, but unless their Jewish status is recognised by religious law, they are prohibited from Jewish marriage or burial rites in the country where they are citizens.

They are not alone in this dichotomy. There was great rejoicing when the Falashas, the black Jews of Ethiopia, were rescued from civil war and famine in that country and 120,000 of them brought to Israel in 1984 and again in 1991. According to legend descended from Menelik, the son of King Solomon's union with the Queen of Sheba, the ancestors of the Falashas probably settled in Egypt in ancient times, from where they moved southwards up the Nile into Ethiopia. Cut off for centuries from contact with other Jewish communities and subject to pressure from neighbouring Christian and Muslim tribes, the form of Judaism they stubbornly maintained was based on Biblical, not Rabbinic Law, of which they were largely ignorant. They were discovered by intrepid medieval travellers, who immediately began the debate that has not been resolved unanimously by the authorities even now. Are they fully Jewish or is there a halachic *safek* (doubt) about their status? Faced by 120,000 new immigrants, *force majeure* compelled the Israeli Chief Rabbinate to issue qualified recognition to the Falashas, subject to ritual immersion, a declaration accepting Rabbinic Law and a symbolic recircumcision for men. A similar *safek* was raised by the same demurring authorities regarding the Jewish status of B'nei Israel Jews from India and, yes, the influx of Russians to Israel in the 1990s. They are good enough for Israeli citizenship but not recognised for Jewish marriage or burial purposes.

This particular anomaly stems from the fact that in 1948 David Ben-Gurion, Israel's first prime minister and a staunch secularist himself, ignored vigorous objections from his Socialist partners and granted control over Jewish status to the religious bloc as its price for entering his coalition cabinet, because he wanted to make the first Jewish government for two thousand years as broad-based as possible. The dispensation has never been rescinded, because the religious parties invariably are an indispensable factor in whichever coalition emerges after an Israeli election and canny in pushing their own agenda. So, for purposes of Jewish marriage or burial in Israel, the outmoded halachic criteria, determined by an unpopular Orthodox rabbinate, still apply, even though less than 20 per cent of the Israeli electorate ever votes for a religious party and in the USA, Israel's staunchest Diaspora ally, about 90 per cent of Jewry is resolutely non-Orthodox. Hence the unseemly horse-trading that regularly ensues when a coalition government needs to strike a deal between religious demands on the one hand and the civic expectations of the overwhelming majority of the Israeli electorate and world Jewry on the other. Rotem's proposed legislation managed to outrage religious die-hards, religious progressives, and civil libertarians throughout the Jewish world.

It must seem baffling for a non-Jewish reader trying to make sense of this complicated saga of why a tiny people, which within living memory lost six million of its number in the Holocaust, should more happily wish to exclude rather than include new adherents, basing that exclusion on strict Rabbinic interpretation of arcane points from an ancient code of law that few born Jews bother with nowadays anyway.

Look at the statistics of Jewish life, with around 50 per cent of the Diaspora young intermarrying; inspect the buzzing beaches of Tel-Aviv and Eilat, where a heterogeneous mix of Israelis and foreign tourists mingle, flirt, fall in love and if they decide to marry do so civilly elsewhere; travel to Cusco in the Peruvian Andes, where backpackers congregate in a kosher restaurant; visit any Jewish community centre in New York, London or Sydney, where the blend of races, colours and ethnic backgrounds is as cosmopolitan as in all modern capital cities. In each place you will see a diverse and multi-faceted group of people, happily sharing Jewish identity, folk memories and culture in common, irrespective of whether or not their maternal grandparents tick all the correct genealogical boxes. Today the great signifier of being Jewish is voluntary identification, a wish to be counted part of *Am Yisrael*, the Jewish people, rather than satisfying genetic criteria that since Hitler will always have an uncomfortable echo of Nazi race laws about them.

Why, then, this punctilious insistence on requiring would-be belongers to jump through Rabbinic hoops, either of the formidable Orthodox kind or the more flexible Progressive variety? Why can they not be allowed to join themselves to the Jewish people and then be taught its history and traditions afterwards – acceptance before study – as was overwhelmingly the way in Talmudic times? What *is* so special about becoming Jewish that it needs to be made so forbidding?

In many minds it is confusedly tied up with the Chosen People concept. To be 'chosen' requires election, a special dispensation, divine favouritism. Each monotheistic religion has traditionally regarded itself as 'chosen'. For Christianity there is no salvation outside the Church; for Islam there is no God but Allah and Muhammad is the last and greatest of the prophets; but Judaism, as the oldest of the monotheistic trinity, has a longer pedigree, going back to the Bible and centrally reiterated in Rabbinic thought, of aggrandising itself as God's chosen people. The 'scandal of particularism' is always a problem for theologians when the idea of a choosing God is examined. Why did God *need* to choose, why not simply convey His truth to all humanity?[8]

It is all the more surprising, therefore, to discover that neither Moses Maimonides nor any other of the great medieval thinkers list 'chosenness' among their basic principles of the Jewish faith. In all likelihood they regarded it as implicit in other dogmas, such as God's special gift of the Torah to Israel. Possibly, though, the influence on them of Greek philosophy, which gave a broader cast to medieval thought, made the particularist notion of a specially chosen people difficult to reconcile with a universalist outlook.

Whatever the reason for their circumspection, it does not alter the fact that, before and since the medieval era, the accusation of an assumed superiority has been regularly levelled against Jews. At times it has been justified. Judah Ha-Levi, a combative twelfth-century apologist on behalf of Judaism, built his defence on the proposition that the Jew belongs to a different category of human being altogether; just as humans are different from animals, animals from plants, and plants from minerals, so Israel is different in kind from the other peoples of the world. And aspects of kabbalistic thought – the Chabad system of the Lubavitcher movement, for example – imply that Jews have a qualitative superiority over other peoples. The Jew alone has two souls: the 'animal soul', the *élan vital* that provides all mankind with its driving force, and the unique 'divine soul', an element of God, as it were, deep in the Jewish psyche.

In mitigation of this racist elitism, it has to be said that the Kabbalah achieved its popularity after the 1492 expulsion from Spain, when the fleeing refugees desperately needed the reassurance that, despite appearances, God still enfolded them in a special providence.

Be that as it may, Jews have always felt the need to justify the doctrine of the Chosen People. By stressing its obligations, the early Reform movement linked it to the idea of Jewish Mission – the Jews had been chosen by God for a special task: to be dispersed among the nations in order to be a light unto them. It entailed not divine favour but extra responsibility. The stock answer to that self-deprecation is that it is patently unjust for the descendants of righteous forebears to be singled out in perpetuity not because of their own merits but because of ancestral merit. And to the mitigating plea that the choice of Israel was not for privilege but for service, Mordecai Kaplan retorted that to consider oneself 'chosen' for service is the greatest privilege of all.

However the Chosen People doctrine is presented, it fails to convince philosophically, is difficult to reconcile morally with the principle that we are all born equal, and is impossible to square theologically with the attribute of God's impartial justice. The same caveats apply *mutatis mutandis* to Christian and Muslim affirmations of special election. For Christianity, it is the Incarnation and the Trinity that make it unique in God's favour. Muslim superiority is emphasised in the Quran's much-cited phrase *umma dun al-nas* – a people distinct from the rest of humanity. Triumphalism is an inevitable corollary of monotheism. As Spinoza acutely observed, 'The holy word of God is on everyone's lips . . . but we see almost everyone presenting their own versions of God's word, with the sole purpose of using religion as a pretext for making others think as they do.'

Until the three monotheistic faiths honestly acknowledge this problem in their own theologies and consider what could be done jointly to modify the continued teaching of doctrines that assert unique chosenness, specialness or superiority – thereby aggravating tensions with other religions – then interfaith dialogue will never advance beyond its current level of banal platitudinising and anodyne declarations calling for world peace and harmony.

So, then, *Who is a Jew*? Bearing in mind that the great majority of people who call themselves Jews nowadays are non-practising, so that for them, unlike ibn Verga's castaway, identity and faith are certainly separable; ergo the most persuasive confirmation of them being Jewish is their own voluntary allegiance to Jewish culture and Jewish peoplehood. Therefore it follows that the simplest, most comprehensive and widely embracing definition one can come up with is to turn on its head Jean-Paul Sartre's acute observation that a Jew is anyone an anti-Semite says is a Jew – which is precisely what Hermann Goering did when he declared, 'I decide who is a Jew' – and affirm that ultimately a Jew *is anyone who says that he or she is one*. Because what can be more self-revealingly true than how you choose to identify yourself?

Someone who should know is Imre Kertész, the recipient of the 2002 Nobel Prize in Literature. Born in Budapest in 1929 of assimilated Jewish parents, he was deported to Auschwitz and then Buchenwald. Although he demurs at being identified as a Jew, he was – as he put it – first rejected by the Hungarians for being Jewish and then, in the camps, rejected by fellow Jews for not being Jewish enough. 'My subject is the freedom of self-definition,' he wrote in 2002, 'which entails the simple idea that each and every member of society has the right to be what he or she is.'

Of course it is *not* a simple idea, but as good a one as there is around in our modern world for defining who is a Jew.

5

God is dead, long live Behaviourism

By making the definition of a Jew more a matter of voluntary self-identification than a question of maternal descent or adherence to a fixed set of beliefs, I recognise that the previously central role of religion in Jewish history is thereby downplayed. But belief is the least significant component in the armoury of the large majority of modern Jews. Perhaps it was ever thus. However, in the past the pressure to conform inhibited Jews from openly expressing their theological doubts, as was the case with Christians until the Age of Reason, and still is the case with most of today's Muslims.

There really is no evidence to suggest – as he seems to think – that atheism was first discovered by Richard Dawkins. One of the difficulties that defenders of religion have in trying to answer him is that he spends most of his time gleefully knocking down medieval 'proofs' for the existence of God that no modern theologian would seriously try to uphold. But, nearly two-and-a-half thousand years ago, the Greek philosopher Protagoras (c.490–c.420 BCE), summed up his scepticism about whether the gods existed with the words: 'Many things hinder certainty – such as, the obscurity of the matter and the shortness of man's life.' In Jewish tradition, Elisha ben Abuyah, a leading rabbi who flourished in the early second century CE, was known as *Acher*, the 'Other

One', because of his heretical views; according to one Talmudic story (*Kiddushin* 39b) he lost his faith after witnessing the death of a child, declaring, 'There is no justice and there is no [divine] Judge.'

Elisha became something of an icon for the leaders of the *Haskalah* (Jewish Enlightenment) movement at the end of the eighteenth century because of his readiness to challenge accepted norms. He was a favourite, frequently cited reference of Isaac Deutscher, the Marxist journalist and biographer of Trotsky. Deutscher grew up in Poland, had a traditional *yeshivah* (Talmudic academy) education and was regarded as a young prodigy until – according to an autobiographical sketch[1] – he 'tested' God by eating a ham sandwich at the grave of a revered rabbi on Yom Kippur. When no punishment struck him down, he promptly became an atheist and a Communist.

In another Talmudic story Elisha is in deep conversation with his pupil Rabbi Meir on a Sabbath day, he on his ass and Meir walking alongside; he ignores the *eruv* (legal limit) for permitted travel on the Sabbath and rides beyond, which Deutscher cites as a metaphor for someone who – like himself – rides beyond the boundaries of Judaism into wider pastures.

Meir stayed safely within the theological *eruv*, as did almost all the ancient rabbis, who questioned neither God's existence nor divine justice and ventured nothing more heretical than the tremulous admission that: 'It does not lie within our power to explain either the well-being of the wicked or the sufferings of the righteous' (*Avot* 4:15).

The generations of rabbis quoted in the Talmud did not compile a systematic theology. Their approach was more haphazard. They studied the Bible in order to explain and justify God's ways to man, not to query His attributes. So they interspersed *halachah* (law) with *haggadah* (lore), in their teachings about the nature of God, good and evil, sin and atonement, reward and punishment. They made no distinction between ethical and ritual ordinances – all were divinely mandated. Their theology encompassed virtually every aspect of the relationship between Man and God and Man with his fellows, but not in any indexed order.

Such a formal treatment had to wait until the medieval period. The first systematic Jewish theologian was Saadia Gaon, whose *Emunot v'Deot* (*Beliefs and Opinions*) was written in Arabic in 933 CE. Many other important works followed, notably Bahya ibn Pakudah's *Chovot ha-L'vavot* (*Duties of the Heart*), written probably in the first half of the eleventh century, also originally in Arabic; Judah ha-Levi's *Ha-Kuzari* (*The Khazar*), composed shortly before he left Spain around 1135, likewise in Arabic; Abraham ibn David (*c.*1110–*c.*1180) wrote *Emunah Ramah* (*Sublime Faith*) as a Jewish Aristotelean; practically all the writings of Maimonides (1135–1204) have theological import, in particular *Moreh Nevuchim* (*Guide for the Perplexed*) and his magnificent Code *Yad ha-Chazakah* (*The Strong Hand*), the first book of which deals predominantly with theological themes; Hasdai Crescas (1340–1416) was a staunch defender of the creator God and opposed, therefore, both Aristotelian notions about the eternity of matter and the efforts of Maimonides and others to synthesise Judaism's teachings with Arab philosophy, as he made clear in his major work *Or Adonai* (*Light of the Lord*); his pupil Joseph Albo (*c.*1380–1435) had been one of the victorious Jewish scholars in a famous debate to 'prove' the superiority of Christianity over Judaism held at Tortosa in February 1413 and attended for a while by Pope Benedict XIII and the King of Aragon. Albo's account of the disputation, subsequently deleted by Church censors, occurs in his *Sefer ha-Ikkarim* (*Book of the Principles*), in which he states that there are only three fundamental principles (as opposed to the thirteen postulated by Maimonides) of Jewish belief, namely: that there is a God; that God gave the Torah to the Jewish people, and that all good deeds would be rewarded and evil ones punished.

It should be noted that all these texts were written by Sephardic Jews, either during the Golden Age of Spanish Jewry or as a consequence of the fruitful interplay between Judaism and medieval Arab thought. Ashkenazi Jews of the Rhineland and Eastern Europe, perhaps reflecting the harsher geographical and cultural background in which they eked out existence, specialised in biblical commentaries and dry legal codifications – prescriptive, not speculative. The study of Jewish law was the characteristic priority of Ashkenazi communities. Their famous scholars – such as Rabbi Gershom ben Judah (*c*.965–1028), remembered for his attainments as 'the Light of the Exile'; Rashi (an acronym of Rabbi Sh'lomo ben Isaac, 1040–1105), and Jacob ben Asher (*c*.1270–1340), whose four-part *Arba'ah Turim* (*Four Rows*) became the model for all subsequent compendia of Jewish religious, civil and criminal law – were concerned with defining proper observance of the commandments, not on dabbling in metaphysics.

With the Jewries of the East in intellectual decline, and those of Eastern and Central Europe narrowing their focus onto ever stricter implementation of the *halachah*, Jewish theological thinking petrified for several centuries.

The radical ideas of Descartes and the Encyclopaedists did not penetrate the ghetto. Spinoza's excommunication by the relatively liberal Amsterdam community went unrecorded. Historically speaking, some Jewries were more theologically inclined than others; the more intellectually vigorous the culture in which they lived, as in the Spanish Golden Age, the greater their tendency to philosophise. Such religious controversies as there were in East European Jewry centred on a correct reading of Rabbinic law or the bitter hostility between the popular new sect of Chasidism and its scholastic opponents, at their head Elijah, Gaon of Vilna (1720–1797), the foremost Talmudic authority of his time.

Moses Mendelssohn, a punctiliously observant Jew by any standard, tentatively led the way towards a reevaluation of Judaism's principles by translating the Pentateuch from its holy tongue of Hebrew into German and then expounding in his major work *Jerusalem* (1783) a well-received apologia of his religion for a Christian audience. In it, he proposed the novel concept that Judaism is unique among religions, in that the law upon which it is based is called 'Torah', correctly meaning 'teaching' or 'knowledge' and not 'faith' or 'belief'. Nowhere in the Torah is there a commandment to believe, writes Mendelssohn; even the Ten Commandments begin with a simple statement of fact: 'I am the Lord your God . . .' According to Mendelssohn, a Jew is not required to believe in anything incompatible with his intelligence (although neither is he permitted to transgress any of Judaism's basic laws). Rather, what the Torah says to Jews concerning God is meant to be *known* and *understood*, not blindly accepted on faith.

Coming after the scandal of defiling the sacred Five

Books of Moses by making them available in the ver-
nacular, this attempt to marry the philosophical ideas of
Gottfried Wilhelm Leibniz (1646–1714) – he who was
parodied by Voltaire as Doctor Pangloss in *Candide* –
with those of the Spanish-Jewish thinkers, particularly
Maimonides, in the defence of Judaism, was greeted with
a storm of protest from traditional Jews.

Their rejection of Mendelssohn's innovative approach
was the time-honoured one of religious conservatism
throughout the centuries when challenged by reformers:
to invoke the thin-end-of-the-wedge argument. Open the
door a crack to reform, and defection, apostasy and as-
similation would surely follow. The rules and tenets of
Judaism never changed, and cannot ever change.

In the decades after Mendelssohn, the key defender
of the status quo and the implacable opponent of religious reform was Moses Sofer (1762–1839), communal
rabbi of Bratislava. He was generally known as *Chatam
Sofer* (Seal of the Scribe) – both a pun on his surname
(in Hebrew *sofer* = scribe) and an acronym from the title
of his major work. His motto was *Chadash asur min ha-
Torah* – 'Anything new is forbidden by the Torah' – a
homiletic wordplay on the biblical law in Leviticus 23:14
that new grains are forbidden to be used before Passover.
This became the defining watchword of Orthodox Judaism, and has more or less remained so until the present.
Therefore those Jews looking for a relaxation of approach from Orthodoxy about allowing women rabbis,
for example, or being more tolerant of homosexuality,
are living in as much pious hope as those Catholics asking the same of the Vatican and will have to wait as long
for a glimmer of concession.

The standard explanation given for the comparative

lack of interest in theology of Jewish thinkers since me-dieval times is that Judaism is a religion of deed not creed. And, anyway, Moses Maimonides had summed up all that needed to be said about Jewish belief in his Thirteen Principles of Faith, which have found their way (albeit with some modification in Progressive liturgies) into every Jewish prayer book.

Like most generalisations, a kernel of truth needs to be hedged by a host of qualifications. For a start, the notion that theology is somehow not a Jewish *specialité de la maison* has not deterred eminent Christian scholars such as George Foot Moore eighty years ago[2] or Hans Kung in our own day[3] from writing comprehensive surveys of Jewish belief. Secondly, the Rabbinic quote usually cited in support of the assumption that in Judaism actions speak louder than words rests on a misunderstanding of the relevant *midrash* (homiletic interpretation of the Bible): 'God said: "Would that Israel had forsaken Me and kept My Torah!"' Contrary to general exposition, this does *not* mean that God would prefer Israel to stop worrying about Him and fulfil His commandments in-stead; rather, that even an uninformed application of the Torah will inexorably lead the people back to Him, because, as the homily concludes: 'The light she [the Torah] contains will restore them to the good [i.e. God]' (*Lamentations Rabbah*, Introduction 2).

As for the Thirteen Principles of Maimonides, they have indeed come to be accepted as normative with the passage of time. But they are by no means conclusive or exclusive. In their own day they provoked controversy and rejection. Other scholars came up with their own versions. We have already mentioned Joseph Albo's three postulates in *Sefer ha-Ikkarim*. His contemporary Simon ben Zemach Duran (1361–1444) advocated the same three, whereas Isaac Arama (c.1420–1494) chose God's creation of the world out of nothing, Revelation and the World to Come. Other thinkers proposed variants such as the Unity of God, the Torah is from Heaven, or Reward and Punishment. On the other hand, Isaac Abarbanel (1437–1508) argued that there are no special principles of the faith but that every part of the Torah is of equal value. For the early Reform movement, Maimonides' eighth principle, that God had given the Torah to Moses 'face to face'; his twelfth, that a personal Messiah would come to redeem Israel; and his thirteenth, that at the end of days there would be physical resurrection of the dead, were deemed unacceptable and have been omitted or reworded in every Progressive prayer book since.

What can be said as a safe generalisation is that although different principles might have received greater or lesser attention at different times, the one basic assertion of Judaism has always been the existence of God. It is this which makes Judaism a religion, and stemming from this core affirmation are certain attributes invariably ascribed to God, starting with His unity. For Judaism, God exists for all eternity; He is One, incorporeal, both transcendent and immanent; He created the universe, is involved in all its processes but is also beyond the universe; He is omnipotent and omniscient; He is wholly good.

There, in a nutshell, you have Judaism's essential premises about God. Because it is austerely monotheistic, Judaism therefore rejects *deism*, the belief that God is only transcendent; *pantheism*, identifying God with Nature (the charge levelled against Spinoza); *dualism*, the belief in two gods, one good the other evil; *atheism*, the denial that there is a God; and *agnosticism*, the assumption that nothing is known, or can be known, of the existence and nature of God.

It should be said in parenthesis that the *via negativa* of agnosticism, meaning that 'silence is golden' when trying to describe God or enumerate His attributes, was a path favoured by many of the medieval Jewish philosophers, especially Maimonides. Joseph Albo in his *Sefer ha-Ikkarim* freely and daringly reworded as 'If I knew Him I would be Him' the quotation of an earlier scholar, Jedaiah Bedersi (*c*.1370–*c*.1430), that: 'The sum total of what we know of Thee is that we do not know Thee.' And Bahya ibn Pakudah recorded approvingly in *Chovot ha-L'vavot* (*The Gate of Unity*, Chapter 2) the saying of an unnamed scholar that only the prophet who knows God intuitively, and the philosopher who has found Him through the process of refined thought, truly worship God; all others worship something other than God.

Such an approach could be defined as *positive* agnosticism. It is the modesty and diffidence of a believer before the immensity of the Prime Cause and Supreme Being, whose attributes are beyond the descriptive limitations of language or human imagination fully to comprehend. The Elizabethan divine Richard Hooker was expressing much the same idea when he wrote in his great work *The Laws of Ecclesiastical Polity* that: 'Where God is concerned, our safest eloquence is our silence.'

Not so nowadays. Only a kabbalist or a fundamentalist would talk in such confident terms about *not* being able to talk about God. In our modern times, most Jews, and I would suspect most educated followers of the other monotheistic faiths as well, adopt agnosticism, in the sense of simply *not knowing*, as their default mode. They subscribe at best to the qualified trust of Pascal's famous

wager that although there is a lack of satisfactory evidence for the existence of God, nevertheless since the expected rewards of theistic belief far outweigh the potential losses should that belief turn out to be erroneous,
prudent self-interest should lead one to place a bet in favour of God.

But even that diffident leap of faith is inhibited by
the chasm between what the ancient rabbis, or Pascal,
believed about God, and what modern, scientific evidence tells us to the contrary. The omnipotent, omniscient,
supernatural Being of traditional belief Who rules His
creation with perfect justice is beyond credibility in the
Age of Science. Whatever the as-yet-unresolved complexities in fully understanding the workings of Nature, most
people apart from scriptural literalists accept that evolutionary theory is a more plausible explanation of our
origins than Creationism or Intelligent Design, which are
medieval 'proofs' for the existence of God that no theologian of repute tries hard nowadays to defend.

Pity the Jewish would-be theologian. In the past, they
required a working knowledge – or accurate translations
– of Hebrew, Aramaic and other cognate Semitic tongues
to understand the Bible and Rabbinic literature, Greek
for the Septuagint and Philo, Latin for the Vulgate and
Aquinas, and Arabic for the medieval thinkers.

The additional disciplines demanded nowadays are
formidable. At the very least, our putative theologian
must be aware of developments in biophysics, genetics,
astronomy, the cognitive sciences, psychology and linguistic philosophy. Astonishing advances in DNA track-
ing, stem-cell research and embryonic cloning are as radical a threat to theistic belief as was Galileo's insistence
that the earth orbits the sun. It is not God's inscrutable

ways but DNA inheritance that determines who shall live and who shall die, who shall be born healthy and who congenitally defective. The human being evolves from its mother's egg cell and its father's sperm cell, through grandfathers and grandmothers and their ancestors all the way back to the first cells, which formed about 3.7 billion years ago and resembled present-day bacteria – 3.7 billion years of constant cell division and cell evolution and, occasionally, cell malfunction, which scientists don't yet fully understand but think could be helpfully investigated by inserting human DNA into an animal egg from which the nucleus has been removed. When, as is inevitable, this takes place, Science will have fully usurped the role of God.

It might be overly complacent of liberal theologians to claim that there is no essential incompatibility between accepting Darwinism and reading the Genesis account of creation as a metaphorical explanation of evolutionary progression. They are overlooking that Darwinism, in placing humanity four square with all other living organisms, implicitly strikes at the tenet – central certainly to Judaism, Christianity and Islam – that our species occupies a unique position in the world as the crown of God's handiwork.

Linguistic philosophy since Wittgenstein has driven a coach and horses through commonly used religious terminology about God and His attributes. Science, we know, can explain what goes on in the universe by discovering the systematic connections among its features and elements, but the existence of the universe as a whole cannot be explained in this way. We must seek an explanation for that in something that is not part of the universe but outside of space and time, an ultimate cause.

Even the Big Bang theory requires reference to some larger reality that contained or gave rise to it. In theology, this role has always been ascribed to God the Creator.

But linguistic philosophers dismiss as unintelligible the hypothesis that at some time in the past God willed the universe to come into existence. To posit that is to employ the concept of an agent producing something, while withholding two of the crucial conditions generally understood in the concept of agency: time and physical causation. The notion that a non-physical God who is neither in space nor time yet might cause space and time to come into being at a certain point is to detach familiar words from their usual application, so that they no longer express rational possibilities. Using words precisely, it could be said that a non-spatial, non-temporal God is logically incapable of doing *anything* in space or time, even allowing for the fact that occasionally religious language cannot help but be anthropomorphic – speaking 'in the language of men' as the Talmud puts it – and metaphorical. The medieval Jewish philosophers were fond of pointing out that not even God can be expected to do the logically impossible, such as squaring a circle or making two and two equal five.

The extent to which believers are willing to be persuaded by semantic theory or scientific advances may vary but, for sure, ever-increasing human knowledge leaves an ever-decreasing space for the traditional deity to function in, reducing Him to 'the God of the Gaps'. That is the dilemma for Jewish believers. It is an unreconstructed theistic view that suffuses all of Jewish ritual and liturgy. There would be little meaning to the Passover *Haggadah* (Narrative of the Passover *Seder* ceremony) if God had not initiated the Exodus; He is solely credited for it in the *Haggadah*, whereas Moses is nowhere mentioned. The solemn fast day of Yom Kippur would lose its cleansing purpose if God did not accept our prayers of repentance. The Feast of Weeks commemorates God giving the Law at Mount Sinai. The Chanukkah festival of lights is predicated on God's wondrous deliverance at the time of the Maccabees. These and all other Jewish observances – even the recently devised services for Israel Independence Day – sanctify God as their instigator, but whatever the reasons why Jews still mark these occasions nowadays, belief in the God of the prayer book would come low down the list.

I must confess that by the time I came to retire from the pulpit, I found it increasingly difficult to lead the congregation in reciting the central prayer of the Jewish liturgy, the *Amidah* ('Standing' prayer), without feelings of intellectual hypocrisy. If that admission is shocking to some, I can only quote the words of a Talmudic sage: 'I will speak that I may find relief.' The *Amidah* extols our great, mighty, exalted God and God of our ancestors, the Creator of all, our Redeemer, Who deals kindly with His children, supports the falling, heals the sick, sets free the captive and keeps faith with those who sleep in the dust. However modern liturgies attempt to reinterpret or gloss those certitudes, empirical experience of wars, disease, famine, natural disasters, wanton cruelty, the Holocaust and everyday examples of casual injustice in what Thomas Hardy called 'this nonchalant universe' must surely lead modern worshippers at least to query them. The more I parroted the words, the more detached I became from them. A story told about Sir Leslie Stephen, Virginia Woolf's father and first editor of *The Dictionary of National Biography*, lodged stubbornly at the back of my mind. It was said of him that he resigned from Holy Orders less because he had lost his faith than because he realised he had none to begin with.

The second paragraph of the *Amidah* poses another problem. In it, God is lauded as *m'chayyeh meitim*, the One Who 'revives the dead'. Physical resurrection of the dead at the end of days was a basic Pharisaic doctrine. It was one of the major points of difference with their opponents the Sadduccees, as it was nineteen centuries later between Orthodox Judaism and the early Reformers.

Many and contorted have been the efforts of Progressive liturgists to deal with this core Rabbinic belief, one that flies in the face of all human reason. To excise it from the Hebrew of the *Amidah* would spoil the rhythm and destroy the flow of a familiar prayer, much as if Christian liturgists suddenly bowdlerised the English of another well-known litany of Pharisaic sayings, the so-called Lord's Prayer. But attempted modifications in translation to the *Amidah*'s meaning while retaining the original Hebrew have neither improved matters nor fortified belief. To cite just a few examples: in *Forms of Prayer* (1977), the previous prayer book of the Reform movement in the UK, God is apostrophised as 'the endless power that renews life beyond death' – which plays fast and loose with the Hebrew and makes little sense in English. In its successor, *Forms of Prayer* (2008), God is 'faithful to renew life beyond death' – which makes even less sense.

My own Liberal movement has fared no better. In our current prayer book, *Siddur Lev Chadash* (*A New Heart*, 1995), we praise God as 'the Source of eternal life' – which invites questions of both accurate translation and meaning, but is marginally preferable to the anodyne and

freely adapted 'all life is Your gift' in its liturgical predecessor *Service of the Heart* (1967).

The worst of all possible worlds is offered by the Central Conference of American Rabbis in its most recent
prayer book *Mishkan T'filah* (*A Prayer Sanctuary*, 2007),
over twenty years in the compiling. The CCAR serves
more than 1.1 million affiliated Reform Jews in the USA,
down from its peak in the 1960s of around 2.5 million, but still the single largest religious grouping in world
Jewry. Evidently its two thousand rabbis found the theological complexities of *m'chayyeh meitim* too difficult to
resolve collectively, because the baffled worshipper can
choose between alternative versions on the same page:
either 'Blessed are You . . . who gives life to all', or next
to it in brackets ('. . . who revives the dead'). Then follows a lame explanation on the facing page to the effect
that thanking God for 'reviving the dead' was a widely
used Rabbinic figure of speech, for example on seeing
a friend after a long absence. Many years ago I had a
colleague who endured a prickly relationship with his
synagogue chairman. When the man entered one Sabbath
service late, my colleague recklessly ad-libbed from the
pulpit that the congregation had just witnessed walking
proof of life after death. Insisting that he had simply been
using an ancient Rabbinic greeting did not save him his
job.

It is probably redundant to mention that Orthodox
liturgies make no attempt to modify the *Amidah* translation for the sensibilities of modern worshippers, just
as they retain every ancient prayer calling for the rebuilding of the Temple in Jerusalem, the restoration of
animal sacrifice and the destruction of Israel's enemies.
The objections that greeted Moses Mendelssohn's mild

innovations are considered just as valid today: if it has been hallowed by time, why bother to fix it?

It has to be said that Protestant Christian theology, on the whole, has been a great deal bolder than its Jewish counterpart in confronting the implications of no longer being able to believe in the powers of a transcendent, interventionist God. From Rudolf Bultmann (1884–1976) and his near contemporary Paul Tillich, to the so-called 'process theologians' influenced by the writings of Alfred North Whitehead and Charles Hartshorne, to post-modern thinkers, the thrust of most contemporary Protestant theology has been to demystify God in favour of an indwelling, non-transcendent Being who is primarily the guardian and arbiter of human ethical conduct. Reinhold Niebuhr, a thoughtful critic of both liberal Christianity and Marxism, charged that Tillich 'presents atheism in theological language'.

It was Bultmann's stated goal 'to make religion logically independent of a supernatural being'. Dietrich Bonhoeffer, the German theologian murdered by the Nazis, whose work became a staple of post-Second World War theological discourse, doubted that God was still needed: 'Man has learned to cope with all questions of importance without recourse to God as a working hypothesis . . . it has become evident (even in religious questions) that everything gets along without "God" just as well as before.'[4]

It was over forty years ago, but I can't actually remember any serious discussions about the nature of God and His attributes at the rabbinical college where I studied. Much study of Rabbinic theology and the medieval thinkers and their ideas, yes, but only the most perfunctory mention of modern belief, which seemed to be taken for granted – a mere twenty-five years after Auschwitz. The college was named after Leo Baeck, the foremost German rabbi and theologian of his era, who had survived Theresienstadt concentration camp and lived in London until his death in 1956. His most celebrated work was *The Essence of Judaism*, originally published in 1905 as a response to Adolf von Harnack's unflattering assessment of the Jewish religion in *The Essence of Christianity*. Harnack's thesis was that Christianity had appeared at a unique historical moment, unconnected to Jewish cultural tradition or Judaism. For many years Baeck's was the standard apologia for Judaism, a bestseller worldwide and an inevitable *bar mitzvah* gift. For all its fame, truth to tell I found it theologically conventional, stylistically ponderous, an opaque mix of neo-Kantianism and existentialism, and very hard going – a reaction secretly shared, I imagine, by my fellow students and those myriads of Jews who reverently dipped into it out of respect for the author.

Baeck was not a theologian to challenge received wisdom. He merely tinkered with the traditional formulations of Jewish belief by the light of then-contemporary philosophical trends. The only recent Jewish theologian to my knowledge, Orthodox or Progressive, who squarely confronted the problem of God and came up with a radical reformulation of the deity was my own favourite, Mordecai Kaplan. Kaplan variously defined God as 'the power that makes for goodness/salvation' (a definition akin to Bonhoeffer's 'the beyond in the midst of our life'), thus firmly locating God in the realm of ethical human aspiration and stripping Him of all transcendent attributes and His guiding role in history. In 'humanising' God, so to speak, Kaplan understood a reality often overlooked by academic theologians or his scandalised Jewish critics: that religion always has to relate to ethics, whereas ethics stand independently of religion. As we have frequently observed in life, an atheist can be quite as ethical a person as a theist. Generations of university-educated, sceptical, otherwise secularised Jews at least could endorse Kaplan's concept of God as an enabler rather than a doer and more concerned with moral conduct than ritual, with the *spirit* of Judaism than its forms.

The great, mighty and awesome God of the Bible and Jewish prayer has lost His potency for ever. 'God' is the catch-all entity we invoke, like a pastor enlisting His support before an American college basketball game, on all the public occasions and festival days when Jews affirm our common adherence to shared ideals about peace, justice and the community of Israel. But after the ritual declaration of loyalty this supernatural Being has little further meaning or influence in our lives. Even those who claim to believe in God resort to imprecision – a sense of wonder at Nature, the 'still, small voice' of conscience, the divinely inspired genius of Mozart, a universe too intricately intermeshed not to have had a guiding hand behind it – when asked to define *why* they believe.

It is a truism that each generation re-creates God in its own image, something recognised by the ancient rabbis in their homiletic comment on the *Amidah*'s opening lines that praise the God of Abraham, the God of Isaac and the God of Jacob. Why, they wondered, the triple repetition of God's name? Surely we are addressing the same deity? And the answer they gave is that the God who appeared unto Abraham was not the God whom Isaac worshipped, or the One who blessed Jacob; to each patriarch He revealed a different aspect of His Being.

As the statistics I gave in Chapter 1 indicate, the overwhelming majority of modern Jews live in a few select urban environments and gravitate towards middle-class occupations: medicine, law, teaching, small businesses, the caring agencies. The God they pray to in their suburban congregations is in their image and likeness. As befits a post-feminist deity, He/She is sensitive to issues of sexual identity and gender and therefore sympathetic to blessing the union of same-sex couples, providing they are in a loving and faithful relationship. He/She hopes for a negotiated settlement to the Israel–Palestine tragedy, with goodwill and understanding replacing hatred and vengeance on both sides. This caring God is shocked by natural disasters such as earthquakes and tsunamis (which He/She did not cause, control of the environment having been quietly dropped from His/Her remit), is enthusiastic for all Green initiatives, upset by Third World famine, and yearns for a speedy end to war, poverty and ruthless dictatorships, so that freedom is enjoyed by all. In other words, our post-modern concept of the Divine Being reflects the concerns of a bourgeois, middle-way social democrat. The all-powerful, decisive God of the traditional liturgy whom nobody can give credence to any longer has been replaced by a celestial social worker who urges us to empathise with the less fortunate and do good deeds. Neither the previous nor the present model is spiritually inspiring.

Instead, to fill the void left by Matthew Arnold's 'melancholy, long, withdrawing roar' of the Sea of Faith, Jews have substituted behaviourism. We practise the traditions of Judaism, while quietly discarding the beliefs that endowed those traditions with their significance. I don't say that disparagingly. It is no small thing still to tell the story after so many generations. There is a Chasidic parable about the movement's charismatic founder, the Baal Shem Tov (Master of the Good Name), who whenever danger threatened his people would go to a certain place in the forest, light a fire and sing a particular melody to God, and the danger would be averted. His chosen successor, Rabbi Dov Baer of Mezritch, would go to the same place in the forest and light the fire, but did not know the melody; still the danger would be averted. Levi Yitzchok of Berditchev, his successor, would go to the same place, knowing neither the melody nor how to light the fire, but still the danger would pass. And *his* successor, Rabbi Israel of Ruzhin, would go to the forest knowing neither the place nor how to light the fire nor the melody, but at least he was able to tell the story.

When people no longer believe in God without quite having the courage to say so, they take refuge in telling the story. They accentuate ritualism and gesture; displacement activities. So old rituals have been reintroduced and new ones invented, even in Progressive Judaism, the supposedly cerebral offspring of Enlightenment reason. At Progressive services – once derided by the Orthodox for aping the decorum of Protestant worship – there is now so much bobbing and bowing before the Ark, and hugging and kissing of the Scrolls of the Law to happy-clappy guitar accompaniment, that a casual visitor might imagine that he had wandered by mistake into some transplanted Polish *shtiebl* (prayer room) from two hundred years ago.

In its early days, Reform Judaism discarded the minor festival of Purim. The biblical Book of Esther which is read in synagogue on Purim has no historical authenticity, does not deliver any religious message, and glorifies the revenge taken by the Jews of Persia on their arch-enemy Haman by hanging him and his ten sons, and killing a further seventy-five thousand of their follow-ers throughout the provinces of King Ahasuerus, who is the love-smitten husband of Jewish Queen Esther. It is a wishful fairy-tale, no more, of a lovely queen delivering her imperilled people, and for centuries was the excuse for jollity, drinking, masques, plays, fancy-dress parties, even cross-dressing, which is strictly forbidden in Deu-teronomy 32:5. On these primly disapproving grounds, Purim was dropped from the Progressive Jewish calendar. In recent years it has made a come-back, and Progressive Jews now celebrate Purim as exuberantly as any Chasidic group. It is a bow to tradition, a way of keeping the story alive, even though it is no more morally elevating than Guy Fawkes Night or Halloween.

At Progressive weddings too, it has become standard for the groom to go through the ritual of solemnly 'in-specting' his bride before the ceremony, a custom that harks back to Jacob in the Bible being fobbed off with Leah instead of Rachel – even though no modern bride is likely to be swathed in all-concealing layers like a desert Bedouin and everyone knows that she and her husband-to-be have been living together for years. Similarly, fake traditionalism decrees that it is obligatory for bride and groom to be hoisted up on separate chairs (a throwback to strict Chasidic rules about keeping the sexes apart) while guests do a lively *hora* (mistakenly assumed to have originated with the early pioneers in Palestine, when in fact it was a Russian peasant dance), before anyone can sit down to eat.

At two recent wedding blessings that I have officiated at between Jewish and non-Jewish individuals, the grandson of Henry Moore the sculptor and the grandson of Count Bernadotte who was assassinated in Jerusalem in 1948 by the ultra-nationalist Stern Gang, have been elevated aloft in bemused deference to their Jewish brides. I recall one wedding reception in a posh hotel a few years ago which dragged on far too long, with precious little to drink or nibble until the toastmaster thankfully summoned us to our tables in the banqueting hall, only for an interminable *hora* to begin. Another guest at my table, echoing a line from the play *Boys in the Band*, groaned under his breath, 'Who does one have to f**k around here to get a cup of tea?'

Other statements of Jewish identity include many men in different branches of Judaism always wearing a skull cap out of doors (a practice copied from Black Panthers in 1970s New York with their Rasta locks) and Jewish women sporting 'Chai' (Life) amulets round their necks. In previous generations, only ultra-Orthodox Jews, who wore unchanged the eighteenth-century garb of their Polish ancestors, would have identified themselves in public by dressing 'different'. The impetus for reform within Judaism was originally social, not theological, to stress similarity with, not difference from, wider society. The early German reformers built their synagogues in the style of Protestant cathedrals, installed organs to accompany newly composed melodies modelled on Bach and Mendelssohn, and prayed decorously without the chanting and swaying of East European worship, in order to demonstrate their compatibility with German culture.

In the UK, the nineteen Sephardi and five Ashkenazi Jews who met to propose the establishment of a reformed synagogue that became, in 1842, the West London Synagogue for British Jews (the adjective more significant

than the noun in how they saw themselves) were motivated by the fact that they now lived in the fashionable
West End and found it irksome to get to services in time
at Bevis Marks or the Great Synagogue in the East End.
Reform Judaism in America, where the first temple had
been erected in Charleston, South Carolina, in 1824, was
likewise the product of acculturation and social advancement. In each country, the aim was to accentuate Jewish
compatibility with the host culture and eliminate any
negative associations that wearing distinctive garb might
have provoked. Today, in contrast, distinguishing markers are shown off by Jews and other ethnic minorities as
a badge of pride. That doesn't bother me in itself; I am
merely suggesting that it is a compensatory gimmick for
the loss of faith.

As actual belief has declined, the popularity of Jewish
education as an alternative way of connecting to Judaism
and the Jewish past has increased. That is a welcome
development, but of course sidesteps any necessity to ex-
amine the theology on which Judaism is based. So adult
Jews can pick from a variety of topics, and study Kabbalah or Spirituality, Yiddish or klezmer music, or the
history of Jews in Hollywood as ends in themselves, all
part of the rich tapestry of being Jewish, without having
to evaluate the subject's intrinsic worth. At my former
rabbinic college, Homiletics – the craft of learning to
preach competently – is now an elective course, but 'Spirituality' (whatever that means) is a syllabus requirement.
As the great Talmudic scholar Saul Lieberman said mis-
chievously when introducing at the Hebrew University
in Jerusalem his friend Gershom Scholem's series of lectures (which would become the celebrated book *Major
Trends in Jewish Mysticism*), nonsense, when all is said

and done, is still nonsense; but the study of nonsense –
ah – that is scholarship!

The teaching of Jewish history is a case in point. At
religion-school level it involves biblical stories about
Abraham, Isaac and Jacob, the Exodus from Egypt, and
stirring tales about King David and the brave Maccabees,
which is fair enough for young children. But for most
Jews, their religious education finishes with *bar mitzvah*
for boys at the age of thirteen; in Progressive synagogues
girls undertake the equivalent *bat mitzvah*, and continue
with the boys to *Kabbalat Torah* (Confirmation) in their
sixteenth year. But if they are Orthodox girls they have
to be content with a watered-down ceremony, not on the
Sabbath and not involving reading from the Torah (for
fear of ritual impurity), called *bat chayil*. And that, more
or less, is the end of their formal Jewish learning.

For a more sophisticated approach to Jewish history
a student has to rely on personal reading, a university
course, or one of the numerous seminars on offer at synagogues and adult-education centres, where the lopsided
Zionist version – Diaspora equals exile, anti-Semitism
and persecution; Israel equals Jewish fulfilment, home-
coming and redemption – is usually taught.

Even with advanced subjects such as Talmud or
Midrash (Rabbinic interpretation of the Bible), the pursuit of knowledge under capable and enthusiastic teachers is undertaken without any expectancy of concomitant
belief from the pupils. In conversation recently with an
observant and deeply committed Orthodox woman who
hosts Talmud study groups in her home, I was startled at
how blithely she dismissed my naive problems with the
God of the *Amidah* by using post-modern terminology to
describe Him as being simply a way of telling a story that

is never definitive or context free – then she happily went off to pray to Him. That is reminiscent of a fable originally told by Eli Wiesel, for which no scrap of evidence in reality has ever been found, about a group of pious Jews in Auschwitz who put God on trial, argued throughout the night whether He was guilty or not, found that He was – and then adjourned for morning prayers. That parable has now found its way into contemporary prayer books – as fact. Such sentimental *bobbe-meysehs* (Yiddish, 'old wives' tales') are the modern substitute for belief.

So it is no surprise that for many years now fundraisers, educators and rabbis have relied on slogans stressing ethnicity and nationhood to rouse the enthusiasm and retain the loyalty of Jews who are otherwise indifferent to Judaism's doctrinal teachings. 'Jewish Solidarity' is wheeled out whenever Israel is being criticised. 'Jewish Continuity' is a favourite one in support of more Jewish day schools. 'Let My People Go' was the rallying cry on behalf of Soviet refuseniks in the 1980s. 'Jewish Survival' was the stark message before and after the Six Day War, coupled with the 614th Commandment added by Emil Fackenheim, a Canadian theologian and Reform rabbi, to the 613 traditionally counted in the Bible: 'Thou shalt not hand Hitler posthumous victories.' Fackenheim made his famous remark at a meeting in New York shortly before the 1967 war, and it was immediately seized on for its catchy publicity value. His next sentence, 'To despair of the God of Israel is to continue Hitler's work for him', was quietly ignored. And when some of Fackenheim's colleagues began to ask, 'Survival for *what*? Or is it merely an end in itself?', and no easy answer was forthcoming, the slogan itself was dropped and segued smoothly into a defiant riposte to all critics of the Jewish state and covert anti-Semites everywhere as *Am Yisrael Chai* – 'The People of Israel Lives On.'

The folkways of tradition and a sense of unbroken Jewish continuity that owes more to the stuff of legend than historical accuracy are what encourage a modern, non-believing Jew in Jerusalem, New York or London to trace a lineal descent from Abraham, Isaac and Jacob in the Bible and therefore, by extension, a 'divine right' to the land associated with the Patriarchs. Of course, the link is more fanciful than real, but it sustained Jews throughout centuries of exile as they prayed to the God of their ancestors to redeem them as He had redeemed His people Israel from Egyptian slavery.

That was before the widespread abandonment of belief. For more than sixty years now, Judaism as the religion of the Jewish people has been sustained by Zionism, its secular alter ego. The early Zionists, led by Herzl, were adept at appropriating the metaphors of faith – the promise of 'a land flowing with milk and honey', the yearning for 'next year in Jerusalem' – and adapting them to their own secular purposes. In that way, Zionism, the newcomer among Jewish responses to modernity, positioned itself in the mainstream of Jewish history as a fulfilment of, not a rupture with, the Jewish past. Under its broad wings and quasi-religious terminology Zionism provided a haven for radical socialists, secular humanists, cultural revivalists, devout Orthodox and classical Reform followers. Everyone disillusioned with the credos of conventional Judaism, from those who wanted to prepare the way for the Jewish Workers' Revolution to those who wanted to prepare the ground for the coming of the Messiah, could find a new set of beliefs in Zionism. Unsurprisingly, the new religion has been no more successful in delivering salvation than the old one was.

In a novel first published in France in 1940 as *Les Chiens et les Loups* and recently translated into English,[5] the writer Irène Némirovsky describes the inhabitants of their unnamed Ukrainian town (probably Kiev, where she was born in 1903) as follows: 'The Jews who lived in the lower town were religious and fanatically attached to their customs; the Jews in the wealthy areas were strict observers of tradition. To the poor Jews, their religion was so completely engrained in them that it would have been just as impossible to extricate themselves from it as to live without their beating hearts. To the rich Jews, loyalty to the rites of their forefathers seemed in good taste, dignified, morally honourable, as much as – perhaps more than – true belief.'

Némirovsky was writing about Ukrainian Jews – probably then the most religiously tenacious and conservative segment of European Jewry – before the 1917 Russian Revolution. She uses the example of 'poor' and 'rich' Jews to categorise the split between true believers and lip-servers to Jewish tradition. One hundred years later, that gap has widened immeasurably and fragmented into further schisms. Nowadays, the religious Jews 'fanatically attached to their customs' are a tiny, albeit instantly noticeable and insistently vocal, minority, around 10 per cent of world Jewry. The Jews who pay respect to ancestral custom but no longer practise 'the rites of their forefathers' or believe in the God of Judaism, constitute the overwhelming majority.

A new category needs to be considered, in addition to the familiar triumvirate of Zionist, Orthodox and Progressive Jew. It is that of the Cultural Jew.

How 'holy' is Holy Scripture?

In *God's Funeral*, his wide-ranging exploration of the decline of faith in Victorian times,[1] A. N. Wilson described Benjamin Jowett, the Master of Balliol, as 'that rather attractive mixture . . . a person of profound religious feeling and a sceptical cast of mind'. The poet W. B. Yeats, born in the Victorian heyday, once summed himself up as 'cursed with a religious temperament but no religion'.

Perhaps it is the lot of any thinking person with spiritual intimations to be torn between an apprehension of wonder at the workings of the universe while remaining unconvinced by religion's deist explanation for them. Any reader puzzled how a rabbi who does not believe in the traditional God can yet be a teacher of Judaism should ponder an anecdote that Gore Vidal tells about his grandfather, Senator T. P. Gore. The senator, who helped to create the state of Oklahoma and was its first elected representative, had a reputation as a powerful orator. After he had given a political speech in Texas, a group of Baptist elders approached him and offered him a fine church and house in Houston if he would become their minister. Gore thanked them and said that the offer was indeed very tempting but he couldn't accept it, as he did not believe in God. The elders replied, 'Come now, Mr Gore, that's not the proposition we made you, is it?'

In other words, to be an effective rabbi, priest or pastor does not automatically require unshakeable belief as a prerequisite. It might further surprise the ingenuous reader to discover, as I have in many a frank conversation over dinner and a good wine, the degree of agnosticism among princes of the church, Catholic as well as Protestant. 'For Blougram, he believed, say, half he spoke' was Robert Browning's estimate of his worldly bishop's apology. Bishop Blougram referred to God as 'The grand Perhaps!' – a description that would find favour with many modern Jews as well, to judge by the only sociological survey on the state of Jewish belief that, to the best of my knowledge, has ever been carried out within a major community, the American one.[2]

According to the survey's findings, 73 per cent of the 5.5 million American adults who consider themselves to be Jewish by religion, parentage, upbringing or affiliation subscribe to the proposition 'that God exists'; the remaining 27 per cent of that core Jewish population (the survey estimates a further 2.2 million persons of Jewish descent or what used to be called 'Jewish extraction', who don't maintain any links whatsoever with Judaism – Madeleine Albright, Secretary of State in the Clinton administration being one such example) either have no religious attachment or hold views that could be classed as 'atheist' or 'agnostic'. And of those 5.5 million adults who do identify as Jewish, nearly 50 per cent regard themselves as 'secular' or 'somewhat secular'. Among all other American non-Jewish adults, the comparable statistics are around 1 per cent who profess to be atheist or agnostic, and 16 per cent who own to being secular. The standard gibe since the Enlightenment against Jews who try to assimilate too avidly has always been that they are bending over backwards to ape the Gentiles. In this instance, far from imitating, they appear to be leading the charge towards godless secularism.

The American Jewish Identity Survey was conducted over a decade ago, before some of the more bizarre manifestations of entering a new millennium had become fully apparent. Strange upheavals seem to affect the human psyche when a climacteric year is imminent. In his seminal work *The Pursuit of the Millennium*,[3] Norman Cohn traced the fantasies and doomsday scenarios that regularly surfaced among mystics, flagellants and revolutionaries in the Middle Ages, and were a precursor, in his view, of the fanatical totalitarianism of Communism and Nazism in the twentieth century. Significantly, his book enjoyed a fresh vogue in the years before the twenty-first century began, confirming for dreamers of the Second Coming, New Age gurus, Apocalypse visionaries, and computer geeks who feared a worldwide systems crash on 1 January 2000, that Armageddon was indeed at hand. Bravely swallowing their disappointment when the earth continued turning much as before, they have fixed their gaze on alternative end-of-days predictions; global warming and ecological disaster are by far the most plausible. As for the more outré end-of-the-world predictions, G. K. Chesterton shrewdly observed, 'Those who cease to believe in God do not begin to believe in *nothing*, they believe in *anything*.'

Instead of the new millennium ushering in the steady advance of Reason and Science at the expense of Religion, the opposite has happened, confounding expectations. Back in 1965, Harvey Cox, until recently Professor of Divinity at Harvard, wrote, not disapprovingly, of the progress of secularism as 'the deliverance of man first from religious and then from metaphysical control over his reasons and his language . . . the dispelling of all closed worldviews, the breaking of all supernatural myths and sacred symbols'.[4]

But in the last decade, pressure on the three monotheistic religions has come as much from extremism within their own ranks as from secularism without. Twenty years ago, Jewish, Christian and Muslim thinkers who shared a universalist outlook were privately aware that theologically they felt more at home in each other's company than they did with the small but shrill band of fundamentalists of their own faith; the future was surely with them in spreading a global ethic that could be endorsed by most of the world's religions. Nowadays, it is the growing number of particularist militants who are setting the religious agenda, and liberals who have to adjust rightwards. I have already alluded in the previous chapter to the neo-traditionalism and behaviourism that has affected the Reform and Liberal wings of Judaism. One sees a similar phenomenon in the rearguard action being fought by progressives in the Church of England against the assertiveness of its evangelical wing. The same tensions are evident within Catholicism and Islam. The internal paradox that the three monotheistic faiths need to resolve is how to cope with growing religious stridency in their ranks on the one hand, and growing secular defection on the other.

Judaism, having characteristically placed more stress on works than faith, and always ranked the community above individual observance, is perhaps better placed than other religions to absorb the widespread secularism among its own adherents. The consequence of loss of faith for a Catholic or a Muslim is that definitionally they are no longer members of the community of believers.

The consequence for a Jew – unless he or she belonged originally to one of the extreme factions – is negligible. He or she can continue to attend synagogue and participate in *bar mitzvahs*, weddings and funerals precisely as before. Kith and kin are paramount in Judaism.

The force of this was again brought home to me a few months ago, when I shared in officiating at a funeral service in the synagogue of a small Jewish community of thirty families in Portugal. The deceased was of Jewish American-Italian lineage, her husband an American Catholic whose paternal grandfather came from a long line of Polish rabbis. Conducting the service in Hebrew, Portuguese and English with me was the community's voluntary prayer leader, a professor of physics at the local university. The synagogue, a tiny gem in Spanish style, had been built before the Second World War by a wealthy Hong Kong Jew and was maintained by the hundred or so congregants and visitors' donations, in the time-honoured Jewish way. Several hundred mourners, mainly employees of the dead woman's large textile factory, were Catholics.

The heavily outnumbered Jewish mourners were a mixture of Ashkenazim and Sephardim, with the addition of a few *Marranos* ('secret' Jews from the Iberian Peninsula forced to convert after 1492) proud to reaffirm their ancestry in today's more tolerant climate. They taught me some words of Ladino, the Judaeo-Spanish lingua franca of Sephardic exiles. They mingled easily and cordially, with no differentiation between believer and non-believer, Jew by birth or Jew by choice, in making up the Orthodox prayer quorum of ten adult men. The unifying factor was that they had come together to express sympathy to a bereaved Jewish family as eclectic in its genetic make-up as they were themselves. I was deeply moved to observe how, on a practical, humane level – like the dozen Jews I met on the Isle of Skye – this small group practise the rituals and maintain the traditions of their Jewish heritage. It had little to do with Jewish belief per se, but everything to do with a shared sense of history, ethnic tenacity and the value placed on community. As Martin Buber observed, 'We Jews are a community based on memory. A common memory has kept us together and enabled us to survive.'

That is why I always prefer to describe Judaism more broadly as a 'culture' rather than narrowly as a 'religion', applying the social-science definition of culture as the shared national tradition, collective memories, predominant language, customs, civilisation, and artistic and intellectual achievements of a particular people. Until the Enlightenment, Judaism was viewed solely as a religion – perforce it had to be; that is how Jews were classified, and treated accordingly. With emancipation and admission into wider society, Jews could express their Jewishness differently and in a variety of ways. Journalism and the theatre were two occupations with a noticeable attraction for Jews in nineteenth-century Europe, as was radical politics. Moses Hess, the confrère of Marx and Engels and a proto-Zionist, was dubbed 'the Communist rabbi'. Inhibited by centuries of legislation against making graven images or indulging in frivolous pursuits, new-found freedom enabled Jews to flourish in art, literature and especially music. A torrent of pent-up Jewish creativity overflowed the barriers previously erected by Rabbinic edict and Gentile exclusion.

What is specifically 'Jewish' about a work of art, piece of music or novel whose creator happens to be Jewish?

With an artist such as Chagall or a writer such as Isaac Bashevis Singer it is easy enough to see; their works are suffused with a Jewish milieu and Jewish themes. They painted and wrote *out of* their Jewishness.

It is less easy with – to pick two modern examples at random – a novelist such as Michael Chabon, author of the quirkily original *The Yiddish Policemen's Union*, or a sculptor such as Anish Kapoor. I was on the small selection committee that chose Kapoor from over a hundred and fifty applicants to design our synagogue's Holocaust memorial twenty years ago, when he was beginning to make a name for himself but was hardly the world-famous artist he is today; it was only afterwards that I discovered he was sixteenth-generation Iraqi Jewish on his mother's side, and not, as everyone assumed from his name, Indian. Earnest interviewers from Jewish newspapers might quiz him or every Hollywood actor with a once-Jewish name (or the late Norman Mailer, who to wary Jewish eyes looked like a quintessential Irish bar-room brawler but boasted he was part Jewish) about their antecedents and upbringing in order to claim them for Judaism; but religion was only a minor element in their overall creative development, unless one makes the dubious claim that being Jewish gives you a unique empathy with, and insight into, certain human conditions, such as the plight of the persecuted, homelessness, or being an outsider. It might well have been true of Jews such as René Cassin who were prominent after the Second World War in developing universal human rights law and the courts and commissions to implement it. But try convincing a Palestinian refugee about this unique Jewish propensity . . .

Still more difficult to pigeonhole is someone such as

Franz Kafka. Is he a Jewish author, a Czech author, or a German author? His case is significant, because a trial is currently taking place in Tel-Aviv to determine who should have stewardship of several boxes of his writings, including primary drafts of his published works.[5] It is well known that Kafka left all his writings to his friend Max Brod, with explicit instructions that they should be destroyed after his death. Brod interpreted his request elastically, publishing *The Trial*, *The Castle* and *Amerika* between 1925 and 1927 and an edition of the collected works in 1935. Thereafter he honoured his friend's wish, and when he escaped from Europe to Palestine in 1939 he stashed most of the manuscripts in suitcases, where they remained until his own death in 1968. In turn, Brod bequeathed the literary legacy to his secretary Esther Hoffe. By now, Kafka was recognised as one of the key writers of the twentieth century. In 1988, financial considerations led Hoffe to sell the manuscript of *The Trial* for $2 million. She died in 2007 at the ripe age of a hundred and one, leaving her two daughters as the beneficiaries of the Kafka material. They want to sell it off, sight unseen, to the highest bidder.

Unsurprisingly, their mother's will is being contested. The first claimant is the National Library of Israel, whose chairman of the Board of Directors declared that: 'The library does not intend to give up on cultural assets belonging to the Jewish people . . .' This proprietary attitude assumes that the State of Israel is indeed the representative of the Jewish people as a whole, and all Jews in Israel and the Diaspora speak as one. A controversial assumption, to say the least; as Antony Lerman put it in a *Guardian* article, if 'the National Library claims the legacy of Kafka for the Jewish state, it, and institutions like it in Israel, can lay claim to practically any pre-Holocaust synagogue, artwork, manuscript or valuable ritual object extant in Europe. But neither Israel as a state, nor any state or public institution, has such a right'[6]

The National Library has a powerful counter-claimant in the German Literature Archive in Marbach, which already owns the largest collection of Kafka manuscripts in the world, including that of *The Trial*, acquired from Esther Hoffe in 1988. Marbach's advocates argue that not only does the archive have superior facilities for preserving the material, but also that Kafka 'belongs' to German literature and, specifically, the German language.

That is an interesting assertion of cultural appropriation based on linguistic osmosis. It could also be used of Polish Joseph Conrad, Yiddish-speaking Isaac Bashevis Singer, Czech Milan Kundera, and all other exiles who express themselves in a language other than their native tongue. Certainly, Kafka's pellucid German prose style has been extravagantly praised by many critics, Hannah Arendt, John Updike and George Steiner among them. But is that any more an indication of where he most truly belongs than his immersion in Yiddish theatre, his efforts to learn Hebrew, his abandoned flirtation with Zionism, or his equivocal relationship with Judaism and the Jewish people?

What clues does Kafka himself give? One of his famous quips about Jews was: 'My people, provided that I have one.' Elsewhere he writes in his diary, 'What have I in common with Jews? I have hardly anything in common with myself . . .' In a 1917 letter to his friend Grete Bloch he says that he is a man who is 'excluded from every soul-sustaining community on account of his non-Zionist (I admire Zionism and am nauseated by it), non-practising Judaism'. Hardly the most ringing endorsement on which to base the National Library's claim that Israel is the only proper guardian on behalf of the Jewish people for the unique cultural asset that is Franz Kafka.

Ultimately, exceptional Jewish artists, however much or little use they make of their homeland, family background and personal experience, are exceptional because they transcend the exiguous confines of religion, nationality, education and upbringing to fashion a universal statement about life. Marcel Proust is a case in point. His older contemporary, the outstanding actress Sarah Bernhardt, was another. She was the daughter of a Jewish *femme du monde* and an unknown father, educated at a convent school and baptised at the age of eleven. Throughout her long career and epic love life she suffered the malicious sniping and venomous abuse of anti-Semitic rivals, who attributed her commercial acumen to her racial identity. She herself said that 'the cherished blood of Israel' accounted for her love of travel, and publicly stood up for Dreyfus during that prolonged national crisis, alienating colleagues, friends and her own son in the process. Yet her sentimental commitment to the Jewish people was clearly a matter of racial identification, not religious belief – shades of Disraeli – and she was as convincing on stage portraying Christian heroines such as Joan of Arc or 'La Samaritaine', a part she played for years in Holy Week, as she was in exotic Byzantine and neoclassical roles.

For many Jews past and present, including, presumably, the 27 per cent of American Jewry who classify themselves as agnostic or atheist, Judaism as a set of religious beliefs is a constraint, not a fulfilment. That, certainly, was the opinion of Achad Ha-Am, the pioneer of Cultural Zionism and Theodor Herzl's arch opponent. In 1891 he paid his first visit to the new Jewish settlements in Palestine and straight away went to the Wailing Wall, the last remnant of Herod's Temple and everlasting symbol of Jewish exile and dispersion. The sight of the Wall and the wan appearance of the pious Jews praying there appalled him: 'I stood and watched them, people and Wall, and one thought filled the chambers of my heart: these stones are testament to the destruction of our land. And these men? The destruction of our people.'[7] For Achad Ha-Am, religious petrification had all but destroyed the Jewish spirit.

The trajectory of Asher Ginsberg's early life – Achad Ha-Am, 'One of the People', was his pen name, chosen for his first essay, published in 1889 – was similar to that of many of his religiously disillusioned Jewish generation. He was the son of a rabbi and tax farmer, and his childhood was so stiflingly pious that his teacher was forbidden to instruct him in the letters of the Russian alphabet, for fear it would lead him astray. Nevertheless, he learned to read Russian by the age of eight from deciphering the signs on shop fronts, taught himself algebra and geometry, and was considered a budding Talmudic prodigy.

The family's move in 1868 to a country estate leased by his wealthy father was Ginsberg's downfall. Not interested in rural pursuits, the young boy shut himself in his room and absorbed the works of medieval Jewish philosophy, particularly Maimonides. From there it was but a short step to the scandalous writings of the Jewish Enlightenment and on to the 'forbidden' books of secular literature in Russian and German. Achad Ha-Am embraced Positivism and abandoned his faith, although not the cultural and ethical values of Judaism, which he always championed.

What repelled him was the unblinking dogmatism of religious Orthodoxy. Its inflexibility stems from the profound – some would say, *excessive* – veneration that Jewish tradition pays to the Torah. 'Torah' is usually translated as 'Law', although more accurately it means 'teaching' or 'regulation' when applied to the entire corpus of biblical laws commanded, it was believed, by God Himself through Moses on Mount Sinai to the Children of Israel. Thus *Sefer Torah* – The Book of the Law – is the designation of the Scroll handwritten on parchment and comprising the Five Books of Moses (Genesis, Exodus, Leviticus, Numbers and Deuteronomy) that is taken from the Ark and read from in synagogue at Sabbath and festival services as the centrepiece of communal worship. Reading from the Law is usually completed in an annual cycle and then immediately begun again at the joyous festival of *Simchat Torah* (Rejoicing of the Law) because, according to the ancient rabbis, there is no beginning and no end to studying God's greatest gift to His people Israel. In the words of a Talmudic sage: 'Turn it again and again, for everything is in it; contemplate it, grow grey and old over it, and swerve not from it, for there is no greater good' (Ben Bag Bag. Mishnah: *Avot*, 5:22). It is Rabbinic interpretation of the laws in the Torah – 613 of them according to their calculation – that gave us the vast repository of enactments and ordinances known collectively as *halachah*.

Strictly speaking, it is only the four books from Exodus to Deuteronomy that contain apodictic laws and regulations. The Book of Genesis is a mythical account of the creation of the world, the first humans, and the adventures of Israel's legendary patriarchs, Abraham, Isaac and Jacob, culminating in the descent of Jacob and his clan into Egypt, where son Joseph had risen to high estate. It may express the first biblical injunction (to Adam and Eve) – 'Be fruitful and multiply' – but not prefaced in the customary prescriptive manner with 'Command the Children of Israel, saying . . .' Nevertheless, tradition ascribes all five books to Moses, given to him directly from God, save for the last verses of Deuteronomy, which describe Moses' death.

Whenever Abraham ibn Ezra (1089–1164), the most astute of the medieval commentators, came across an anomaly in the Torah text, such as the different wording of the Ten Commandments in their Exodus and Deuteronomy versions, he would brush away the discrepancy with the enigmatic sentence: 'The wise man will understand.' He did not dare to suggest openly that human hands might have been involved in compiling the Torah. For Moses Maimonides, *all* of the Pentateuch (its English title, from the Greek root for 'five') was of equal sanctity; there was no difference between verses such as 'The sons of Ham: Cush, Egypt, Put and Canaan' (Genesis 10:6) and the Ten Commandments.

This insistence on the Torah's divine nature is so deeply embedded in Jewish dogma that as recently as 1963 Rabbi Dr Louis Jacobs, Anglo-Jewry's outstanding scholar, was denied the principalship of Jews' College, at the time Orthodoxy's foremost rabbinical seminary, because he did not accept literally the doctrine of *Torah min ha-shamayim* – the Law given from heaven by God on Mount Sinai. His willingness to rely on the evidence of biblical scholarship that has agreed for over two centuries that the Five Books of Moses were drawn together and redacted from different literary sources created a scandal that split the Orthodox community in the UK and had worldwide repercussions.

Orthodoxy is relatively relaxed about biblical scholarship that corrects dates or authorship of other parts of the Bible, such as the prophetical books and the court histories of Samuel, Kings and Chronicles. If it doesn't actively *encourage* research that confirms that David did not write the psalms attributed to him, nor Solomon the Book of Proverbs, and that the long Book of Isaiah comprises the words of two different prophets given the same name but living over a hundred and fifty years apart, then at least these are manifestly the writings of human hands, not God, therefore subject to human fallibility. Orthodoxy draws its line in the sand when the divine authorship of the Torah is queried. Torah is God-given, therefore immutable. The Revelation at Sinai is as fundamental a creed of Judaism as the Resurrection is for Christianity or the archangel Gabriel dictating God's words of the Quran to Muhammad is for Islam.

Even Progressive Judaism – usually so decisive in modifying or excising traditional custom when the Orthodox liturgy still prays for the restoration of the Temple and animal sacrifice or the *halachah* perpetuates sexual inequality in its treatment of women – treads coyly when dealing with the Torah's provenance. Naturally, as befits a post-Enlightenment religious movement, it accepts biblical scholarship and that the Five Books of Moses are of human authorship. Therefore it stops short of calling the Torah 'divine', but extols its unknown writers and editors for being 'divinely inspired' –

whatever that woolly phrase means; as in 'the divinely in-spired Mozart', presumably.

It is easy enough to claim that the commandments to be impartial in applying justice or to protect the poor, the widow and the orphan are examples of 'divinely inspired' and eternally valid legislation; but what about those nu-merous other injunctions to avoid a menstrual woman, to subject a suspected adulteress to the waters-of-jealousy ordeal in which the priest administers to her a potion that will make her barren if she is guilty, to exclude the leper, or to blot out the Amalekites, men, women and children, for ever? Progressive Judaism's answer is that such laws are no longer applicable, but to be viewed in the context of their time and place, and therefore as unacceptable by modern standards as deporting a child to Botany Bay for stealing a loaf of bread would be. Which invites two questions: firstly, *who* decides what is a timeless, universally valid law and what is merely a time-bound, context-restricted one? And, secondly, surely 'divinely in-spired' laws – unlike ordinary human ones – should be *above and beyond* time, place and historical context, not circumscribed by them?

Already then, non-fundamentalist exegesis concedes that the Five Books of Moses are divinely inspired only *in parts*. So why have many Progressive synagogues in Is-rael and around the world gone back to the traditional custom of reading excerpts from *all* of the Torah, animal sacrifice, ritual purity, warts and all? In its early, radical days, Progressive Judaism barely bothered with the Book of Leviticus, which, apart from the sublime so-called Holiness Code in chapters 19–25, is largely devoted to laws of priesthood, sacrifice and bodily secretions. In-stead, the rabbi would choose what was euphemistically called 'a timeless passage' from elsewhere in the Torah for the weekly Scroll reading and moral edification of his congregation.

Nowadays, young rabbis of either sex, schooled in Progressive seminaries by neo-traditional teachers, read the unsavoury portions by choice. It gives them the opportunity, as they explain to worshippers when introducing their selected passage of Torah, 'to struggle with the text' of our sacred Book, as Jacob wrestled with the angel at the ford of Jabbok. In my experience since retirement, as a suffering Jew in the pew, what that usually means is that the rabbi's sermon will be devoted to discovering new and ingenious insights, mystical, anthropological and psychological, into the laws of leprosy, or why a menstrual woman is forbidden to approach the Tent of Meeting in the wilderness until she has thoroughly cleansed herself for seven days and brought two turtle doves as an atonement offering. And the rabbi will then conclude this abstruse exposition by saying that this is what the ancient Israelites believed but, of course, as modern Jews, we reject all such superstitiously arcane regulations. Which leaves me to sigh inwardly and groan: then why bother to talk about them in the first place, instead of using sermon time for a *positive* message?

The reason why is because we no longer trust in the motto of Progressive Judaism's founders that Reason with a capital R is the gateway to faith. Even if we know rationally that God did not descend on Mount Sinai to give Israel the Law – any more than He gave Muhammad the Quran – centuries of our ancestors venerating the Torah and poring over it as the Tree of Life has left its indelible mark on us, so that we too accord it quasi-divine sanctity. We bow to the Sefer Torah as it is processed

around the synagogue, adorn it with bells and costly ac-
coutrements, house it in an Ark, and before and after
reading from it recite blessings thanking God for having
chosen us from among all the peoples to give us His true
Torah. And then we listen, if the weekly reading is from
Leviticus, to a lengthy recitation of the laws of animal
sacrifice . . .

This is not said in denigration of the Torah. The Torah,
along with the other books that make up the Hebrew
Bible, is at the heart of the Jewish people's sense of
identity and shared destiny. It is our foundational document, as powerfully evocative today as ever. Taken as
a whole, the Pentateuch is a magnificent narrative of Israel's earliest folk memories, God's election of them as
His covenant people, slavery in Egypt, and the miraculous deliverance leading to the unique theophany at Sinai
and entry into the Promised Land. It has its longueurs
(all those 'begats' and census takings; 'Begin the Begat'
– a lyric Cole Porter might have written) and unedifying sections. It was Evelyn Waugh, I think, who told the
story about Randolph Churchill, Winston's son, deciding
to read the whole of the Bible while in the army during
the Second World War and throwing it aside after a few
pages of Genesis with the exclamation, 'God, what a s**t
God is!'

But as well as examples of God's arbitrary and terri-
fying decision-making, the Torah also contains uncompromising exhortations to private and communal behaviour of the highest ethical norms, and the Ten Commandments (more accurately in the original Hebrew the
'Ten Words'; they fitted on two stone tablets) are
routinely hailed as the cornerstone of Judaeo-Christian
civilisation. The unknown biblical writers repeatedly in-

sist that Israel's covenant with God had to be actualised through a body of cultic regulations, regularly performed with accompanying rituals, and the Israelites needed to submit to and obey a corpus of general law governing persons, property, social obligations and moral conduct if they were to merit their special relationship. Although it is a moot point whether all of the wilderness-given laws – for example, the ones concerning the Jubilee year, in which land is neither sown nor harvested, slaves go free and debts are cancelled – were actually implemented once the Promised Land had been conquered and the kingdom of Israel settled, as Robert Alter observes in the Introduction to his superb recent translation of the Torah, the effect of these lengthy legal passages, cultic, civil and criminal, 'is to bridge the distance of the epic *illud tempus*, the time-back-when, of the narrative and bring the text into the institutional present of its audience'.[8] Always observing the Law throughout the generations is an existential condition of Israel's continuing election, just as the Passover *Haggadah* (Narrative) reminds us annually to regard ourselves as though we personally had been redeemed from Egyptian bondage.

Apart from laws and statutes, in the Joseph saga we have one of the gems of the storyteller's art in all of literature, so subtle and cunning and building to such a riveting climax that an admiring Thomas Mann expanded it into his tetralogy *Joseph and His Brothers*, without improving on it. And the Genesis account of Creation is still compelling, for all that we know it didn't really happen in that way, and the final paragraphs of Deuteronomy about the death of Moses still bring tears to the eyes. After all the textual analysis and assessment of Moses by scholars, historians, archaeologists, believers, debunkers and Sigmund Freud, it is still probably Thomas Mann in his, to my mind, superior foray into the Pentateuch with his novella *The Two Tablets of the Law* who most convincingly catches the essence of Moses and his mission. Mann uses an extended metaphor of the sculptor patiently moulding and shaping a piece of recalcitrant marble to illustrate the achievement of Moses in painstakingly working on the rebellious Children of Israel to make them worthy of becoming God's Chosen People and receiving His Law at Sinai.

But that said and having paid tribute to the depth, scope, variety and solemn purpose of the Pentateuch and the enduring influence it has had on the Jewish religion and Western civilisation generally, it must be reiterated that the Torah is a human document. Prefacing every ordinance with the words 'And God commanded Moses, saying . . .' no more makes that commandment 'divinely inspired' than being born in a barn makes one a horse, as the Duke of Wellington reprimanded the man impudent enough to call him Irish. For the ancient rabbis, the Torah was coeval with and as momentous as Creation itself; at the giving of the Law 'no bird chirped, no fowl beat its wings, no ox bellowed, the angels did not sing, the sea did not stir, no creature uttered a sound: the world was silent and still and the Divine Voice spoke' (Midrash, *Exodus Rabbah* 29:9). But for all that, it is still a work of literature and in that respect no different in ambition from other monumental literary epics of the ancient world by Homer or Virgil, although different in purpose. And just as we are not inhibited from recognising when Dante or Milton – two other writers with the lofty aim of justifying God's ways to man – are sometimes freewheeling and going through the motions in the more turgid passages of the *Divine Comedy* and *Paradise Lost*, or that *King Lear* is probably the greatest tragedy ever written, whereas *All's Well* is a pleasant trifle, so too we should feel free to judge the contents of the Pentateuch strictly on their merits, and rate an ethical commandment to care for the stranger because once you were strangers in the Land of Egypt above a ritual commandment to bring a guilt offering before the High Priest. To give equal weight to *all* of the Torah regardless, and respect it indiscriminately, is to abandon our free will and moral judgement.

There was a joke going the rounds in Israel during Menachem Begin's obdurate premiership. President Carter visits Jerusalem to try to revive the peace process. Begin takes him to the Temple Wall and says, 'Mr President, this wall is the holiest site in the world for Jews. For millennia all our hopes, dreams, tears and yearning for restoration to our homeland have been centred on it. Tradition says that from here a sincere prayer goes directly to God. Now, Mr President, you can have three prayers to send to God.'

Carter says, 'First, I pray that Jews will live in peace and security in their restored homeland.'

Begin replies, 'Mr President, from your mouth to God's ears.'

Carter continues, 'Second, I pray that the close friendship between Israel and the USA will grow even stronger.'

Begin replies, 'Mr President, from your mouth to God's ears.'

Carter says, 'And third, I pray that one day the Palestinians too will live in peace and security in their own homeland.'

Begin shrugs and replies, 'Mr President, what are you asking for? It's only a wall!'

So too with the Torah. At the end of the day, unique though it is in all of world literature, it is only a book. 'Its ways are ways of pleasantness, and all its paths are peace,' the congregation sings, quoting Proverbs 3:17, when the Scroll is returned to the Ark after the weekly reading. If only that were altogether true. The Torah contains much that is malign as well as benign. As we know, its words are used by religious fundamentalists and secular hardliners alike, to justify Israeli retention of West Bank land and subjugation of the indigenous population – as God commanded the Israelites before they crossed the Jordan. Its language is called in evidence to fob off those women looking for greater equality before the religious law. Deuteronomy 24:1–4 states specifically that a man 'gives' and the woman 'receives' a bill of divorce – she is not allowed to institute proceedings herself. And as for those Orthodox women perhaps dreaming of one day becoming rabbis – the Torah text always refers to the 'sons' of Levi as priests, never the 'daughters'. The same specious excuse of linguistic construction is favoured by diehard Christians opposed to women clergy; the Greek word for 'godhead' in the New Testament is masculine, not feminine.

Religions that claim their validity from a holy text are ultimately in thrall to that text. Islam with the Quran has the same difficulty as Judaism with the Pentateuch, Christianity less so, because although the New Testament is hallowed, the Gospels and other writings that it comprises are attributed to their authors by name. Matthew, Mark, Luke, John and Paul are disciples retelling the story; they have presumptive authority for Christians in that they report the ministry and teachings of Jesus, who they believed was the Son of God. But they make no claim of divine authorship for their words. The New Testament is read for inspiration, instruction and edification about the life and death of Jesus, God's only be-gotten son. Unlike the Pentateuch or the Quran, it is not read as God's *ipsissima verba*.

According to Matthew's Gospel (5:17), Jesus said that he had come not to destroy the Law but to fulfil it. The argument that too close attention to the letter of the law can detract from its spirit was one that the ancient rabbis also acknowledged. The tractate in the Mishnah known as *Ethics of the Fathers* begins by cautioning that one should 'make a fence around the Torah' in order to safeguard its proper observance. A little further on, the rabbis suggest that Tradition – the time-honoured way of doing things – provides that fence. But then they warn against the danger of building the fence higher than the Torah itself. When a law hedging the Law becomes an object of ritual sanctification in its own right, then the original purpose of what it is supposed to be safeguard-ing has long since been forgotten.

When that happens it is due to the over-elaborate re-spect and a priori acceptance granted to the Torah by all branches of Judaism. Instead of considering its teach-ings individually and sifting the wheat from the chaff, we give them nodding assent *in toto*, even those that are grossly offensive to modern sensibilities. We have al-lowed ourselves to be lulled into paying lip service to the metaphor of the Torah's divine or 'divinely inspired' au-thorship.

The proper response of reformed religions should be neither instinctively to rebel against their canonical texts nor uncritically to submit to them, but constantly to evaluate them by the light of fresh evidence and modern knowledge. As A. E. Harvey, distinguished Christian scholar and a former canon at Westminster Abbey, put it, 'We believe that there is an irreplaceable source of knowledge and guidance in Scripture, but that it is a perennial task to interpret that in the light of our own circumstances and conditions of life.'[9] The Torah should be viewed similarly. In the words of a great Reform teacher and master of Rabbinic literature about the *halachah* generally, 'It can guide us without governing us to the extent of limiting precious liberty and modern conscience.'[10] If there was a greater readiness on the part of Judaism's teachers to adopt such a tempered approach, the lesser would be the inclination of those Jews who reject the premiss of a divine author to discard the Torah altogether, thereby throwing out the baby with the bathwater.

So what prompts all those Jews – the majority today – who define themselves as non-believers or predominantly secular, nevertheless still to call themselves Jewish? The answer lies in something additional to religious teachings alone and can best be summed up as Jewish culture or, more amorphously, Jewish values. The four-thousand-year-old link that a modern Jew in Jerusalem, New York, London or the Isle of Skye traces back to the biblical Abraham might be genetically fanciful, the result of a resolutely transmitted myth over hundreds of generations more than a historical reality backed by any convincing evidence; but it and the national narrative that evolved from it over the centuries in all its infinite variety, customs, folk memories, intellectual efflorescence, tragedies and achievements still has the power to retain the loyalty of the overwhelming majority of men and women in the world today who classify themselves as Jewish. That is the legacy of tradition that binds together the heirs of a diffuse culture in which religion is a major component but not the only one. Jews are a *religious people* – certainly neither a 'race' nor a 'nation' – with the adjective describing the beliefs that originally defined them, the noun connoting their diversified cultural and geographical backgrounds. Adherents can choose where and how they wish to opt in, what on the menu takes their fancy and those dishes they would rather decline, including, for many, the chef's religious recommendations.

Rejecting Judaism's beliefs would have been shocking in the past; less so today. We have noted before that modern Jewish identity is fluid and made up of several components. When historians talk about Hellenism as the dominant influence in the Mediterranean and Near East after the conquests of Alexander the Great, they are not referring only to the 'high' culture of Herodotus and Thucydides, Sophocles and Euripides, Plato and Aristotle; they mean also the demotic spread of Greek architecture, Greek notions of citizenship, Greek science, philosophy, theatre, art and dress, the Greek *Gymnasion* in which to educate the young and instil ideals of physical beauty and grace. All this was not achieved by scholars alone. Its main standard bearers were the soldiers, merchants, traders, entrepreneurs and artisans who poured into the lands of the Orient to take advantage of economic opportunity, speaking Greek as the common language of diplomacy, commerce and daily communication. That is the way with culture. Hellenism was broad enough to embrace the plays of Aristophanes for the elite, temples to the gods for the devout, elected assemblies for the legislators, market places for business, bath houses for male friendship, and circuses for *hoi polloi*. Out of it all emerged the social, artistic, civil and moral values that made up what we call Hellenistic culture. Religion was but one of several ingredients.

So too with Judaism as a culture. When Abraham ibn Ezra, not only a great biblical commentator but also a distinguished poet, philosopher and grammarian, wrote the lines:

> The Arabs write of love in boasts
> and the Romans of vengeance and battles
> the Greeks of wisdom and cunning
> and the Persians of fables and riddles;
> but Israel sings – in psalms and hymns –
> of God, the Lord of hosts

– it was not the whole story. Spanish-Jewish poetry, permeated with the heat and landscapes of Andalusia, was also sexually explicit and attuned to physical and natural beauty. The medieval Jewish communities of Poland and the Rhineland were indifferent to Nature – there are only a few words in Yiddish that stand in for the abundant variety of birds, plants and flowers – but once the *Haskalah* had taken root, Jewish poets and novelists dealt with secular themes as readily as their Christian counterparts.

It is easy enough to list the values, originally religion-based, that have expanded to become normative secular traits among Jews since emancipation and our entrance into wider society. An insistence on Justice is the first, even more rooted than the ideal of peace. Peace is an elusive yearning, but justice is practical and instantly available to deal with conflict and redress wrongs. Due perhaps to that inbred Talmudic gene that loves to pore over, analyse and tease out every nuance of meaning in a Torah commandment, Jews are prominent in the legal systems of most democratic countries. Whether in the 1960s civil rights movement in the American South or in the campaign against apartheid in South Africa, secular Jews were in the vanguard and often braver than their circumspect religious leaders in speaking out for freedom. The memory of Egyptian slavery and the Exodus still resonated for them.

Alongside the passion for justice goes – or should go – the principle that all are created equal and therefore accorded equal treatment under the law, home-born and stranger alike. Although this instinct for justice and equality appears to have been blunted for many Jews nowadays when it comes to the question of justice for the Palestinians, the brightest and best among the Israeli and Diaspora young are in the forefront of campaigns for human rights in the Occupied Territories and against legislation – proposed by the same David Rotem who wanted to change the conversion law – that would require a loyalty oath from Israeli Arabs.

A second core Jewish value is *tikkun olam* – 'improving the world'. Good deeds are more important than beliefs. Thanks to its use as a postscript in Steven Spielberg's film *Schindler's List*, the Rabbinic statement that he who saves a single human life, it is as if he saved the whole world, has become probably Judaism's best-known ethical maxim (adding to the wry amusement of those of us needled by the fact that 'Love your neighbour as yourself' is usually misattributed to Jesus, when actually he was directly quoting Leviticus 19:18).

There has always been a certain urgent Jewish impulse to improve society, to better the lot of the needy, to care for the widow and the orphan. The Bible, the Talmud, the Rabbinic Codes and the moralistic literature all stress the duty of helping those less fortunate by giving to charity. The *Sefer Chasidim* – the Book of the Pious, a thirteenth-century ethical tract – instructs us that a community that has not yet built itself a synagogue must first provide for the poor. Maimonides' eight degrees of charity are famous. The lowest step is to give reluctantly. Next comes giving cheerfully but parsimoniously, rising through gradations of giving when asked, giving voluntarily, giving anonymously, giving communally rather than individually, until the highest rung of all is reached, which is to deflect poverty by providing someone with a loan or a job so that they can become self-sufficient. As the proverb says: Give a man a fish and you feed him for a day; teach him how to fish and you feed him for life.

A striking aspect of Jewish civic legislation was its practical realism. Ordinances about communal health and safety, a property owner's responsibilities to the public, the correct way to treat employees, or the alleviation of poverty by means of taxation, start from the premiss that such measures are not only beneficial in themselves but are also aids to harmony between different groups in the wider society. 'We feed the poor of non-Jews, comfort their mourners, and bury their dead with the dead of Israel *mipney dar'chei shalom* – for the sake of peace,' admonishes the Talmud (*Gittin* 61a).

There is no shame for Jews in being rich – but it does come with the injunction that there should be moderation in affluence, and giving a proportion of one's wealth to good causes. The motives for philanthropy are varied and complex and not always altruistic, as we know. But whatever the reasons for patronage, every major Diaspora Jewish community is admired for taking care of its own elderly and needy as well as having benefactors who donate munificently to the arts, universities and public facilities of the countries where they live.

A third Jewish cultural characteristic is the emphasis on education. In the Rabbinic social hierarchy, the scholar stood on the top rung of the ladder, and a learned poor man took precedence over a wealthy ignoramus. For the ghetto Jew, study was the means to escape from the restrictions and dangers of everyday existence. Since emancipation, it has been the path to social and material advancement. 'My son the doctor' is a stock line in any Jewish-mother joke, but it does highlight the respect accorded in Jewish tradition to learning over wealth, and why Jews are disproportionately represented in academia, medicine, the professions and the sciences. Before Hitler's rise to power, Einstein was merely the best known of thirty-nine leading German-Jewish scientists, ten of whom had won Nobel prizes. That expertise was largely inherited by the USA and the new State of Israel, both world leaders in medicine, the sciences and technology.

Attachment to family and community is not a unique Jewish concern, but one shared with most other minority groups in an alien environment. Even so, it is a deeply ingrained and constantly reiterated Jewish value. As with other minorities, family and communal cohesion has become strained with the transition from immigrant status to fourth- and fifth-generation citizenship. Today's rates of marital breakdown and divorce are not markedly different in Jewish communities from those in wider society, whereas, in the past, fear of communal disapproval had a deterrent effect. But it is still unusual to come across a

Jewish father who abandons his family without making financial provision, or a Jewish husband who physically abuses his wife and children. In the bleakest days of Soviet Communism, when Jews were routinely discriminated against by the authorities, Russian women still preferred a Jewish husband, given the choice, because Jewish men tended not to get drunk and beat their wives. The family home is the 'little sanctuary' of the prophet Ezekiel (11:16) that replaced the destroyed Temple, and warnings against separating oneself from the community are a constant Rabbinic admonition. Mutually sustaining family and community as the twin pillars of Jewish survival is a lesson that has percolated down through centuries of historical experience.

There are those who might argue that commendable though the values of justice, bettering society, charity, education and family may be, without the stiffening of religion they represent merely the aspirations of a secular ethic and have nothing specifically Jewish about them. My counter-argument would be better that Jews continue to lead their lives by the ethical commandments of Judaism while rejecting empty affirmations of belief and the paraphernalia of ritual than that they keep minutely to every aspect of the dietary laws and Sabbath observance but disregard their civic obligations to wider society.

In fact, though, that is an artificial apposition, because for Judaism both universal ethical principles and particularistic ritual scruples are perfectly tenable together. My concern is for those Jews – the majority – who no longer feel in tune with the religious beliefs and practices of Judaism but would be happy to identify themselves as culturally Jewish, even if that means little more than attending the annual Passover *Seder*, enjoying Jewish cuisine, reading the books of Jewish writers and laughing at Jewish jokes. While they still call themselves Jews, they contribute to the continuity of the Jewish people. Irreligious, non-believing doctors, scientists, social workers, teachers, artists, actors, trades people who still respond in however attenuated a fashion to some echo of their Jewish heritage and try, in however modest a way, to make the world a slightly better place for their being in it are in my view as much part of the wide canvas of Jewish culture as the most devoutly observant Talmud scholar.

That is the advantage that culture has over religion. The Jewish religion is specific in its beliefs and the demands it makes on adherents. Jewish culture is eclectic and tolerant of all shades of diversity. Judaism the religion – like all religions – finds it easier to exclude than include. Judaism the culture – like Walt Whitman – is vast and contains multitudes.

Judaism and Jewish culture

For many years until his death I had a dear friend and colleague who was one of the most respected leaders of Progressive Judaism worldwide. Blessed with a powerful intellect and great personal integrity, he thought deeply and wrote, preached and lectured extensively about all aspects of Judaism. His theology had been moulded by the classical principles of Progressive Judaism's founders: belief in a creator God who demanded ethical conduct above ritual observance from His children and was encouraging mankind's (later 'humankind's') steady progress towards a better world of justice, morality and harmony between nations. History, steered by God and however many its terrible digressions along the way, was leading us towards the messianic age (replacing the personal messiah) of love, peace and friendship, when all would acknowledge God's unity and do His will.

Such sanguine optimism about human progress under a paternalistic deity, moulded by the Victorian vision of seemingly unlimited scientific, industrial and material advancement, was dealt a savage corrective by the slaughter of the First World War, followed in the 1920s and 1930s by economic collapse and the rise of ruthless totalitarianisms; its death knell sounded when the scale of the Holocaust was revealed after the Second World War. My friend, himself a German survivor, had modified his theology in the light of sobering experience, rediscovering both an intensified respect for the traditions of the Jewish past and a closer identification with fellow Jews in the present. Essentially though, he always maintained his twin beliefs in a God who is constantly engaged in the lives of individuals and that, despite its vicissitudes, Jewish history is purposive, unfolding towards the messianic age in a divine master plan that we humans can glimpse but dimly.

I was never wholehearted about either proposition. Deference to my friend's learning and the conviction with which he expressed his beliefs always inhibited me from engaging too combatively with him in theological debate. But, after he retired, perhaps I did begin to express my questions and doubts more freely and publicly. A product of the British empirical school, I find it logically untenable to derive 'ought' from 'is' or value from fact. After one sermon in which I argued both against the notion of an interventionist God and the notion that Jewish or indeed any history has an ultimate purpose, he turned to his neighbour in the congregation and lamented, 'David has just demolished two of Judaism's main pillars!' Naturally, the congregant was quick to tell me.

But the warm response to the sermon from other congregants afterwards did suggest that I had touched a nerve and they were grateful to me for frankly voicing their own reservations. *They* had doubts that God intervenes in human affairs, whatever my colleague taught; and despite the popularity in Old Testament studies since the 1950s of what German theologians called *Heilsgeschichte* (Salvation History) – reading the Bible as the narrative of God's redeeming acts in history – they, like me, wondered more prosaically whether history is not simply, as a pupil in Alan Bennett's play *The History Boys* puts it, just 'one f***ing thing after another!'

The belief in God's redemptive role in Jewish history is everywhere in the prayer book. 'Rock of Israel', 'Shield of our salvation', 'Redeemer of Israel', 'We have no Redeemer but You' are some of His most frequent appellations. A new prayer co-authored by my friend for the 1967 prayer book *Service of the Heart* began: 'We see God's guiding hand most clearly when we look back on the history of our own people. Delivered from Egyptian bondage, bound to God by the covenant at Sinai, inspired by prophets and instructed by sages, we survived oppression and exile, overcoming time and again the forces that would have destroyed us . . .'

That was the prayer I quoted in the sermon that questioned God's interventionist role in history. Rather than rehash my own objections about the many times when God's guiding hand has *not* been clearly seen in Jewish history, I would prefer to summarise the admirably succinct reasons that John Rawls (1921–2002), the most influential liberal political philosopher of the last century, gave for his loss of belief. He had intended originally to become an Episcopalian priest and had submitted his doctoral thesis entitled *A Brief Enquiry into the Meaning of Sin and Faith*. In 'On My Religion', an essay written when he was seventy-six, Rawls elegantly disposes of the God-in-history proposition. First, he recounts how appalled he was as a soldier in the Second World War to hear a padre preach that God was aiming bullets at the Japanese while protecting Americans from Japanese fire. Private Rawls upbraided the first lieutenant padre for these 'falsehoods about divine providence'. Secondly, in an episode of arbitrary contingency, a friend with whom he had shared a tent was chosen over him for a mission that proved fatal. And, thirdly, after learning about the Holocaust he wondered, 'How could I pray and ask God to help me, or my family, or my country, or any other cherished thing I cared about, when God would not save millions of Jews from Hitler?' The passage continues: 'To interpret history as expressing God's will, God's will must accord with the most basic ideas of justice as we know them. For what else can the most basic justice be? Thus, I soon came to reject the idea of the supremacy of the divine will . . .'[1]

The larger question of whether or not history has a teleological 'purpose', an end towards which it is striving, is one that historians and philosophers have long argued about and disagreed over. Personally, as befits a sceptical cast of mind, I endorse Hegel's brisk statement in his introduction to *Lectures on the Philosophy of World History* (1830) that: 'What experience and history teach us is this – that nations and governments have never learned anything from history, or acted upon any lessons they might have drawn from it.'

But even if Hegel was absolutely correct (and over time he did change his mind and philosophy about history's purpose), it does not alter the fact that for Judaism – and for Christianity and Islam too – God is the guiding intelligence behind the ebbs and flows of world history that will end in universal salvation, however differently the three monotheistic religions may interpret the ultimate manifestation of the divine will.

So what of the friend who thought that by querying that credo I had demolished two main pillars of Judaism? I was confident that Judaism would survive my mild iconoclasm, but he and I did what we usually did after a doctrinal difference of opinion; we went for a long walk with our dogs on Hampstead Heath to talk through our views. By the end of the walk we agreed that our difference was largely a semantic one. Where I had carefully used only the word 'intervene' in my sermon when talking about God's role in history, my friend was using 'intervene' or 'influence' interchangeably, although there is a considerable difference in meaning. I was willing to concede that God more passively 'influences' history rather than actively 'intervenes' in it, and for the sake of peace gritted my teeth and refrained from adding that from empirical observation His 'influence' seemingly can be, on occasion, as much for evil as for good.

This has particular import for Judaism. If we have already divested God of omnipotence and omniscience and if in the argument between Intelligent Design and Darwinism we lean heavily in favour of evolution, would stripping away this last vestige of at least *indirect* divine influence on history not be a step too far, effectively leaving us with a godless Jewish culture that has insufficient resources to survive on its own?

At first sight, it is a question heavy with negative implications for the future of the Jewish people. Every act of public worship, every custom, ceremony and ritual in which Jews participate collectively, from giving thanks for food to mourning the dead, is prefaced by a rubric praising God; the God who has a special partiality for His chosen people and maintains watch over its destiny. In the words of *Mi-pi El*, a popular Sephardic Sabbath hymn, 'By God alone, by God alone shall Israel be blessed.' Remove that comforting support, openly question whether God actually does work through history or indeed is a concept anything more potent in our lives than an occasional reminder to behave charitably towards the poor and needy, and the whole edifice of Judaism, laboriously constructed over three thousand years, would come tumbling down. So say conservative guardians of the Torah, whether they define themselves as religiously Orthodox and therefore resistant to innovation, or as Progressive and receptive to it.

In reality, I don't think that much would change. The ultra-Orthodox will continue believing what they have always believed, unaffected by the discoveries of science or the insights of modern knowledge. The nominally observant will tweak, but not discard, their usual compromises, from serving kosher food at home but eating in non-kosher restaurants outside, to riding in their cars rather than walking to synagogue on Sabbaths and festivals. Progressive Jews have never been overly concerned by Sabbath restrictions or the dietary laws anyway, although in recent years most of their synagogues have allowed only fish or vegetarian dishes on their premises, as part of the wider neo-conservative trend to compensate for loss of belief with greater emphasis on ritual. And secular Jews, who constitute the majority, will still initiate their male children into the 'Covenant of Abraham' with the ceremony of circumcision (as Abraham Geiger (1810–1874), the leader of German Reform Judaism, did with his sons, although denouncing it as 'that barbaric rite') and continue marrying in synagogue 'according to the law of Moses and Israel', with the groom breaking a glass at the end of the ceremony, and being buried or cremated with a Jewish funeral service. I doubt that even as vociferous a non-Jewish Jew as Isaac Deutscher went to his final resting place without having the mourners' *Kaddish* recited over his coffin. The *Kaddish* is, in fact, a doxology, a hymn of praise, mainly in Aramaic, not Hebrew, extravagantly lauding God's mighty attributes, recited in accord with the Rabbinic principle that one should praise God in sorrow as in joy. The first concern of a Jewish son, no matter how secular or alienated he claims he is, is to be able to recite *Kaddish*, in transliteration if needs must, at a parent's funeral, as has been the custom for almost two millennia.

A gently amusing series on TV's Channel 4 recently, called *Friday Night Dinner*, nicely caught the secularised *mores* of modern Jewish family life. Father and mother live in a clearly identifiable London suburb. They are archetypal. He is anxious, hen-pecked, slowly being defeated by life, like Willie Loman in *Death of a Salesman*, although Arthur Miller didn't quite dare to make Loman explicitly Jewish. She is the classic *kvetch* of emasculated-Jewish-husband jokes (e.g. Why do Jewish men die before their wives? Answer: Because they want to), pretty once as her husband once must have had a certain vitality to win her, but settling down now into discontented middle age. The viewer just knows that whatever sexual activity went into producing their two bright, verbally sharp, unathletic boys has long since been replaced by twin beds. Friday-night dinner is a sacrosanct institution. The boys must come back home for it, a meal also attended by grandma, another staple of Jewish comedy, the doting, forgetful, artlessly foot-in-mouth *buba*. Eating is regularly interrupted by a nerdy Gentile neighbour who likes to think that he is taking a keen anthropological interest in the customs and traditions of the exotic family next door. But while the Friday-night meal together is the centrepiece of their week, as it has been for Jewish families since time immemorial, they do not observe a single Sabbath Eve ritual on it; no Sabbath candles, no blessing over the wine and bread. In one episode, after father has ruined the meal he cooked because his wife is on crutches and demanding sympathy for a minor accident, they blithely go out instead to the local Chinese restaurant. Even while smiling at the situation, I thought what a far cry it was from my parents' day, when going out on Friday night would have been unthinkable, and in my maternal grandmother's house Sabbath was purgatory, with no lights allowed to be switched on during Sabbath hours and toilet paper thoughtfully torn off the roll beforehand and neatly stacked, so that no visitor needed to infringe the laws against doing any manner of work on the seventh day.

Tradition, family and community are unlikely to lose their conformist hold on Jewish behaviour. The grip may weaken with succeeding generations, but wherever Jews are a minority, they will stubbornly retain, like all minorities, the religious symbols and traditions of their past, even if they no longer give credence to the beliefs behind them. The Jewish calendar and its arcane workings is a case in point. It is a lunar calendar, so that a normal year consists of twelve months, each running from new moon to new moon. To keep it in line with the solar year, the annual shortfall is made good by the intercalation of an extra month seven times in every nineteen years. In ancient times, the Sanhedrin in Jerusalem confirmed the sighting of the new moon with fire signals on hilltop stations, or by sending out messengers to far-flung communities. Because it was often impossible to let Jews in Egypt, Asia Minor or Greece know in time, a second day was added to new moon and festival observances as a precautionary safeguard.

The astronomical calculations for fixing the calendar in perpetuity were settled under the Palestinian Patriarch Hillel III (300–330 CE). Henceforth, everyone anywhere could know when new moons and festivals were due to fall. However, Rabbi Jose of the Sanhedrin, in a move to reaffirm the customary precedence of Palestinian Jewry over the Diaspora, wrote to the Babylonian and Alexandrian communities cautioning them not to abandon the ways of their forefathers but to persevere with the old system of setting aside both days. And so it has continued to the present for Orthodox Jewry. The 'second day of the Diaspora' is tagged on to the festival calendar, although fewer and fewer synagogue-goers bother to observe it and attendances are embarrassingly meagre. With a similarly exaggerated respect for tradition, the reckoning of the years takes as its starting point the supposed creation of the world. Combing the biblical data and genealogies with literalist exactitude, medieval Jewish scholars came up with the calculation that creation had occurred in the year 3760 BCE. While this kind of dating is hardly borne out by modern cosmology, it is still the quaint custom to open the service on the Jewish New Year, in Orthodox and Progressive synagogues alike, with a prayer asking that the coming year, starting on the first day of the seventh lunar month of Tishri 5771 (i.e. 9 September 2010) may be for us and all Israel a year of good and blessing.

Over the course of time, commemorating the festivals has undergone a process of secularised reinterpretation and reinvention, most markedly in Israel itself, the cradle of the religion but also the place where Jews are least diffident about rejecting Judaism in favour of a cultural and nationalist Jewish identification. I was on my pioneer desert kibbutz in 1958 for the annual Passover Seder. It was led by David Ben-Gurion, Israel's recently retired prime minister. This was a left-wing kibbutz where I had spent the day of Yom Kippur seven months previously out in pasture with the horses, working and eating, not fasting, and wondering, like Isaac Deutscher, whether I would be stricken down for my flagrant impiety. The Passover *Haggadah* we used was a socialist version that followed the traditional order of retelling the Exodus story interspersed with drinking four cups of wine, to highlight four key promises of miraculous divine intervention, but all references to God were omitted and the from-slavery-to-freedom journey of the Children of Israel had been transformed into a from-winter-to-spring homily about Diaspora degradation giving way to Zionist redemption in making the soil of the homeland bloom again. The medley of songs recounting God's wondrous deeds and acts of deliverance that exuberantly conclude the Seder meal in most *Haggadah* liturgies had been replaced with pioneer work songs about rebuilding the land of milk and honey in order to be rebuilt by it.

What was new to me over fifty years ago has since become normative. The gay and lesbian movements, feminists, Greens, civil rights groups, all have appropriated the customs and rituals of *Pesach* to draw attention to their own particular concerns. A good example is the orange that now appears on Seder plates in many households, alongside the traditional five symbols of parsley, bitter herbs, a sweet paste called *charoset*, a roasted shank-bone and a roasted egg, whose meanings are explained during the course of narrating the Passover story. Adding an orange started only in the mid-1980s, but already it has become the stuff of almost as many legends and misapprehensions as the Exodus itself.

According to Susannah Heschel, Professor of Jewish Studies at Dartmouth College and the daughter of Abraham Joshua Heschel (1907–1972), a leading American scholar, theologian and civil rights activist, she was the author of the custom – although even her own words have undergone transformation and variant readings in her subsequent retellings of the episode. In her original account (April 2001), she had been invited to participate on a panel at Oberlin College and Conservatory in the early 1980s. While there, she came across a feminist *Haggadah* that had been compiled by some of the students. They had devised a ritual of adding a crust of bread to the Seder plate as a sign of solidarity with Jewish lesbians, because 'there's as much room for a lesbian in Judaism as there is for a crust of bread on the Seder plate'.

Heschel appropriated the symbol for her next family Seder, but substituted an orange instead of the crust of bread. For her, an orange was suggestive of the fruitfulness of Judaism when gays, lesbians and others marginalised by the Jewish community become active, contributing members – whereas the startling presence of bread on the Seder plate would reinforce the negative association of homosexuality with a transgressive violation of Jewish values. Instead, she asked everyone at the Seder table to take a segment of orange, recite the blessing over fruit, and spit out any pips as a sign of repudiating homophobia and empathising with Jewish gays and lesbians.

Among the urban myths that in less than thirty years have accreted around this pleasing little gesture of solidarity is the story that it all started in response to a man who stood up after a Heschel lecture and declared angrily that a woman belongs in synagogue leading prayers as much as *an orange belongs on the Seder plate*. How little time it takes for a factual occurrence to be magnified into a fanciful story, the story into a myth, and the myth into a historical tradition!

Chanukkah too has undergone the same process. It has metamorphosed from a festival that celebrates God's saving power in miraculously keeping the Temple lamp alight for eight days into a nationalist commemoration of the Maccabees, the band of brothers who fought off repeated attempts by the Seleucid dynasty to conquer Judea in the second century BCE. The Maccabees were a favourite role model for early Zionists and Diaspora advocates of a 'muscular Judaism' that stood up defiantly instead of meekly accepting anti-Semitism's blows. (Purim's transformation from a bloodthirsty revenge story into an acceptable children's carnival, even in Progressive synagogues, has already been mentioned.)

It was Ben-Gurion, having begun his career as a rigid small-town Marxist full of dismissive contempt for the opiate of the Jewish masses, who in later life led the crusade for reading the Bible not as a restrictive summary of religious rules and regulations but as a vivid historical document relevant for teaching new Israeli citizens about their past. Reputedly the IDF, the Israel Defence Forces, would consult the Bible to learn the routes taken by Joshua and the Children of Israel in their conquest of the Promised Land as part of their desert training to thwart potential Arab invaders. Israelis are keen archaeologists, and an intensive module of every school curriculum is familiarisation with the geography and topography of the Bible. It is studied as I would prefer my rabbinic colleagues to study it – not with excessive reverence as 'divinely inspired', but by the canons of secular literary criticism, which view it as a unique work of literature, probably the greatest ever written, and of irrefutably human authorship.

Recently, and for the first time in a long time, I sat as one of the three members of a Rabbinic Board interviewing six would-be proselytes to Judaism. I found some of their written statements on why they wanted to become Jewish extremely moving and quote in part from the reasons given by a young Greek Orthodox Serbian woman with a Jewish fiancé: 'I want to convert and be part of his religion and its amazing four-thousand-year-old traditions. Although I wasn't very religious, I was amazed with Judaism's values on life, its traditions, and the large focus on family . . . I was aware that the process [of becoming Jewish] would require me to explore many aspects of my spiritual, cultural and social identity . . . To feel authentically Jewish will require patience, courage, a sense of humour, a desire to learn, and a willingness to ask some hard questions . . . Being Jewish means everything to me. The spirituality, the never-ending desire for learning, the varying cultures of Jews around the world, the community, the importance of the family, Shabbat, food, tradition, customs and way of life in every possible aspect are all areas that I have learned about and hope to grow with me so I can pass them on to my children.'

It is testimonies such as these, catching the essence of modern Jewry's blend of culture, tradition and practice, that make me confident about Jewish continuity, even in a future of declining religious belief. I know a London-based philanthropist who is an indefatigable propagator of secular Judaism. He has endowed chairs and educational programmes in secular Jewish studies at Israeli and American schools and universities. Some of these institutions were set up to teach Judaism as a religion. That has not deterred them from suddenly discovering an interest in non-religious Jewish culture, thereby making them eligible to benefit from his largesse. They remind me of the joke about the wealthy businessman who goes to an American Reform rabbi and asks him if he will bury his dead dog with a proper Jewish funeral service. That is too much even for a Reform rabbi. He splutters that it is a disgusting blasphemy and asks the businessman to leave. 'What a pity,' says the bereaved owner. 'I had been planning to make a large donation to your Temple rebuilding Appeal.' 'Wait a minute, wait a minute,' the rabbi hastily replies. 'You didn't tell me that your dog was Jewish . . .'

My philanthropic acquaintance gave a speech at the Hebrew University in Jerusalem over a decade ago that conveys the gist of secular Judaism's philosophy. In it he said, 'Secular Jews believe that Judaism is the historic culture of the Jewish people. This culture is much broader than religion and includes everything significant that the Jewish people have created over the last three thousand years. Secular Jews participate in this culture and engage in a continuing dialogue with Jewish values, memories, books, customs and traditions. They also engage in a significant dialogue with other cultures as well.' Elsewhere he added, 'All civilisations, if only to carry on heritage and tradition, require symbolic and sentimental forms and ceremonies – even if not fully believed!'[2]

No one who is concerned for the survival of Judaism would cavil at those remarks. They are even more pertinent to the Jewish situation today than they were when first delivered more than ten years ago. Since then, secular, or humanist, or cultural Judaism – the terminology varies but its meaning is broadly similar – has become more widespread, while religious Judaism is steadily declining.

Paradoxical though it may sound, the growing involvement of Jews in their culture at the expense of their beliefs could prove to be the salvation of Judaism, especially in the Diaspora. In Israel, the symbols and reminders of Jewish religion, culture and history are ever present: in street names, monuments, signposts, Sabbath as the day of rest, public holidays on festivals and, above all, the revived Hebrew language. If the overwhelmingly secular majority of Israel's Jewish citizens needs the services of religion for any reason, such as the rituals associated with birth, marriage or death, granting a religious divorce or regularising Jewish status according to the *halachah*, they have thousands of state-funded Orthodox synagogues and rabbis to choose from. Despite Orthodox hostility, even Progressive Judaism is making strides in its fight for recognition, equal treatment under civil law and state funding for its institutions. Most Israeli Jews can ignore religion most of the time, but it is there for them when they need to call on it.

It is different in the Diaspora. There, religion is a private affirmation and only tangentially the state's concern. In liberal democracies where Jews are citizens, the business of forming congregations, paying rabbinical salaries and maintaining facilities such as old-age homes, day schools and charities relies largely on voluntary contributions from the Jewish community. Countries such as the UK, Germany and France provide some government funding (as they do to other ethnic minorities) for recognised educational and social projects, but these depend on additional Jewish support for anything above the basic requirements.

In the Diaspora, the synagogue still remains the focal point of organised Jewish life. But its hold is loosening. All the available statistics show that in every major centre of Jewish population around the world, synagogue membership is ageing and declining for every branch of Judaism save the ultra-Orthodox sects. According to a UK survey jointly published by the Board of Deputies and the Institute for Jewish Policy Research, the number of households belonging to a synagogue dropped by 16.8 per cent between 1990 and 2010.[3]

Any variations in the downward trend that is affecting mainstream Orthodox, Conservative and Progressive synagogues alike tend to be temporary blips and localised, depending on demographic factors. For example, the congregation in which I began my rabbinic career forty years ago was then a thriving one, with over a thousand adult members. It closed down recently; its former members mostly live elsewhere and have joined their nearest Progressive synagogue, while few new Jews have moved into the catchment area to replace them.

It would be tempting to claim on behalf of my rabbinical colleagues in what I liked to call my 'vocation' (but which my wife referred to more prosaically as 'your job') that the arrival of a charismatic new rabbi – who is loved by the elderly and a hit with the young; who has the knack of delivering sermons of enviable scholarship and wit that never last longer than five minutes; who combines this with ten pastoral visits a day while not forgetting weddings, funerals and representing the community at official functions; and who always looks smart and well dressed on a salary of £50 a week – would have a galvanising effect on synagogue membership. But I have to admit that no matter how successful some rabbis are, or how incompetent and dull others are, their personal effect on synagogue enrolment or defection is negligible – perhaps a dozen members either way in any given year. Familiarity and location are the strongest motives for members to stay put in their present synagogue. They might like to criticise the rabbi, the council, the choir, the uncomfortable seating, or the quality of the *Kiddush* wine, but it would take something exceptional to stir them from their habitual quiescence to go and join another synagogue. As with Church of England and Catholic congregations, that sense of social obligation, of needing to be seen at public worship, has steadily eroded over generations. Nowadays, it rarely extends beyond attendance at the two main festivals of Rosh ha-Shanah and Yom Kippur. But most elderly congregants still stay faithful to the *shul* they rarely attend.

It is different for the young married. With them, synagogue affiliation falls year on year, especially in economically straitened times. If balancing the family budget ever came down to a choice between paying the annual subscription of a synagogue I rarely used and, when I did, having to listen to an uninspiring rabbi lamely defending a theology I no longer believed in or keeping myself and the family healthy by renewing our membership at the local sports centre and swimming pool, it would take a strong sense of Jewish duty to opt for the synagogue. 'The *shul* with the pool', as it was dubbed, was the experiment tried by American suburban congregations in the 1970s. Instead of just being open for Sabbath worship and Sunday morning Religion School, they developed into community centres, providing weekday clubs, lunch-time guest speakers, counselling services, adult education and sports facilities, as enticements to tempt people into coming to services on Sabbath. It made little difference to attendances. People used the amenities during the week, and stayed home at weekends. 'I'm in charge of a religious megalopolis,' an American Reform rabbi boasted to me, describing his huge synagogue complex in Los Angeles.

But he and his community centre with a synagogue attached were no more immune from fluctuations in the property market, falls of the Dow Jones Index and population shifts than are Jewish congregations in London, New York, Toronto, Sydney or Johannesburg. In the USA, if a neighbourhood declines and the middle classes move away, a synagogue's likely response would be to explore the viability of selling its premises and relocating to the new suburban magnet. In the UK, Jews are stubbornly attached to familiar surroundings. For the worried honorary officers of a declining congregation, upkeep of the building and paying salaried staff is costly, and income does not keep pace with expenditure. So they come up with various schemes to augment income; exiguous imitations of the American model. A nursery school is one possibility, if the premises meet health and safety standards. Hiring out the community hall for outside functions is another. Letting classrooms to bridge clubs, dance classes, film societies, yoga, pilates and keep-fit groups have all been tried. But the core problem remains: more members are leaving than joining synagogues, and raising subscription levels even higher might prove to be self-defeating, because belonging to a congregation is optional; having to pay council tax and utility bills isn't.

Since they first proliferated in response to the destruction of the Temple in 70 CE, synagogues have had a threefold designation as houses of prayer, houses of study and houses of assembly. Jews would gather at the synagogue in all lands of their dispersion in order to pray to the One God, educate their children, and meet with fellow Jews. One feature common to all branches of modern Judaism (always excepting the ultra-Orthodox) is that most young people in their late teens and early twenties don't bother with synagogue. They are noticeable by their absence unless dutifully attending with their parents on the High Holydays, which I take to be a healthy sign that they are more interested in their studies, the other sex, and exploring the great world outside than in Judaism. It is only when they settle down and have children of their own that, in time-honoured fashion, they look to the synagogue to provide their offspring with a Jewish education. That is when they take out membership. It is children who prompt their parents to come back and join.

Decades ago – meaning when I was being taught in Religion School or taught there myself as a student rabbi – the standard of instruction was frankly appalling. Worthy, usually unqualified volunteers struggled to instil the rudiments of the Hebrew alphabet in recalcitrant pupils or tell them the same stories each year about the festivals when they came around. Any Israeli in England for more than a few weeks was guaranteed a job, on the mistaken assumption that, whatever their pedagogical ability, at least Hebrew was their native tongue and surely they must know *something* about Judaism. Years of disappointing experience to the contrary confirmed that most of them were no better than native teachers at getting the children enthusiastic about Hebrew home-work, and Israelis in any case harboured a perplexed and condescending incomprehension about Jewish life in the Diaspora.

But at least advertising a Religion School on its pro-spectus helped to keep synagogue income ticking over. Every year it brought in a new generation of parents as members. And, in recent years, Jewish education has caught up with the techniques and teaching methods and technological skills of secular education. Teaching was always an esteemed Jewish occupation – but at the exalted level of the rabbis named in the Talmud, or, since European emancipation, of professors holding a university chair. The humble schoolteacher, like his *shtetl* predecessor the *melamed* in the village *cheder*, was not ranked high in the social hierarchy. The dire standard of Religion School teaching in the past once prompted me to the wry observation that the miracle of Jewish survival had been *in spite of*, not because of, the quality of Jewish pedagogy. But the scope and diversity of modern educa-tion has made teaching not just a nice job for a Jewish boy (and girl) but also a respected one. Religion Schools now can provide a stimulating and happy environment, unlike the sullen and joyless experience of my memories.

It seems strange, then, that most synagogues have signed up to the current vogue for state-funded faith schools, thereby endangering any viable future for their own in-house religious education. The push for more faith schools in the UK came from the government's re-sponse to the race riots in Burnley, Oldham and Bradford in the summer of 2001. Tony Blair and the Labour Party had already pledged to provide more faith schools in their manifesto for the June general election that year, but it was the official Cantle report into the street violence and rioting, published in December 2001, that galvanised the government into action. In a telling phrase, the report described white and Asian communities as leading 'parallel lives'. The report made bleak reading. It catalogued the inner-city deprivation, high unemployment, polarised enclaves of whites-only or Muslims-only, virtually segregated schooling and the fear of being 'flooded' by Asian immigrants that had fanned racial tension. Instead of the integrated tolerance that multiculturalism was meant to engender, it had provoked exclusion and a retreat into ethnic ghettos – the ideal breeding ground in both communities for fomenting racism and paranoia about the 'other'.

I never understood why one of the major initiatives that the government came up with in response to the report was to call for the building of more state-funded single-faith schools – the very policy that the report had criticised for entrenching deeper divisions. The ideal of multiculturalism, earnestly preached by liberals such as myself from our predominantly white and middle-class London neighbourhoods, had manifestly failed to translate to the grim conditions in decaying northern towns. Offering parents the chance to have their children educated in schools where three-quarters of their fellow pupils were required by law to be of the same religion was either recognition of reality or an admission of defeat, depending on one's point of view.

Whatever considerations prompted them, religious communities were quick to recognise an opportunity and to extol the virtues of faith schooling over secular education. Faith schools instilled abiding values, not trendy humanist ones; they taught the eternal truths of their own faith while also inculcating respect and tolerance for other religions; by taking in a set quota of different-faith pupils they exposed their own children to diversity and multiculturalism, thus fitting them to take their place in society as good Christians/Jews/Muslims/Hindus/Sikhs and responsible citizens of a modern, multi-ethnic United Kingdom. Or so we were asked to believe.

Who can blame the faith communities for trying to win back a little influence over our vulgarly materialist and brashly atheist country? But some of their claims are contentious and others speculative. For example, no convincing evidence exists that people brought up in faith schools become 'better' Jews, Christians and Muslims or more responsible citizens than their peers educated at secular schools. Parental and home example counts for at least as much as daily indoctrination at school. Some children will be positively influenced by religious instruction and remain abidingly loyal to their ancestral faith; others will be positively turned off by it and reject the religious beliefs that were forced on them when young. And much as one wants to hope that in faith schools respect and validity is accorded to the tenets of other religions in a spirit of Enlightenment forbearance, the innate triumphalism of Judaism, Christianity and Islam would suggest otherwise. If the aim is to teach that all religions are equal and have been equally endowed with a portion of God's truth, then why set up faith schools in the first place, rather than letting secular schools get on with spreading the message?

But for parents worried by constant chopping and changing in the national curriculum and unmistakable evidence of lowered standards, faith-based schooling has a seductive allure. In the words of a *Jewish Chronicle Education Supplement*, 'We have probably never had it so good in Jewish education in this country. The Jewish school system has expanded beyond what anyone could have imagined twenty years ago.'[4]

Having its own faith schools has always been a necessary ingredient of Orthodox Judaism. But Progressive Judaism too, founded on the principle of being a Jew at home and a patriotic citizen in public, has also succumbed to the siren song of faith schooling. In September 2010 a new, purpose-built and magnificently equipped Jewish Community Secondary School, JCoSS for short, opened its doors in a London suburb. Ostensibly a cross-communal venture for 'Jews of all backgrounds', its admissions criteria make clear that the ethos and guiding spirit behind the school is Progressive, not Orthodox. First priority will be given to 'Jewish children', defined as 'children who demonstrate, or of whom at least one parent demonstrates, commitment to the Jewish faith or involvement in recognised Jewish faith activities'. The school has been financially supported and enthusiastically endorsed by every Reform and Liberal community in the UK; all Progressive Jews have welcomed the creation of a school that deliberately rejects the rigid Orthodox definition of who is a Jew when vetting would-be pupils.

In the face of so much excitement and admiration for the dedicated efforts that turned the school into a reality, with others to follow, it seems churlish to mention that a few Progressive Jews, me included, still harbour doubts about the desirability of extending faith schooling at the expense of a state system and universal curriculum. A key tenet of liberal ideology is that all children, regardless of their religious or ethnic origin, should be taught together the common values of citizenship and national identity.

But I and every parent know from personal experience that vague ideals about equal opportunity and shared values usually succumb to the special needs of our own children. And as every Jewish grandmother will tell you, *their* grandchild is uniquely special. Over 50 per cent of Jewish children in the UK are now educated in faith-based schools. Jewish parents are notorious for the sacrifices they will make and the lengths to which they will go in order to achieve the best education for their children. If the local church primary school, a Church of England grammar school established after Henry VIII's break with Rome, or a fee-paying public (i.e. private) school is considered the best in its field, Jewish parents will skimp and save or move house to send their child there. Given the fractured and variable condition of state education, especially in inner-city areas where even head teachers and local education authority officials will let slip remarks about 'bog-standard comprehensives' and 'sink schools' it is no surprise that so many parents, Jewish ones among them, are desperate to find a better alternative for their children.

That is where faith schools score. They tend to insist on the wearing of uniforms and have stricter discipline, higher standards and less ethnic diversity. Catholic, Protestant and Muslim parents have all been caught out on admission forms dissembling their place of residence or exaggerating the frequency of their attendance at services in their anxiety to get their children into the faith school of their choice. Jewish parents are required to produce similar proofs of domicile and practice, but they get caught out by different and more contentious criteria, as a Court of Appeal ruling in the summer of 2009 demonstrated.

The Jews' Free School (JFS) in London, originally founded in the East End in 1732, is a centre of academic excellence. It is a prestigious, heavily oversubscribed and taxpayer-funded faith school on a large campus in North London. Its standing in the top tier of national league tables is duplicated by the success of other Jewish schools in the capital and provincial centres of Jewish population such as Manchester, Birmingham, Liverpool and Leeds. As with their faith-school counterparts in other religions, the admissions policy of Jewish schools is to give first priority to Jewish children.

So far so good. But the definition of Jewish status applied at the JFS and almost all other Jewish schools in the UK with the exception of the Progressive JCoSS is that of Orthodox Judaism's main bastion, the United Synagogue, whose Chief Rabbi is Lord Jonathan Sacks (who himself, to his exquisite embarrassment, attended a school called Christ's College) and whose Rabbinical Court, the London *Beth Din*, is the most stringent in the world.

A child, known in court as 'M', born of a Jewish father and a mother who had converted to Judaism under non-Orthodox auspices, was refused admission to the JFS on the ground that the Chief Rabbi did not recognise the mother's Jewish status. M's father promptly sued the United Synagogue, and was joined in the action by another couple who had been married in an Orthodox synagogue in New York. The wife had converted under the auspices of the Chief Rabbinate in Jerusalem and is herself a teacher at the JFS, but her children would not be eligible to attend the school because Lord Sacks and his *Beth Din* do not recognise her conversion.

After a lengthy and expensive case that garnered much unwelcome publicity and has depleted the United Synagogue's coffers by hundreds of thousands of pounds in legal costs, the Court of Appeal ruled that the Chief Rabbi and the JFS had been in breach of the 1976 Race Relations Act by refusing M admission. Under the provisions of the 1976 Act, Jews are categorised as an ethnic group entitled to its protection. The Act has been of previous benefit to the Jewish community, for example in enabling persons of Jewish identity to bring successful cases against employers who deny them jobs on the ground of their religious practices, such as taking time off for Sabbaths and festivals. According to the Court of Appeal's decision, subsequently upheld by the new Supreme Court in one of its first judgments, in relying on an investigation of M's parental descent rather than on a consideration of his – or his parents' – religious practice, the Chief Rabbi and the school had infringed the Act and been guilty of ethnic prejudice.

Because we Jews are a litigious people, it is an odds-on bet that where M's parents first trod, others are sure to follow. Nor should future schools that decide to follow the broader JCoSS definition of Jewish status regard themselves as immune. Some bright lawyer is bound to discover grounds on which even its generous definition of Jewish status can be challenged on behalf of a rejected applicant. Abstruse legal byways certainly weren't the first consideration of Progressive congregations when they unanimously endorsed the establishment of JCoSS and generously supported it.

But they should have asked themselves about its likely

knock-on effect on their one steady source of income, the Religion School. Wild horses won't be able to drag children who attend a faith school five days a week into synagogue Religion School at the weekend. The threat of cancelling their *bar* or *bat mitzvah* unless the child attends extra synagogue classes is an empty one; they can learn their Scroll portion and any other requirements just as well at day school. So enrolment and attendance will decline drastically in all those synagogue Religion Schools where parents choose faith schooling for their children. And when the main reason why parents join a synagogue – for it to provide a Jewish education for their children – no longer applies, membership defection will accelerate. It is already happening. A rabbi at one of the largest Progressive synagogues in the country told me recently that formerly having been antipathetic to *bar* and *bat mitzvah* ceremonies, because they overshadowed Sabbath morning worship, he is now grateful for them, because at least they bring a decent-sized attendance to services; on a non-*bar mitzvah* Shabbat he will get hardly any children and their parents attending, and perhaps a hundred mainly elderly worshippers – from a congregation of over *two thousand adult members*.

The percentage of faith-educated children will rise still higher in future as more Jewish schools are built and parental concerns about the poor quality of state education are not allayed. Synagogues will become a hive of secular activity on weekdays, with all their adult clubs and societies and maybe also a kindergarten and Tiny Tots group, but mausoleums at weekends. The synagogue is declining in importance as a house of prayer or study, while still fulfilling its function as a house of assembly.

It would be more sensible for religious Judaism to

face the realities of modern Jewish life, with attendance at worship spasmodic and children's education being farmed out to faith schools, and actively engage instead with cultural Judaism in all its secular, non-religious manifestations, rather than regarding it fearfully as a threat. Synagogues, like churches, will always be there to cater for those who find comforting reassurance and consolation for life's exigencies in the familiar tropes of prayer, worship and ritual. For those Jews no longer impressed by the affirmations of faith, synagogues will still evoke historical memories and loyalty to tradition. To hear the haunting melody of Max Bruch's *Kol Nidrey* on Yom Kippur Eve is a spiritual experience, even if one can no longer accept the premiss that on this day God judges all human actions and decides our fate for the coming year. It was Julian Barnes who regretted his lack of familiarity with religion's consolations by saying, 'I don't believe in God but I miss Him.'

Religion is about aesthetic impressions as much as belief. In a Christian context, it would be a stony-hearted materialist who failed to be moved by the grandeur of Chartres Cathedral, George Herbert's poem 'Love' or Verdi's *Requiem*, whether or not subscribing (as one suspects Verdi didn't) to the central tenets of Christianity. Those three random examples among many – without even beginning to consider Renaissance art – demonstrate how, in earlier times, cultural creativity was a fruitful corollary of Christianity.

The same can be argued of the relationship between Jewish culture and Judaism. Hellenistic mosaics scattered throughout the Galilee and the extensive wall paintings discovered at the Dura-Europos synagogue (at first mistaken by scholars for a Greek temple, because of the artwork), or the long tradition of illuminated religious manuscripts such as the priceless Sarajevo *Haggadah*, show that however rigid the prohibition against graven images might appear to be, it did not deter Jewish artists in the past, and if they needed a defence against outraged zealots, they could have quoted the Rabbinic concept of *Hiddur mitzvah*, 'beautifying the commandment' by sanctifying God in the choicest, most creative way possible.

But in modern times, as the religious element in Jewish self-identification has steadily diminished, religious Judaism has tended to view secular Jewish culture not as complementary but as a worrying alternative. Symptomatic of this ambivalence was the review by a young rabbi of a book by the Israeli scholar Eliezer Schweid called *The Idea of Modern Jewish Culture*.[5] On the one hand, the reviewer wondered about 'the apparent lack of an intellectual underpinning' for cultural Judaism; he questioned whether Jewish culture outside of Israel 'has a place within modern Jewish institutions'. On the other hand, he recognised that the ubiquity of cultural Jews represents 'a significant challenge for those of us who work in synagogues, or indeed in Jewish schools'. His uneasy compromise was to call on synagogues to become more accessible to 'those seeking the broadest of Jewish cultural life' while lacking religious belief, and on religious believers to become 'increasingly vocal that even where it is not based on theological belief, Jewish religious practice and prayer can be a rewarding form of cultural expression . . .'

On the principle that if you can't beat them, join them, and with synagogues having lost their indispensability as houses of prayer and study, my more robust conclusion would have been that their survival will depend on a strategy of keenly embracing cultural Judaism, not keeping it at arm's length. Moving in their own cosy, like-minded circles, rabbis and educators are often unaware of the antipathy felt by secular Jews towards organised religion. They are happy to identify with Jewish art, literature and music, but are turned off by anything that smacks of the community at prayer.

My experience over many years as the senior rabbi of a high-profile 'cathedral' synagogue was that when I invited well-known rabbis such as Lionel Blue or distinguished Christian clerics such as the Bishop of London as guest preachers, it would add maybe seventy worshippers to the regular Sabbath morning attendance. When I invited a Jewish stage and film director such as John Schlesinger or Nicholas Hytner to be interviewed on a weekday evening about their work and the Jewish influences on it, or cellist Steven Isserlis to conduct a masterclass with a promising Jewish musician, audiences of four to five hundred people would happily buy tickets for the event. Controversial public meetings about Israel and the Middle East were equally well supported. The bulk of those Jews at such meetings were probably secularists and their attachment to Judaism was solely cultural, but it pleased me that they would step inside the synagogue with no sense of incongruity, and without feeling uncomfortably that their humanist principles were at variance with the religious principles taught from the pulpit. A bolder approach to advertising the synagogue as a Jewish Cultural Centre embracing the range of Jewish creative expression from prayer and worship to dance and Wittgenstein's linguistic philosophy would attract back many otherwise alienated secular Jews inside its doors.

When all is said and done, it is impossible definitively to separate the Jewish religion from Jewish culture. One gave birth to the other; they overlap, and their proximity makes them mutually dependent. Eliezer Schweid writes in his appraisal of Achad Ha-Am, 'Despite the fact that his religiosity had been replaced by a scientific world-view, he remained a Jew in his way of life, his world outlook, and his values. Even without religious belief, he found that his former way of life still held a positive personal and universal significance for him as it related to family, society and nation.'[6] Way of life, world outlook and values: we are back to that loose-knit but widely recognised amalgam of moral teachings, ethical conduct, societal obligations, family ties and responsibility for one's fellow humans that goes by the name of 'Jewish values'.

Are such values sufficiently 'thick', in sociological jargon, to sustain the distinctive identity of a Jewish people that for the most part has discarded belief and swapped it for Zionism? Nietzsche, having announced the death of God, was scornful of those thinkers – particularly in England – who tried to preserve Christian morality while denying the Christian faith. He directed his sharpest vituperation at that 'moralising little woman' George Eliot, clinging on to respectability after being emancipated from theology. For him, the idea of a moral law without belief in the lawgiver was vacuous.[7]

Despite Nietzsche's bromides, I am optimistic that Jewish moral law *can* still resonate and provide inspiration, even when most of its followers no longer believe in a divine lawgiver. For one thing, Judaism is a much smaller, more compact religion than Christianity; it can be policed more effectively. The spur to ethical conduct may come from a belief in God, personal morality, Kant's categorical imperative, or communal pressure. Whichever it is, Jews are self-consciously aware that their individual behaviour has repercussions and ramifications beyond their own tiny orbit. It reflects on Jews as a whole. A rueful Yiddish maxim put it that when a Jew does something meritorious, he is praised in the singular; when a Jew does something illegal or immoral – all Jews are the same!

Taken collectively, Jews are no better or worse than any other people. There are rotten apples as well as upright human beings in every race, faith and nation. But it is a unique admixture of history, homelessness, stoicism in the face of persecution, religious teachings, and the faintly recalled biblical exhortation to be 'a kingdom of priests and a holy people' that over two millennia has developed in Jews a particular emphasis on justice, right conduct and improving the world. The Russian-Jewish historian Simon Dubnow (1860–1941) wrote in his essay 'Jewish History', 'Men must beware of looking upon Religion as an ideal to be yearned for; it should be an ideal to be applied.' To its followers there has always been a pleasing practicality and specificity about Judaism's teachings, with their insistence that an hour of good deeds in this world is more important than worrying about the world to come; the practical application of religion.

This brings us back to where we began, the ancient triad of Jews, Judaism and their relationship with Israel. Nowadays the three are badly out of kilter, linked in a partnership that has subordinated the dictates of Jewish conscience to the tawdry manoeuvrings of Israeli politics. Trying to put the relationship back on an even footing will determine how – or even *whether* – the Jewish people will continue to add its own distinctive contribution to civilisation.

8

Jewish ethics and the State of Israel

In his great book *A Fire on the Moon*, about the first lunar landing, Norman Mailer is present at a press conference that Armstrong, Collins and Aldridge give to the world's media before blast-off. A BBC reporter dares to ask the one question that hovers, unarticulated but palpable, in the air: 'What . . . will your plans be in the extremely unlikely event that the lunar module does not come up off the moon's surface?' Asked to comment on the emotions he might feel when facing death, Armstrong gives a tight smile and replies, 'Well, that's an unpleasant thing to think about.' Mailer ponders the surreal situation of pressing three men – in what otherwise, with all its bland talk and PR jargon, could have been any other press conference at which a company had unveiled a new product – to contemplate the prospect of being stuck on the moon for ever. He sums it up with a profound aphorism: 'The horror of the Twentieth century was the size of each new event, and the paucity of its reverberation.'

Repetition dulls the shock of novelty and therefore the sharpness of our reaction to it. It coarsens our sensibilities. The Nazi genocide, horrific in its day and held up as a unique warning to future generations, has been imitated in its intent if not yet in its scope several times since, in Asia, Africa and the Balkans. The first time in the 1960s that the Soviet Union accused Israel of using 'Nazi tactics' against Palestinians, the tasteless *chutzpah* of comparing the victims to their worst persecutors prompted an outburst of revulsion throughout the Jewish world; forty years on, it has become a routine insult applied indiscriminately either to Israel by its enemies or by right-wing Jewish settlers confronting the police. The very word 'Holocaust', once handled with caution and reserved only to refer to the enormity of that particular Nazi genocide, is now carelessly bandied about after some trivial incident of mindless violence such as a street fight; so too with the word 'tsunami', first brought to general notice after the Indian Ocean disaster of Boxing Day 2004 that killed over two hundred and thirty thousand people, now used to describe any mound of paperwork submerging a civil servant.

'Compassion fatigue' is the glib phrase to excuse our tired reaction to yet another appeal for earthquake victims or starving children. It is not only the *size* of each new event but the frequency with which they occur and capture the headlines for their brief fifteen minutes that anaesthetises our senses. In a few days in early 2011, the 'Arab Spring' that toppled despots in Tunisia and Egypt and threatened regimes in Algeria, Syria, Jordan, Saudi Arabia, Yemen and the Gulf States was overtaken in news headlines by Japan's nuclear disaster in the wake of earthquake, which in turn gave way to a civil war in Libya that was dubbed a 'stalemate' after it had lasted all of two weeks. When Harold Macmillan was asked to name the biggest problem he had to cope with as prime minister and allegedly replied, 'Events, dear boy, events', he was talking about an era that appears positively Edwardian in its leisureliness compared with ours.

The dwindling reverberation from yet another vast

new event quickly following in the footsteps of its predecessor blunts our moral responses. What caused heart-
searching the first time around prompts barely a ripple
by its tenth repetition. Moral slippage oozes in widening
circles like an oil slick. It is instructive in this respect to
contrast the reactions in Israel and the Diaspora to the
1983 Kahan Commission of Enquiry into the Sabra and
Shatila massacre in the wake of Israel's 1982 invasion of
Lebanon with the response to the 2009 Goldstone Report of the UN Human Rights Council into alleged war
crimes committed by Israel and Hamas during Operation
Cast Lead in Gaza.

The Kahan Commission's report contained a shrewd
and objective analysis of the situation in Lebanon since
the civil war of 1975, along with a detailed résumé of the
military and political calculations leading up to the decision to send Christian Phalangist militia under Israeli
surveillance into the Palestinian refugee camps of Sabra
and Shatila. Above all, it was a document of unwavering
moral principle. Chaired by the President of the Supreme
Court, Yitzchak Kahan, alongside Supreme Court judge
Aharon Barak and Reserve Major-General Yonah Efrat,
the Commission found Israel indirectly responsible for
the massacre of between seven and eight hundred camp
residents (according to the Israeli army's own intelligence
estimates) by Phalangists itching to avenge the recent assassination of their leader Bashir Jemayel and atrocities
committed against them by Palestinians since 1975. The
Commission recommended the dismissals of Arik Sharon, the Defence Minister; Chief of Staff Lieutenant General Rafael Eitan, and Director of Military Intelligence
Major General Yehoshua Saguy, as well as sundry less
senior personnel.

The Commission's scrupulous determination to un-
earth the truth while refusing to be deterred by political
pressures or arguments about state security went some
way towards restoring Israel's battered reputation at the
bar of world opinion. The predominant response in Israel
and the Diaspora was one of gratitude that, however
grim the report's findings, no whitewash had been used
to conceal them. There was something of a cleansing
ritual to the report's fastidious unpicking of what had
happened in Sabra and Shatila, after the most traumatic-
ally self-inflicted damage in the young state's history.

Having been a vocal critic of Israel's misconceived and
disastrous foray into Lebanon (some irate Likud supporters from Ilford phoned the synagogue to threaten they
were coming to burn it down, but evidently got lost on
their way into Central London), I remember writing an
article in *The Times* saying how proud I was of a report
that demonstrated Jewish moral values at their most enduring.

In finding Israel guilty of indirect responsibility for the
massacre – the sin of omission rather than commission
– the three enquiry members did not cite rulings from
the Geneva Convention or other treatises on warfare, but
instead went back to the Bible and gave the example
from Deuteronomy chapter 21, verses 6–7, with its Rabbinic interpretation. The elders of a town within whose
boundaries an unknown corpse had been found are commanded to sacrifice a heifer and pronounce over it the
formula: 'Our hands have not shed this blood, neither
have our eyes seen it.' The Talmudic rabbis puzzled why
innocent townsfolk nevertheless were required to make
an expiation offering for the dead man. The answer they
came up with, in the name of Rabbi Yehoshua ben Levi,

was that although the town was technically blameless, had its citizens offered the unknown stranger help and sustenance he might not have died (*Sotah* 38b). The Kahan Report added that when pogroms had been visited on Jews in the past, responsibility for them was blamed not only on the perpetrators but also on those who had failed in their duty to ensure safety and public order. It concluded its findings with the admonition: 'But the end never justifies the means and basic ethical and human values must be maintained in the use of arms.'

Fast forward almost three decades to the Goldstone Report into the Gaza campaign, and Jewish reactions to it. The mood in Israel and the Diaspora had darkened in the meantime, and the ethical nuances of the Kahan Report had become blunted – confirmation of Mailer's maxim about the size of each new event and the paucity of its reverberation. Too much had happened in the intervening thirty years, mainly bad. Sharon's refusal to resign, supported by Prime Minister Begin, whose first response to Sabra and Shatila had been that '*Goyim* (gentiles) kill *goyim* and Jews are blamed', prompted a large protest rally at which a grenade was thrown, killing Emil Grunzweig, a reserve combat officer, and wounding six others.

Since 1982, the cultural divide between Ashkenazi and Sephardi Israelis, as between hawks and doves over the future of the West Bank, has grown steadily wider. The first Palestinian *intifada* shocked Israel out of its complacency about indefinite retention of territories captured in the Six Day War. A Brooklyn-born West Bank settler went on a murderous rampage at the Tomb of the Patriarchs in Hebron, killing twenty-nine Muslims at prayer; his burial place has become a revered site for settlers.

Then the prime minister himself, Yitzchak Rabin, was assassinated by a fanatic for having signed the Oslo Accords with the PLO. Arab terrorist attacks continued, causing greater carnage, attacks of a ruthlessness and frequency worse than anything yet endured by the Israeli civilian population. Almost as shocking as Sabra and Shatila – although by now Israel's diehard defenders were inured to the escalating scale of retaliation and those of us who believed we were loving but critical supporters of the Jewish state were in despair over the unimaginative and grossly disproportionate military response to every terrorist atrocity – was the shelling of the village of Cana in Lebanon which killed a hundred and five innocent civilians, after Hezbollah had launched rockets across the border. The Israeli apology for its deadly mistake was grudging and formulaic.

A quick skim through each major event and the paucity of its reverberation since the turn of the century would reveal: a virtual breakdown of what is still laughingly called the 'peace process'; a second *intifada*; the increasing influence of the settler movement in Israel, reflected in government policy and backing from the army's top echelons; the growing McCarthyism of successive right-wing coalitions, typified most recently by the Knesset Bill outlawing public use of the Arabic word *naqba* 'tragedy' – the Palestinian term for their dispossession in 1948; indictment on charges of fraud and corruption against two serving prime ministers and several other cabinet members; the conviction on charges of rape and sexual harassment while in office of a former state president; a bungled second Lebanon war against Hezbollah in the summer of 2006 that left the military keen to apply lessons learned there to Gaza in December

2008; a frantic last-days-of-the-Roman-Empire hedon-
ism among an electorate enjoying material prosperity
but cynical towards its political leaders, nervous about
a nuclear Iran, fearful for its children waiting to serve
in an army conflicted about its policing mission against
the Palestinians, aghast at the assertiveness of the ultra-
Orthodox, convinced that the world is instinctively
against Israel, and pessimistic about ever knowing peace.

The least lovely football club in London is Millwall
FC, whose bellicose supporters' favourite chant is
'Nobody likes us, we don't care'. That tone of truculent
self-pity just about summed up the mood in which Israel
awaited the Goldstone Report. With Israel already heavily criticised by the international media for having used
excessive force in Gaza and deliberately destroying its
civil infrastructure, a fact-finding mission from the UN
Human Rights Council, with which Israel refused to co-
operate, preferring to launch its own investigation into
alleged war crimes, did not augur well. As the *Guardian*
journalist Jonathan Freedland pointed out, the UN Human Rights Council does seem to have an excessive interest in Israel. Thirty-two of the sixty-seven resolutions
it had passed up to 2010 related to Israel, with not a
single report on such bastions of human rights as Sri
Lanka, Congo and Darfur, let alone any investigation
into tyrannies such as Belarus, North Korea and Saudi
Arabia.[1]

So when Judge Goldstone admitted eighteen months
after its publication that the final report of the Council
was flawed and partially repudiated his own handiwork
in an op-ed piece in the *Washington Post*, his article
reverberated around the world.[2] Needless to say, his carefully qualified reservations were filleted to leave only

the snappiest sound bites of the 'Goldstone retracts' or 'Judge confesses he was wrong' variety. His rejection of the charge that civilians in Gaza were *intentionally* targeted 'as a matter of policy' was avidly seized on by Israel's and Diaspora spokespeople as decisive refutation of a blood libel against the Jewish people. The Israeli Foreign Ministry received instructions from Benjamin Netanyahu's government to lobby UN members to have the report cancelled, as eventually had happened with the notorious General Assembly resolution of November 1975 that condemned Zionism as a form of 'racism'. Israel's jubilant supporters took Goldstone's partial concession as evidence that the army had been cleared of all allegations of misconduct during the Gaza campaign.

Which was not quite the case. In a thoughtful op-ed piece in the *Washington Post* four days after Goldstone's, Jessica Montell, Director of *B'Tselem*, the highly respected Israel Information Centre for Human Rights in the Occupied Territories, pointed out that at least 758 Palestinian civilians had been killed in the hostilities, of whom 318 were children. More than 5,300 civilians had been injured and over 3,500 houses destroyed. Banned white phosphorous bombs and inherently inaccurate mortar shells had been used in densely populated areas. Public buildings and electricity, water and sewage plants were targeted. Ambulances were prevented from tending to the dying and wounded. Of the 52 criminal investigations Israel opened into Operation Cast Lead, only 3 had led to indictments; nearly three years later, the status of the other investigations was still unclear and, anyway, they concerned incidents allegedly committed by individual soldiers, not the broader issue of government policy and its bearing on orders issued to troops by their commanders in the field.[3]

Then came, to my mind, the most telling paragraph of Montell's article. Unsatisfactory though it was, she wrote, Israel had done far more than Hamas to investigate its crimes, giving rise to 'perhaps the most disturbing aspect of Goldstone's opinion piece and the Israeli spin of it: the measuring of Israel against Hamas. Israel did not wilfully target civilians; Hamas did. Israel initiated investigations; Hamas did not. *When the bar is set so low, Israel easily clears it.*' (Italics mine.)

How are the mighty fallen! For the first fifty years of the state's history it was taken for granted that Israel occupied the moral high ground, the one democratic country in the Middle East – as its spokespeople unfailingly reiterated – governed by the rule of law and therefore never stooping to the behaviour of neighbouring Arab regimes or the terrorist tactic of deliberately targeting civilians. Perhaps unreasonably, higher standards *were* expected of Israel. I know that I and most other Jews in the Diaspora did look to Israel to set a better example and uphold civilised norms. And now it has come to this; that we are supposed to be proud when Israel scores higher than Hamas in a moral evaluation test.

Certain human rights organisations – Christian Aid and Amnesty International, for example – and Israel's inveterate critics (the two are sometimes synonymous) hold an unrealistic view of what happens when soldiers are fighting for their lives. As anyone who has been under fire knows, troops commit deeds in the heat of battle that horrify them afterwards. Rules of engagement and Just War doctrine were formulated precisely to refute the proposition that because war is hell the usual morality of peacetime no longer applies and anything goes. It is an attempt to affirm humane standards even in the brutality of combat. Israel has always imbued its citizen army with the concept of 'purity of arms' and in the past could reasonably lay claim to being the most moral fighting force in the world (ultimately as meaningless a boast as the routine claim of every president or prime minister that his country's soldiers are 'the finest in the world'), if we discount the candidature of parade-ground armies such as those of Scandinavia or Lichtenstein.

In October 1967, after the Six Day War, a book was published in Israel by the kibbutz movement under the title *Soldiers' Talk*. It was a transcript of personal interviews and group discussions with kibbutz members who had fought in the war. They talked honestly about death, fear, for some 'the sweet smell of war', their feelings towards the enemy and 'the tragedy of becoming victors' as little David took on the stature of Goliath. Officers and the higher echelons of the IDF were predominantly kibbutz-bred in those days, and they figured disproportionately too among the dead and wounded. Twenty thousand copies of the book were printed – enough for each family in the kibbutz movement. It became a sensation in Israel, with copies passed from hand to hand. A second edition was snapped up within weeks. A third reprint for the general public sold 100,000 copies – a runaway bestseller for the small-book market in Israel. An English translation appeared as *The Seventh Day*[4] and was equally successful in the USA and Great Britain. The disarming frankness of the *kibbutznik* interviewees whose rigorous moral and social values had been inculcated by their ideological upbringing, was a persuasive advertisement for the image of the Israeli soldier-citizen as a reluctant warrior who when forced to fight did so with valour and magnanimity towards the enemy, then laid down his arms and returned to his civilian occupation.

It is a sign of changing times and more ambiguous values that towards the end of 2010 the Israeli non-governmental organisation *Shovrim Shtika* ('Breaking the Silence') released a book with the cumbersome title *Occupation of the Territories – Israeli Soldier Testimonies 2000–2010*, to mark the tenth anniversary of the outbreak of the second *intifada*. The organisation's mission statement says it is there as a forum for soldiers returning from tours of duty to 'discover the gap between the reality they encountered in the Occupied Territories and the silence they encounter at home'. Over seven hundred former conscripts and reservists who have dared to break the silence and speak out against military infractions in Gaza and the West Bank have been branded cowardly traitors and risk ostracism by their platoon comrades – a heavy price to pay in a society that values *esprit de corps* above all other virtues. E. M. Forster's troubling remark in *Two Cheers for Democracy* that if he had to choose between loyalty to a friend or country he hoped that he would have the guts to betray his country would be incomprehensible to an Israeli; in terms of loyalty, friend and country are inseparable. But every year, despite intimidation and threats of court martial or imprisonment, a steady number of soldiers refuse to serve in the Occupied Territories and request other duties.

Occupation of the Territories contains the lengthy (431 pages) testimonies of 101 male and female soldiers and is organised into four chapters according to the four key principles used by the military authorities to define

Israeli policy in the Territories: 'Prevention [of terror]', 'Separation', 'Fabric of Life' and 'Law Enforcement'. The testimonies reveal what lies behind those innocuous connotations. For example, 'Prevention' encompasses not only the deadly pursuit and targeted assassinations of suspected terrorists, but also – in military jargon – 'searing the consciousness' of the civilian population into recognition that resistance is futile, by using tactics of mass arrests, forcible beatings of bound detainees, intimidation of families, commandeering and deliberate destruction of houses and property, and what is known as 'demonstration of presence'. Night patrols in Palestinian towns and villages will regularly shoot into the air, fire off sound bombs and flares, conduct random house searches in the early hours and aggressively question unlucky bystanders, as 'demonstration of presence'. Field-level commanders write up their reports about these provocative patrols under standard euphemisms about 'harassing activity' and 'disruption of normalcy'.

The consistency and similarity in detail of these soldiers' testimonies cannot be brushed off as the imaginative reconstructions of malcontents with a grudge against the army. Rather, they corroborate the assertion by the Executive Director of 'Breaking the Silence' that the last decade of Israeli presence in the Territories 'demonstrates the moral deterioration of Israeli society as a whole – not just its actors on the ground, the soldiers. We hope that the book . . . will stimulate a frank public debate on the moral price of ongoing control of another people.'

It is scant comfort to know that, despite the Nazi slur, occupying armies from long before the IDF or the Wehrmacht and the SS have employed similar tactics to cower civilian populations. But Jews don't like a Jewish army to do such things. It disturbs our ideal of the citizen-soldier and that iconic photo from the Six Day War of the boyish paratrooper gazing up in wonder at the captured Western Wall, on either side of him two swarthy, equally rapt, probably Moroccan or Iraqi-born soldiers, in a potent image of Israel the melting pot for Jews from East and West. We prefer to remain in ignorance of the army's brutality in the Territories, or to take on trust the boast of Israeli generals and politicians for many years after 1967 that theirs was the most benign occupation in history – which is like boasting about being only a little pregnant. No occupation leaves the vanquished praising the victors for their benevolence, and the longer it goes on with no diplomatic solution in sight – forty-four years now and counting – the less benign an occupation it becomes in order to restrain an increasingly restive native population.

Probably we Jews all suffer from selective moral vision about Israel. Eli Wiesel, Nobel Prize winner and keeper par excellence of the Holocaust flame, was never shy of lecturing the Soviet Union on its misdeeds, or reprimanding President Reagan in 1985 for honouring German war dead, including forty-nine members of the Waffen-SS, buried at Bitburg cemetery; but whenever it came to taking a stance about some controversial Israeli action he would loftily declare that only those who lived in the country had the right to criticise it. Isaiah Berlin was similarly resolute in declining to speak out publicly.

With all due respect to two such distinguished Jewish figures – and many others of equal stature whose silent support for Israel must have been stretched to breaking point on occasion – ethical values are absolute, not relative. They may make allowances – like Justice – for extenuating circumstances and human frailty, but apply equally to all. A perplexing passage in Anthony Julius's *Trials of the Diaspora* contains a lengthy excursus on the 'humiliations inflicted on the occupied population' by Israeli military rule over the Occupied Territories. With a lawyerly precision that was all the more devastating for its restraint, Julius listed the burdens of 'checkpoints, curfews, closures, permits, and all those other limitations of movement that are imposed without accountability' on the Palestinian population. He catalogued targeted assassinations that have killed innocent bystanders, the shootings, beatings and tear gas that have injured thousands of civilians, the punitive destruction of private property, the uprooting of orchards and fields, the demolition of workshops, factories and hothouses, the confiscation of vehicles, the house searches, the demands for production of identity papers, the examination of personal effects, the shaming of parents in the presence of their children, the land grabs, the separation of families, neighbours and fields by the looming ugliness of the Security Wall, settlements connected to each other by roads Palestinians are prohibited from using, the building of homes for Jewish citizens on land confiscated from non-citizens who are then expected to share it peaceably 'in conditions of the grossest inequality' and concludes: 'None of these criticisms, in my view, is anti-Semitic. Many of them seem to me simply to be true, and what is true cannot be anti-Semitic.'[5]

An unflinching moral pronouncement, which Julius instantly vitiates by the subtle special pleading he then proposes in mitigation. The inadequacies of the Palestinians' own political leadership; the institutionalised thievery and violence of the Palestinian Authority

under Arafat; maximalist Arab posturing; the 'deform-
ing burden' carried by Israel on account of its neighbours' refusal to accept its existence in 1948 and leaving
1 per cent of its Jewish population dead in the ensuing
war, leading to the conviction that 'Israel cannot afford
to lose any battle (let alone, war) and that its security
must be pursued above all other considerations'; Arab
rejection of the Peel Commission partition proposals; the
collaboration of Palestinian leaders with the Nazi cause
during the Second World War and therefore, by implicit
extension, with the Holocaust; all circling back to the
prevalence of modern Arab anti-Semitism and the refusal of extremist factions such as Hamas and Hezbollah to
recognise Israel.

All this may be persuasive in explaining *why* Israel is
suspicious about Arab intentions and therefore imposes
repressive control over West Bank Palestinians but, from
a moral perspective, it does not *excuse* it. Turning a blind
eye has become second nature for most Israelis and their
Diaspora supporters. They are outraged – and rightly so
– by the gruesome murder of civilian families with young
children on their West Bank settlements or barrages of
indiscriminate shelling against towns near the Gaza border. But they respond to each new revelation of settler
provocation, police tardiness in investigating Palestinian
complaints and the army's favouritism towards the col-
oniser as Weimar Germans did in the 1930s to Hitler's
step-by-step erosion of civil liberties and the rule of law
– by lowering their heads and walking past on the other
side of the street. And, anyway, they say, we still rank
higher than Hamas, Syria or Saudi Arabia in a human-
rights test.

It is academics, clergy and lawyers who are often

among the worst culprits, both in Israel and, less ex-
cusably, the Diaspora, where distance should grant the
benefit of clearer thinking. Instead of adopting an un-
ambiguously moral stance, they hover behind equivoca-
tions and a pose of 'objectivity'. Taken as a whole, the
intellectual classes have never been renowned for their
bravery. Under whatever regime in history, they always
seem to rub along and get by. Pastor Martin Niemoller's
mantra about the inactivity of German intellectuals following the Nazi rise to power – 'First they came for the
Communists and I didn't speak out because I wasn't a
Communist. Then they came for the trade unionists and
I didn't speak out because I wasn't a trade unionist. Then
they came for the Jews and I didn't speak out because
I wasn't a Jew. Then they came for me and there was
no one left to speak for me' – is justly celebrated and
frequently quoted, but it doesn't seem to have encouraged the present generation of Israeli intellectuals to step
down from their ivory towers and show a concerted lead.

In a joint review of *What Is a Palestinian State Worth?*,
the latest book by philosopher Sari Nusseibeh, president
of al-Quds University, and *Occupation of the Territories*,
David Shulman, a Humanities professor at the Hebrew
University of Jerusalem, delivered a damning indictment
of the supine passivity over the last forty-four years of
his academic peers and their failure to mount a sustained
and politically significant campaign against the occupation and blatant annexation of swathes of the West Bank
by Jewish settlers.[6] Although the government is probably
right in being suspicious of Israeli universities as a natural breeding ground of leftist and peace-oriented opinion,
academics as a group have, for the most part, managed to
live within the system and tolerate its injustices – yet an-

other example in the long litany of *trahison des clercs* and a particularly shaming one, since Israel does still have a robustly independent press and jealously guarded freedom of speech. In their hardly outspoken opposition to the general policy of fragmenting, isolating and fencing in all Palestinian communities within the territories controlled by Israel, the intellectual classes are clones of the Kissinger-like character in Joseph Heller's novel *Good as Gold* whose favoured political strategy was one of 'fiery caution and crusading inertia'.

In the days of the Mandate, standard bearers such as Martin Buber and Judah Magnes would provide the uncomfortable moral touchstone against which to judge Zionist actions; until his death in 1994, the Orthodox scholar Yeshayahu Leibowitz fulfilled the same role regarding continued occupation of the Territories and its corrupting effect on the Israeli psyche. Nowadays, with the sporadic exception of writers such as Amos Oz and David Grossman, the intellectual establishment is more concerned to fight off the threat of an academic boycott from strident left-wing sociology lecturers in minor UK and European universities than to bring unified pressure to bear on its own government about ongoing military control of the Palestinians and appropriation of their land. The widespread apathy on the part of most Israeli academics, artists and public intellectuals about the daily situation fifty miles from where they meet to gossip in their favourite Tel-Aviv sidewalk cafés and expensive restaurants is shaming. Probably *Les Héros sont fatigués*, as the title of the gloomy 1955 Yves Montand film put it, worn out by a reality that never ameliorates, or perhaps there is always the possibility of a lecture tour sponsored by Jewish communities abroad if one doesn't make the

Diaspora uncomfortable by straying too far from the official government line.

Obviously, it is as one-eyed to blame Israel for causing all the problems in the region as it is to portray the Palestinians as the innocent, downtrodden victims of Israeli expansionism. In the past both sides have been culpable of exploiting the festering situation to their own short-term advantage. Israel's obsession with security and the Palestinian refusal to assuage it by giving up revanchist dreams and accepting that partition is the least bad compromise when two peoples claim the same piece of land have been key factors. But the tide turned after first Egypt, then Jordan, signed peace treaties with Israel and the PLO abrogated its Charter calling for the elimination of the Zionist state and recognised Israel. Since then, the diplomatic onus has been on Israel, as the overwhelmingly more powerful protagonist, to offer the Palestinians enough hope to induce them away from violence and towards moderation. This Israel has signally failed to do; instead, the pace of settlement building and land confiscation has accelerated over the last fifteen years.

The Arab League's peace initiative of 2002, reaffirmed at the Riyadh summit of 2007, is still lying on the table, comatose but not yet officially declared dead. The plan called for an independent Palestinian state; Jerusalem as a joint capital; Israeli withdrawal from the Occupied Territories to pre-1967 borders; a 'just solution' based on negotiated agreement to the thorny Palestinian refugee issue, and a peace treaty between Israel and the Arab states and the normalisation of relations. Had such a deal been offered to Ben-Gurion in the 1960s he would have regarded it as a messianic vision come true. According to various opinion polls it would be broadly acceptable to most of the Israeli electorate today, subject to satisfactory negotiations about border adjustments, the future of the settlements and the status of Jerusalem. Yet the plan has been persistently rubbished by Israeli government ministers and never once formally discussed at a cabinet meeting.

It baffles and angers Israel and Diaspora supporters that no matter how wanton the Palestinian terrorist atrocities or horrific the suicide bombings, ultimate blame always seems to fall on the Jewish state when its armed forces respond over-vigorously to attacks against its citizens. The world's reaction is 'poor Palestinians'. That is the paradox of asymmetrical power. As Alexander Solzhenitsyn observed in *The First Circle*: 'You only have power over people as long as you don't take *everything* from them. But when you've robbed a man of *everything* he's no longer in your power – he's free again.'

The Palestinian leadership on the West Bank is beginning to realise this. Alongside the creation of a civil infrastructure with all the apparatus ready to govern a Palestinian state-in-waiting (a lesson learned from the example of the Zionist leadership in Mandate Palestine), non-violent resistance to Israeli occupation is spreading as an organised tactic. In his *NYRB* review Professor Shulman cites villages such as Al-Nabi Salih, where the nearby Israeli settlement of Halamish has taken over nearly half of the village lands and a precious freshwater spring, and Budrus and Bil'in, where there have been weekly confrontations after Friday prayers between protesting villagers and the army. There is a staged, almost choreographed quality to these protests. The demonstrators advance, to be repulsed by water cannon,

tear gas, rubber-coated bullets and sometimes live am-
munition. In Bil'in, which has lost a third of its land to
the Security Wall, two villagers have been killed, many
wounded and hundreds arrested over the last six years.
Sometimes, depending on the tenseness of the general
situation, the mood of the villagers and the aggression
of the military response, clashes occur, with futile stone-
throwing from the Palestinian side. Generally though, the
demonstrators manage to maintain non-violent discipline
in the face of the guns. In al-Nabi Salih a huge sign in Arabic and English reads: 'We believe in Non-Violence. Do
you?'

And that is leading to a transformational change in the
relationship between oppressors and oppressed that Nusseibeh points to at the conclusion of *What Is a Palestin-
an State Worth?* Moral leverage to bring about change
through the non-violent exercise of innate freedom and
holding fast to universal values belongs with the weaker,
not with the stronger, party. If 'one defines power as the
ability to cause political change to one's advantage, it
is the *Palestinians* who hold this power even though (or
precisely because) they are being held down by a mighty
military force'.

The powerlessness of power to suppress natural justice
indefinitely is a truism well understood by Judaism and
exemplified many times by Jewish history. Therefore a religious lead would be valuable in instructing the Israeli
public and its politicians to show moral sensitivity in
their dealings with the Palestinians. But it is no more
forthcoming than an intellectual lead. The best that
Orthodox rabbis can come up with are *halachic* pro-
hibitions against selling property in the Holy Land to
Gentiles and actively endorsing the settlers' holy mission

in reclaiming every place name mentioned in the Bible. My own rabbinic colleagues in Progressive Judaism, usually at the forefront of initiatives for improving the world when it comes to poverty in Africa or deprivation of human rights elsewhere, are uncharacteristically diffident when the spotlight falls on Israel's systematic mistreatment and disenfranchisement of the Palestinians. At most, they might mildly criticise behaviour that goes against unspecified 'Jewish values' and offer up a prayer for greater understanding and true peace between the two peoples, speedily and in our days, Amen. As the proverb says, fine words butter no parsnips. An uncompromising statement of moral principle just might.

Instead, the headquarters in Jerusalem of the World Union for Progressive Judaism – to remind you again, the largest religious grouping in world Jewry with nearly two million members – regularly sends out mailings to its constituents about supporting 'Women at the Wall'. This is a group of Progressive women who want to be allowed to worship at the Western Wall. Now if these women feel a compulsive need to don head covering and prayer shawls in order to assert their inalienable right to pray near to scandalised Orthodox men at an ancient relic, all well and superstitious, but I would have been happier if just once in the past four years a message had come from them, or World Union headquarters – or indeed *any* Jewish religious body, Orthodox or Progressive, male or female – offering a response based on teachings from the classical Jewish sources to the continuing blockade of Gaza, which does not differentiate between Hamas followers and innocent civilians in a population of one-and-a-half million people and therefore is contrary to the fundamental principles of morality and justice first articulated by Abraham when he asked God concerning Sodom and Gomorrah, 'Will You indeed sweep away the righteous with the wicked? . . . shall not the judge of all the earth do justly?' (Genesis 18:23, 25).

The curse of the Internet to offset its many blessings is the amount of unsolicited material that pours in. Recently I received a sermon from the portentously titled Director of the Interreligious Coordinating Council of Israel, an American rabbi who has lived in Israel for thirty-two years. He was preaching on the most famous verse in the Bible, 'You shall love your neighbour as yourself' (Leviticus 19:18), which is repeated in slightly different form a little further on in the chapter: 'When a stranger resides with you in your land, you shall not wrong him. The stranger who resides with you shall be to you as one of your home-born. You shall love him as yourself, for you were strangers in the land of Egypt' (Leviticus 19:34–5).

Few biblical verses could have greater relevance to the neighbourly relationship between Israel and Palestine. The preacher recognises this: '. . . because of our history as a persecuted minority in someone else's land throughout our history, we Jews should have a special sensitivity to the non-Jewish citizens in our midst.' And what is the lesson he gleans from this? That 'we ought to give this issue higher priority. It ought to be more central to our Jewish identity today . . .' Moreover, says the preacher as he builds to his anodyne peroration, if Israel is to remain both a Jewish and a democratic country, 'the way that we relate to this issue will be critical for the future of the state, both for Jews who live in Israel, and for Jews who support Israel all over the world'.

It is the – at best – worthy *feebleness* of such religious

responses and at worst the crude self-interest of Torah-true fundamentalists in promoting their agenda for a Greater Israel that confirms secular Jews today in their view that Judaism – meaning the religion of the Jews – is an optional extra when it comes to defining what makes up their modern Jewish identity. Neither pious platitudes from religious liberals in lieu of frank speaking nor an aggressive evangelism from the ultra-Orthodox that goes against the grain of Enlightenment ideals about tolerance between different religions and peoples have much to offer towards solving urgent contemporary problems. Furthermore, it plays into the hands of Jewish and Muslim extremists. They *want* to resolve the Middle East impasse by means of a holy war; an already obdurate geopolitical conflict is being further exacerbated by this malign intrusion of religion. When in September 2000 Ariel Sharon went on his inflammatory walkabout in the Temple Mount area to assert Jewish claims to worship there, and ignited the second *intifada* as a consequence, it would have been hard to dream up a less likely *religious* champion than the corpulent ex-soldier rancher, unless John Wayne had still been around to play the part.

Religion has discredited itself as a force for peace in the Middle East and will remain discredited for as long as its practitioners insist on citing from their holy scriptures to prove their priority in God's favour and exclusive rights to the land. The problem of selective quotation applies equally to Judaism, Christianity and Islam. Until it is resolved by an understanding between the mainstream followers of the three monotheisms voluntarily to omit from general usage and the instruction of their young those passages that are derogatory and offensive about other faiths, religion cannot expect to play a mediating role in the conflict. In current circumstances, religion in-flames hatred in the Middle East rather than damping it down. But that is a different problem, for another time.

All fair-minded people, Jewish or not, would probably accept the following broad résumé: that in June 1967 Israel conquered the Territories in a justified war of self-defence. The Israeli government and military assumed that peace negotiations would take place and occupation of the West Bank, Gaza and the Golan Heights would not last more than a few weeks or months, at most. Rebuffed by the Arab States meeting in Khartoum in August 1967 and issuing a communiqué of Three Noes – no peace with Israel, no recognition of Israel, no negotiations with Israel – settlement building began almost by default, as a tit-for-tat retaliation: 'If you won't budge, neither will we.' Besides, retention of Arab lands provided Israel with security in depth from attack and strategically sited settlements would act as an early-warning system.

Soon though – at Passover 1968, to be precise – religious zealots overturned the likelihood of selective settlement construction based on military requirements. Like Fortinbras claiming the throne of Denmark, the zealots invoked 'rights of memory in this kingdom' going back to the Bible. Rabbi Moshe Levinger and his *Gush Emunim* (Block of the Faithful) refused to vacate the hotel in central Hebron where they had celebrated Passover until they were allowed to build a new settlement, *Kiryat Arba*, near by at the Tomb of the Patriarchs, a site venerated in both Jewish and Muslim tradition. Ever since then, settler pressure groups either of the aggressively nationalist or the religiously fundamentalist variety, or a combination of both, have been the tail wagging successive government dogs. The natural order has been overturned. It is not the government but the settlers who drive policy. In the words of a French radical about the 1848 Revolution: 'I am their leader. I had to follow them.' As a result, an original settler population of a few hundred on the West Bank in 1968 has grown to around 230,000 today.

If that is an acceptable reading of the course of settlement expansion over the last forty years, what I am about to say won't receive anything like the same general endorsement. It is that Israeli politicians of all hues have backed themselves into a corner from which they don't know how to extricate themselves, after years of lazy acceptance of the status quo, sneaky admiration for the new breed of Zionist pioneers planting the Israeli flag on remote West Bank hilltops, overt encouragement of more settlement construction, and military intelligence assessments that the Arab population could be monitored and controlled by a tight system of mobile patrols, movable road blocks, fragmentation into non-contiguous enclaves, expropriation of land for 'security purposes' and physical separation from the settlements by the construction of Jews-only roads and a Security Wall.

That worked for the first twenty-five years of 'the most benign occupation in history'. Now, though, politicians across the party spectrum face a quandary. They know that the impetus for a Palestinian state is inexorable; most of them have paid lip service to it. Should their distaste for the idea and tardiness in paving the way for it become too obvious, it will provoke the ire of the USA, Israel's one staunch ally, and international condemnation. But a mass evacuation of settlers would precipitate deep unrest, even civil war, in Israel. That, certainly, is the settlers' threat. (Personally, I think it is largely sound and fury. If the settlers want to stay they could do so subject to Palestinian law, just as one-and-a-half million Arabs live in Israel under Israeli law. And as the majority of the 230,000 settlers were tempted to the Territories by favourable loans, cheaper housing and tax concessions, so too they could be tempted back inside Israel by similar inducements.)

The alternatives for any Israeli government appear to be stark: either bow to the settlers and their brand of apocalyptic messianism; batten down the hatches and stay put; defy hostile world opinion and await the next, possibly terminal, war with the Arabs. Or, take the plunge, face down settler posturing and convince a dubious public that a solution to the Israel–Palestine conflict is at last attainable; that it is in Israel's best interests to have for a neighbour a stable, demilitarised Palestinian state in which growing prosperity, pride in self-government and awareness of how easily the Israeli army could reoccupy the territory marginalises the irredentist agenda of extremist factions such as Hamas.

That is the choice. No coalition government, by definition a compromise between competing platforms, could propose evacuating the settlements and survive. Of the two Israeli political leaders of the present generation who were conceivably powerful enough to have pushed through such a proposal in return for the opportunity of peace, one was assassinated for his efforts and the other survives in a permanently vegetative state on his Negev ranch. So the drift, hesitancy and indecision continue, encouraging the settlement movement to push on. And all the while Israel's international standing deteriorates and her diplomatic vulnerability grows. The new buzz word of the Israel PR Lobby is 'de-legitimisation'; it

has replaced 'anti-Semitism masquerading as anti-Zionism' in the lexicon of dangers facing the state from a
hostile world. After discounting the hyperbole and them-
against-us mentality, it is the case that after more than
sixty years of statehood Israel's acceptance is still dis-
turbingly *provisional* in the eyes of some; being held
responsible for not solving the Palestinian problem is the
root cause of that provisionality.

So what might coax Israel to accept that holding on
to the Territories is counter-productive? That a policy of
pragmatism – especially if it is seen to have failed – can
never be morally justified? Persuading a sceptical public won't be an overnight process. No sudden conversion
will change the mindset of a Jewish people within and
outside Israel indoctrinated for decades to believe that all
Arabs are bent on destroying the state and that all Israel's genuine peace efforts in the past have been turned
down by an untrustworthy enemy. It was a Talmudic
rabbi who declared of the coming of the Messiah, 'All the
promised ends of the world have been and gone. Now
everything depends on repentance and good deeds' (*Sanhedrin*, 97b); how much more so is that true of trying to
alter a deeply ingrained national narrative, change popular perceptions of the 'other' and encourage a kiss of life
for the moribund peace process.

It can be done. But it will require that leap of the imagination which according to Shelley is the great instru-
ment of moral good. It offers a chance to those apathetic intellectuals, ineffectual academics, disengaged artists
and tremulous rabbis who until now have failed to break
the silence to rediscover their moral compass by giving
an unequivocal lead to the idealistic Jewish young; it
presents the alienated Jew with an opportunity to asso-

ciate with an initiative that makes him feel proud of, not embarrassed by, being Jewish, and it reassures the humanist Jew that Jewish values are strong enough for Judaism to survive as a cultural identity without the need to believe in God.

A start would be a mass petition from Jews worldwide to the Israeli prime minister's office under the slogan 'Passover for the Palestinians'. Even Eli Wiesel might have difficulty in refusing to sign it. All of Judaism's ethical teachings are based on and derive from the concept of Freedom. It is the *sine qua non* of Jewish values. The exodus from Egyptian slavery is the folk memory above all others that is embedded in our collective unconscious and unites religious, secular, atheist and only-just Jews in nominating the Passover Seder as their favourite celebration. It was Heine, in many ways the epitome of the post-Enlightenment Jew adjusting to the temptations of modernity without forfeiting Jewish distinctiveness, who wrote in *Germany to Luther*, 'Since the Exodus, Freedom has always spoken with a Hebrew accent.' The journey of the Hebrew slaves to freedom has been the inspiration for most liberation movements in Western history and 'Let my people go' the battle cry that has urged them forward. Liberty is a universal yearning, shared by all peoples everywhere.

In an era of global communication, when images on Facebook can start a popular revolt against tyrannical regimes and the first reaction of fearful despots is to ban foreign journalists and shut down the Internet, several thousand Jews around the world have already signed up to organisations such as J Street that call for an alternative approach to the wearing, brutalising occupation by Israel of another people's land. Views on how this can be achieved differ widely, but that is the stuff of healthy political debate. One value on which all Jews surely agree is the indivisible nature of freedom, a right due to all, including the Palestinian neighbour.

If that basic Jewish value is reiterated often enough and forcefully enough to whichever Israeli government is in power, by a partnership of its own citizens and Diaspora Jews on whose behalf it claims to act as guarantor, then undoubtedly it would be galvanised into a more visible and energetic search for peace. The collective expression of the Jewish people's will to stay true to its core values would force the government to take heed, squarely confront the dangerous illusions of the settlers, and respond positively to diplomatic overtures for ending the conflict. It can work. Herzl's father Jakob, when his son's plans for a Jewish homeland were getting nowhere, advised him to write a popular pamphlet that would inspire the little men to band together like a mighty river. Herzl listened and produced *Der Judenstaat* (*The Jewish State*), the seminal text that brought Zionism to public notice.

That would become the first step in a process of Jewish self-liberation; freedom from always choosing to see ourselves as the perennial victims of persecution and anti-Semitism; from wallowing in the self-pity of being misunderstood; from imagining that we are 'owed' by the rest of the world and should be granted special leeway because of the Holocaust; from subordinating the universal dictates of conscience to the tawdry manoeuvrings of Israeli politics.

Jews and Judaism today face the challenges common to most societies and religions. In Judaism there is a widening rift between the ultra-Orthodox who carry on regardless, the religious moderates who search for a synthesis of tradition with modern knowledge, and the growing secular constituency who have no patience for ancient beliefs but wish to express their Jewish identity in a tolerant multiculturalism.

The argument between Zionism and Diasporism is set to run for as long as the majority of Jews freely choose to live outside Israel. Whether a Jewish state was the solution to the 'Jewish Problem' or merely the new Jewish problem has yet to be decided. Teaching Jews to accept the Bible as the work of human authors and the *halachah* derived from it as our guidance not our governance will require a lengthy educational process. Persuading all Jews of the advantages in redefining Jewish status more liberally on the basis of upbringing and identification, not maternal descent, is a principle that needs to be widely debated and publicised. It will take time and patience to reassure religion's sceptical guardians that Judaism's ethical values and cultural legacy are a compensation for the loss of faith and a bulwark against mass Jewish defection, and therefore should be advocated positively as part of the total Judaic experience.

These are important debates for the future direction of the Jewish people and their religion of Judaism. Whether in Israel or the Diaspora, we are a stubborn, stiff-necked, disputatious, energetic, adaptable, resilient, enormously talented people – *my* people. We have to recognise that any attempt to impose the discarded beliefs of a religious past onto a secular present and expect Jews to stay loyal is futile. 'This is not the way.' But if we stay receptive to all manifestations of the Jewish spirit, religious and secular, while holding fast to the moral teachings that have been the mainstay of our infinitely diverse culture throughout its long history, I am confident that Judaism won't die out as the 'fossilised religion' of Arnold Toynbee's controversial description, but will continue to add its own distinctive and valuable contribution to civilisation and improving the world.

Notes

Chapter 1: Zionism triumphant, the Diaspora subservient

1 North American Jewish Data Bank, 2010.
2 'World Jewish Population, 2008', *American Jewish Year Book* (2008).
3 'The Economic Downturn and the Future of Jewish Communities', Institute for Jewish Policy Research, September 2009.
4 Salo Baron, 'Ghetto and Emancipation', *Menorah Journal* 14 (June 1928).
5 Marcus Dysch, 'Aliyah Soars as Crunch Bites', *Jewish Chronicle*, 4 June 2009.
6 David Goldberg, *The Divided Self: Israel and the Jewish Psyche Today*, I. B. Tauris, London, 2006; paperback edn, 2011.
7 Isaiah Berlin, *The Hedgehog and the Fox: An Essay on Tolstoy's View of History*, Weidenfeld & Nicolson, London, 1953.
8 Anthony Julius, *Trials of the Diaspora: A History of Anti-Semitism in England*, Oxford University Press, Oxford, 2010.

9   Uri Avnery, 'In the Knesset', *London Review of Books*, 5 August 2010.

Chapter 2: Creating Israel's foundation myth

1   Peter Novick, *The Holocaust and Collective Memory*, Bloomsbury, London, 1999, p. 147.

2   Novick, *The Holocaust and Collective Memory*, p. 147.

3   See, for example, Jeremy Bowen, *Six Days: How the 1967 War Shaped the Middle East*, Simon & Schuster, Chicago IL, 2003, pp. 52–3, and Shlomo Gazit, *Trapped Fools*, Frank Cass, London, 2003, p. xiii.

4   Richard Rubenstein, *After Auschwitz*, Bobbs Merrill, Indianapolis IN, 1966.

5   Novick, *The Holocaust and Collective Memory*, p. 296, n. 31.

6   David Vital, 'After the Catastrophe: Aspects of Contemporary Jewry', in Peter Hayes (ed.), *Lessons and Legacies: The Meaning of the Holocaust in a Changing World*, Holocaust Educational Foundation, Skokie IL, 1991.

7   Avraham Burg, *The Holocaust is Over; We must Rise from its Ashes*, Palgrave Macmillan, Basingstoke, 2008.

8   Benyamin Natanyahu, *A Place among the Nations*, Davar Books, Tel-Aviv, 1993.

Chapter 3: Anti-Semitism and anti-Zionism

1   Mordecai Kaplan, *Judaism as a Civilization*, JPS and Reconstructionist Press, Philadelphia, 1981.

2   George Steiner, *The Portage to San Cristobal of A.H.*, Faber and Faber, London, 1981.

3   Bernard Lewis, *Semites and Anti-Semites*, Phoenix, London, 1997, pp. 121–2.

4   Bernard Lewis, *The Jews of Islam*, Routledge & Kegan Paul, London, 1984, pp. 32–3.

5   Lewis, *The Jews of Islam*, p. 85.

6   Lewis, *The Jews of Islam*, p. 190.

7   Julius, *Trials of the Diaspora*, pp. 582–3.

8   Martin Gilbert, *In Ishmael's House*, Yale University Press, New Haven CT, 2010, chapter 14ff.

9   Al-Musawwar, 4 August 1972, translated by Norman A. Stillman in 'New Attitudes toward the Jew in the Arab World', *Jewish Social Studies*, vol. 37 no. 3/4 (summer–autumn 1975), p. 197.

10   'The Jewish Holiday of Purim', *al-Riyadh*, 10 March 2002.

11   '"Taliban rule" at British university', *The Sunday Times*, 17 October 2010, p. 17.

12   Phyllis Chesler, *The New Anti-Semitism: The Current Crisis and What We Must Do About It*, Jossey-Bass, Hoboken NJ, 2003.

13   'No Joke, Silvio!', *Jewish News*, 7 October 2010.

14   'How a judge's Gaza tirade led to uproar', *Jewish Chronicle*, 23 July 2010.

15   'Julius Leaves Me Punch-Drunk', *Manna*, summer 2010.

16   Martin Gilbert, *Churchill and the Jews*, Simon & Schuster, London, 2007, quoted in Julius, *Trials of the Diaspora*, p. 39.

17   Diana Pinto, 'Asemitism', keynote lecture, European Region for Progressive Judaism Conference, Paris, February 2010.

Chapter 4: Who is a Jew?

1 Solomon ibn Verga, *Shevet Yehudah*, translated by M. Wiener, 1855, p. 90.

2 Hannah Arendt, *Rahel Varnhagen: The Life of a Jewess*, East and West Library, London, 1957.

3 Tzvetan Todorov, *In Defence of the Enlightenment*, Atlantic Books, London, 2009.

4 Max Hastings, *Did You Really Shoot the Television?*, HarperPress, London, 2010.

5 See Shlomo Sand, *The Invention of the Jewish People*, Verso, London, 2010, or Arthur Koestler, *The Thirteenth Tribe*, Random House, New York, 1976.

6 See John Davis, *The Jews of San Nicandro*, Yale University Press, New Haven CT, 2010.

7 Isaiah Berlin, 'The Life and Opinions of Moses Hess', in *Against the Current*, The Hogarth Press, London, 1979.

8 See Louis Jacobs, *A Jewish Theology*, Darton, Longman & Todd, London, 1973, pp. 269–75.

Chapter 5: God is dead, long live Behaviourism

1 Isaac Deutscher, *The Non-Jewish Jew & Other Essays*, Oxford University Press, Oxford, 1968.

2 George Foot Moore, *Judaism in the First Centuries of the Christian Era*, Harvard University Press, Cambridge MA, 1927.

3 Hans Kung, *Judaism*, SCM Press, Norwich, 1992.

4 All quotations from Mitchell Silver, *A Plausible God*, Fordham University Press, New York, 2006, p. 8.

5 Irène Némirovsky, *The Dogs and the Wolves*, translated by Sandra Smith, Chatto & Windus, London, 2009.

Chapter 6: How 'holy' is Holy Scripture?

1   A. N. Wilson, *God's Funeral: The Decline of Faith in Western Civilization*, John Murray Publishers Ltd, London, 1999.

2   Egon Mayer, Barry Kosmin and Ariela Kaysar, *American Jewish Identity Survey 2001*, Center for Jewish Studies of The City University of New York.

3   Norman Cohn, *The Pursuit of the Millennium: Revolutionary Millenarians and Mystical Anarchists of the Middle Ages*, Oxford University Press, Oxford, 1970.

4   Harvey Cox, *The Secular City: Secularization and Urbanization in Theological Perspective*, 25th Anniversary Edition, Collier Books, New York, 1990.

5   Judith Butler, 'Who Owns Kafka?', *London Review of Books*, 3 March 2011.

6   Antony Lerman, 'The Kafka legacy: who owns Jewish heritage?', *Guardian*, 22 July 2010.

7   Achad Ha-Am, *The Truth from the Land of Israel: Complete Works of Achad Ha-Am*, in Hebrew, Tel-Aviv, 1946.

8   Robert Alter, *The Five Books of Moses: A Translation with Commentary*, W. W. Norton & Company, New York, 2004, p. xiv.

9   A. E. Harvey, in e-mail correspondence with the author, January 2011.

10 Solomon B. Freehof, Introduction, *Modern Reform Responsa*, The Hebrew Union College Press, Detroit MI, 1971.

Chapter 7: Judaism and Jewish Culture

1 See Kwame Anthony Appiah, 'Religious Faith and John Rawls', *New York Review of Books*, 9 December 2010.
2 Felix Posen, 'Alternative Judaisms', Hebrew University, Jerusalem, May 2000.
3 *Jewish Chronicle*, 21 May 2010.
4 *Jewish Chronicle Education Supplement*, 8 April 2011.
5 Josh Levy, '"Cultural"' Jews Are No Laughing Matter', *Manna*, autumn 2009.
6 Eliezer Schweid, *The Idea of Modern Jewish Culture*, Academic Studies Press, Brighton MA, 2008, p. 161.
7 See Anthony Kenny, *A New History of Western Philosophy*, Oxford University Press, Oxford, 2010, p. 990.

Chapter 8: Jewish ethics and the State of Israel

1 Jonathan Freedland, 'Comment is Free', *Guardian*, 6 April 2011.
2 Richard Goldstone, 'Reconsidering the Goldstone Report on Israel and war crimes', PostOpinions, *Washington Post*, 1 April 2011.
3 Jessica Montell, 'Beyond Goldstone: A truer discussion about Israel, Hamas and the Gaza conflict', PostOpinions, *Washington Post*, 5 April 2011.
4 Avraham Shapira (ed.), *The Seventh Day: Soldiers' Talk about the Six-day War*, André Deutsch, London, 1970.
5 Julius, *Trials of the Diaspora*, pp. 500–502.
6 David Shulman, 'Israel and Palestine; Breaking the Silence', *New York Review of Books*, 24 February–9 March 2011.

Index